SHOOT!

CELEBRATING THE BEST OF THE PREMIER LEAGUE YEARS

Published in 2020 by Welbeck

An Imprint of Welbeck Non-Fiction Limited, part of Welbeck
Publishing Group.

20 Mortimer Street London W1T 3JW

A CIP catalogue record for this book is available from the
British Library

ISBN 978 1 78739 495 7

Editorial Director: Martin Corteel
General Editor: Adrian Besley
Project Editor: Ross Hamilton
Design Manager: Luke Griffin
Assistant Designer: Eliana Holder
Page make-up design: Tim Anderson
Picture research: Paul Langan
Production: Rachel Burgess

The publishers would also like to thank the following
sources for their kind permission to reproduce the
photographs in this book.

Getty Images
Page 5: Ross Kinnaird; 6: Ben Radford; 7: Simon
Stacpoole/Offside

PA Images
Page 4: (top left) Matthew Ashton/EMPICS Sport, (bottom
left) Owen Humphreys/PA Archive

Every effort has been made to acknowledge correctly
and contact the source and/or copyright holder of each
picture and Welbeck Non-Fiction Limited apologises for any
unintentional errors or omissions, which will be corrected in
future editions of this book.

Printed in Dubai

10 9 8 7 6 5 4 3 2 1

SHOOT!

CELEBRATING THE BEST OF THE PREMIER LEAGUE YEARS

**NOSTALGIC GEMS
FROM THE VOICE
OF FOOTBALL**

WELBECK

INTRODUCTION

The late 1980s were a period of doom and gloom for English football thanks to ancient stadia, violent hooligans that kept many fans off the terraces, and a game that was stagnating.

But then Greg Dyke, at the time head of London Weekend Television (and ironically a former local newspaper colleague of mine) had an idea… to form a super league made up of the top teams. Their fixtures would all be on TV and his company would broadcast them and make loads of money.

Dyke, who later became Football Association chairman, saw his idea blocked, but two years later, with the not-insignificant help of sports agent Jon Smith, England's Premier League was formed. *Shoot* was there to witness the final days of the old First Division in 1991-92, when Leeds United, under Howard Wilkinson, lifted the title… and then report as big-money transfers and mind-boggling wages proceeded to change English football forever.

With the advent of the Premier League, many of the biggest names in world football arrived in England to enhance the game, help generate massive TV income and swell crowds in brand new all-seater grounds. Nowadays, the league is said to be approaching an annual income of around £10 billion, with something like 1.6 billion fans watching around the planet. In the early years, however, it remained a much more humble affair, despite the influx of new money and talent. The same goes for the players of the era.

I recall one of my first face-to-face interviews with a rising Premier League star since taking over the editor's role at *Shoot*. It was late summer on the lawn outside of a posh hotel, and into the car park drove Shay Given, the Newcastle United and Republic of Ireland goalkeeper, who greeted us with a typical Irish smile and welcome.

'Ah, but we need some props for the photo shoot,' said the photographer. No problem – Shay jumped back into his Audi TT sports car, drove to the club's nearby training centre and arrived back with some balls to go with his gloves and club shirt. The painter giving the hotel a spruce up butted in with: 'Good keeper, shame about the club… I'm a Sunderland fan.' Given, who had had a previous loan with the Mackems, laughed and the pair shook hands.

Above left: The arrival of the Premier League signalled the dawn of a new era for Manchester United – and for *Shoot!*

Above: A young John Terry playing for Chelsea. Even as a teenager, he was showing the qualities that would help make him the club's most successful captain and a Premier League titan.

Left: Alan Shearer and Sir Bobby Robson, two legends of the Premier League era, and a couple of absolute gentlemen to boot.

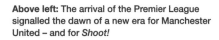

There were plenty of suggestions even then that some star players were out of touch with reality, but not Shay, who even signed an autograph for a supporter of his team's biggest rivals.

A couple of weeks down the line, future England and Chelsea captain John Terry – then with just a handful of games under his belt on loan at Nottingham Forest and still a teenager – agreed to visit a village junior school with me.

It just so happened that a lot of the locals were Chelsea fans, and they were already aware of the rising star. The plan was for two classes to meet him, have a kick about, and then for an autograph session but news of the 'secret' visit got out and parents, grandparents and a whole host of other classes turned up. I glanced at JT's agent, who looked back at me wide-eyed. The headmaster, sensing something wasn't going to plan, decided to step in and try to cut back the crowd.

'No, don't do that,' said JT. 'I'll sign something for everyone.' Cue football shirts, shorts, books, pieces of paper… and even one school shirt!

It's not just players who appeared on the pages of *Shoot*, there were also some amazing managers – and not just Sir Alex Ferguson and Arsene Wenger.

Former Everton striker and manager Joe Royle, then boss of Ipswich, was due to call me so I could interview him, but as the clock ticked past the agreed time the phone stayed silent. Finally, it rang: 'Joe Royle here. Sorry I'm late, I got held up in training. I hope it's still OK to call.' A gent and a legend.

Another late caller was former Newcastle and England striker Alan Shearer, the Premier League's record goalscorer and now BBC *Match of the Day* pundit. Although I'd interviewed him previously, it was still a bit surreal for the phone to ring and the voice at the other end say: 'Hello, Alan Shearer here.' His reason for being just a few minutes late dialling in? There'd been a big horse race on the TV and he'd wanted to see the result. He never did say if he had a winning bet…

Two questions I nearly always get asked about my years in football, which stretch back more than two decades before I joined *Shoot*, are: Have you ever interviewed David Beckham? Who is the best player you have ever interviewed?

The answer to the first is: sort of! I fired off some written questions for him and got the answers back. We did get other interviews with Becks, although he was always pretty busy…

The second answer is Sir Bobby Robson. Of course, many years ago, he played for Fulham and West Brom but most fans will remember him as boss of England, Ipswich, PSV Eindhoven, Sporting Lisbon, Porto, Barcelona and finally Newcastle, the club he supported as a boy. It was in his final post that I was lucky enough to interview Sir Bobby for *Shoot*. It's impossible to recreate in words the aura around the man – you had to experience him walk into a room and talk to you to understand.

I'd defy anyone not to like him! He was the type of person who felt like he was your friend. His knowledge of the game was immense. His ability to get the best from players was huge. This guy quite simply loved football. He lived and breathed the game until cancer cruelly took his life.

I remember almost every minute of every interview with Sir Bobby, but the stand-out moment was when he was involved in publicity for the launch of a computer game. The young lad from the games company handed over a copy of the game to Sir Bobby, who put it down on a table and went off to have a chat with me and get a few pictures taken. When we returned, he was aghast that the disc was not where he put it. He was so apologetic to the lad and was hunting for the package.

I whispered in the lad's ear to pick up one of the other games – like the one he had given to the boss, they were all sealed – say he'd found Sir Bobby's and hand it over. When he did, there was a massive air of relief from the manager. He was delighted – even though he was only going to give it to his secretary for one of her family's younger members.

Sorry for fooling you a little Sir Bobby! I know you will forgive me.

Colin Mitchell
Former Editor of *Shoot*

FOREWORD

It has been such a privilege to commentate on the Premier League right from its very first weekend back in 1992. It is also a real pleasure to be part of this nostalgic look back at many of those years through the pages of *Shoot*!

I was an avid reader of, and very occasional contributor to, a magazine which was both fun and informative. Many a time I found an article about a player which provided fresh details which I could use in my broadcasts.

The Premier League coincided with the growth of specialised TV Sports channels and Sky Sports in particular. The partnership has flourished for almost three decades now. The first 'live' game was at the City Ground in 1992: Nottingham Forest, managed by the late, great Brian Clough, against Liverpool under the guidance of Graeme Souness, now a friend and colleague at Sky.

It was the start of a massive adventure for football and for television, though it was not my first Premier League commentary. A day earlier I had covered the defending champions from the last season of the old First Division, Leeds United. Their first game in the new structure was at home to Wimbledon. Those memories will come flooding back now top-flight football has returned to Elland Road.

In these pages, *Shoot* reflects on a long period of domination by Manchester United; the Jack Walker-bankrolled Blackburn Rovers, who became champions in '95; and the challenges to Alex Ferguson's great managerial skills from the likes of Arsene Wenger's Arsenal and the ever-improving Chelsea. And there is much, much more besides!

The best way to recall your favourite football moments, players and teams is to check what was actually written about them at the time. *Shoot*, in its own inimitable style, was there.

Read on…

Martin Tyler, Sky Sports

Right: Premier League Executive Chairman Richard Scudamore presents Martin Tyler with the award for Premiership Commentator of the Decade back in 2003. Nearly 20 years later, Martin – and the Premier League – are still going strong.

Opposite: Martin's voice has become inextricably linked with some of the defining moments of the Premier League era. It's impossible to imagine watching the league without him.

McG

Durrant is the comebac

He's a midfield player with exceptional talent and the ability to excite the crowds.

He had the soccer world at his feet when he suffered an horrific knee injury which threatened to end his career.

Now he's on the comeback trail and aims to lead his country's World Cup qualifying campaign in style.

No, we're not talking about Gazza. But for Ian Durrant the comparisons are obvious.

The 25-year-old Rangers ace is finally back in business after more than three years out of the big time. And, just like Gazza, he's got his sights set on next Wednesday's World Cup qualifier as his next step along the recovery road.

"It's been hard enough getting a game at Rangers lately, but I'll be really delighted if I make the starting line-up against Portugal next week," he says.

Yet one look at the Durrant Diary shows just how close he came to quitting.

October 8 1988
Shatters right knee ligaments in horror tackle by Aberdeen's Neil Simpson. Career looks over.

October 9 1988
The first of many hours in the operating theatre trying to piece his knee together.

November 1988
More meetings with the surgeon's scalpel.

February 1989
Begins rehabilitation work at Lilleshall.

December 1989
Back at Ibrox to start weight training.

June 1990
As doubts about his comeback grow, he travels to the USA for the first of two revolutionary operations to try to save his career. Each op costs £25,000.

Jan 19 1991
His first game back for Rangers reserves. 10,000 turn up to watch.

April 6 1991
First team return as sub against Hibs.

August 1991
The start of a season of frustration as he is still unable to pin down a regular first team place.

March 1992
Finally returns to regular action, making 14 appearances by the end of the campaign.

May 1992
Collects his first Scottish Cup winners medal as Rangers beat Airdrie.

August 22 1992
Scores in his first Old Firm game for four years.

September 10 1992
Wins his sixth Scotland cap - and his first for four years - as sub in Switzerland.

8

AZZA!

King of Scotland

Durrant's injury cost him seven major honours. During his time on the sidelines Rangers won four League titles and three Skol Cups

GIVE HIM A GO!

That's the advice for Scotland boss Andy Roxburgh on the eve of next week's crunch World Cup qualifier with Portugal.

And it's not just Rangers fans who believe comeback king Durrant is the man to lead Scotland's challenge.

Midfield rival Murdo MacLeod also reckons that Ian is the man for the job next Wednesday, when Scotland will break with years of tradition to play a major match away from Hampden.

The 34-year-old Hibs skipper, still battling to shake off the injury which cost him his place in Scotland's European Championship squad, says: "Ian has proved that he is back to his best...and he knows the way to goal.

"He made an immediate impact when he came on as sub in Switzerland last month and gave them all sorts of problems with his pace and power."

Durrant was back in action for Scotland against Switzerland last month

ANDY ROXBURGH is ready to gamble on Durrant at Ibrox next week in an effort to make up lost ground.

Last month's 3-1 defeat in Switzerland was a serious setback to Scotland's hopes of qualifying for the 1994 World Cup and Roxburgh knows his team can't afford to drop any points against the Portuguese.

That's why he is ready to use Durrant in his starting line-up and says: "Ian is a player with real talent.

"We were introducing him gradually before his injury and his potential is still there.

"His greatest gift is the way he times those forward runs. He knows exactly when to burst into the box."

Roxburgh even wanted to take Durrant to Sweden as part of his European Championship squad but reveals: "Ian felt it was too early for him.

"But now he has broken the barrier and is back in the frame.

"We didn't lose any of the five games in which Ian has started - but the last thing he needs right now is any extra pressure from me!"

HOW THEY COMPARE

DURRANT		GAZZA
Glasgow. 29.10.66	**Born**	Gateshead. 27.5.67.
25	**Age**	25
5ft 8ins	**Height**	5ft 10ins
9st.7lbs	**Weight**	11st.7lbs
146	**Lge games**	205
21	**Lge goals**	40
4	**U21 caps**	13
6	**Full caps**	20
Scottish Champion 1987, Skol Cup winner 1987, Scottish Cup winner 1992	**Honours**	FA Cup winner 1991

SHOOT

YOU'LL NEVER WALK ALONE
LIVERPOOL FOOTBALL CLUB
100 YEARS
1892 — 1992

Steve McManaman

STAND BY YOUR McMANAMAN

He's on the verge of becoming a superstar yet is still only 20-years-old. He was voted man of the match in last season's FA Cup Final as Liverpool beat Sunderland at Wembley but was sidelined for the start of the Premier League campaign by injury. Now he's back in action and Liverpool already look a better side for his presence.

* Steve McManaman was born in Liverpool on February 11, 1972 and supported Everton as a boy. He later rejected an offer to join the Goodison Park club as well as Manchester United, West Brom, Bolton and Luton in order to sign for Liverpool.

* He once won the North-West schoolboys cross-country championship.

* He started his first game for Liverpool on the opening day of the 1991-92 season, a 2-1 home win against Oldham. He had already made his debut for England's Under-21 side eight months earlier.

* His stunning FA Cup Final performance in May wasn't his first game at Wembley. He'd already played there for England's Under-18 team against Spain.

* His Liverpool room-mate is Mike Marsh and his favourite pastimes are playing pool and golf. Marco Van Basten is his favourite player.

* His dislikes include playing against Wimbledon (wonder why?), Emmerdale Farm and country and western music.

HE SAYS

Obviously I'm glad that I chose Liverpool. It was suggested that I should sign for a smaller club as I would get a better chance to get in the first team. But it has worked out better than anyone ever imagined for me here.

I get fed up with Liverpudlians being portrayed as thick layabouts. We are warm-hearted, easy going people with a great sense of humour.

I've put on a bit of weight since the start of last season and now feel a lot stronger. It's getting harder for people to knock me off the ball.

I want to do enough to get into the England senior squad regularly and earn a place in the 1994 World Cup. I've already been to America but it would be great to go back there as a World Cup competitor.

THEY SAY

Steve is a young man who has everything going for him. Whenever he's been asked to do a man's job in the first team he has never shirked it and he has always been selected on merit. I'm sure he is going to develop into something special.
Graeme Souness

THEY SAY

He is not far away from an England senior place. He showed in the FA Cup Final that he is not troubled by big occasions and I see no reason why he cannot become one of English football's real favourites.
Graham Taylor

THEY SAY

He has been compared with our own Ryan Giggs and that is fair enough, though neither deserves to be compared with anyone else at the moment. Steve is a very bubbly character and should develop into an outstanding individual.
Terry Yorath

OVER THE TOP

WE'RE NOT BIASED - WE'LL HAVE A GO AT ANYONE

RONNIE & RENATA

The news that Ron Atkinson sent his Villa team out onto the pitch for the recent game against Manchester United to the sound of Rene (the little fat one of Rene & Renata fame) singing 'Nessun Dorma', set us thinking. How about these footballing anthems...

Wimbledon - WAR by Edwin Starr

Blackburn - MONEY, MONEY, MONEY by Abba

Nottm Forest - THE ONLY WAY IS UP by Yazz

Rangers - SIMPLY THE BEST by Tina Turner

If you think you can do better, send us your suggestions to the usual OTT address.

FANZINE CHOICE

THIS WEEK: SW6 CHELSEA

A fair minded look at the goings on at The Bridge, the authors of SW6 don't simply slag people off for the sake of it. It's a good mixture of humour and serious issues and, at 50p, well worth a read.

Q. What's the difference between Leeds and Mickey Mouse?

A. Mickey Mouse is still in Europe!

Heaven sent

They say that God moves in mysterious ways...

Gillingham, the League's bottom team, having sacked manager Damien Richardson after six successive defeats, turned to the Reverand Kevin McElhinney for 'spiritual guidance'.

And so, it came to pass, that Gillingham did win their next game - 3-1 against Hereford.

But the modest clergyman insisted: "The players must take the real credit."

We're so pretty, oh so

WHERE ARE THEY NOW?

10 things that haven't been seen for a while

1. John Barnes' afro comb

2. Ron Atkinson's shampoo

3. Tony Adams' car keys

4. Vinny Jones' Fair Play award

5. Alex Ferguson's sense of humour

6. Chris Waddle's passport

7. A Manchester United Golden Boot winner

8. Wimbledon's fans

9. Kenny Dalglish's stress

10. A Luton win

Dalglish is Keane on Roy

How to make friends and influence people...

Barnet chairman Stan Flashman says of his club's fans: "The supporters don't matter as far as I'm concerned. They just pay their entrance fee. I don't care whether they come to Barnet or not."

Nice to know you're appreciated, isn't it?

Generous Torquay fans travelled 300 miles with a food handout... for a cat. They took dozens of tins of grub to their Third Division game against Halifax, after Town manager John McGrath said the club were so skint he could not afford to feed club cat Benny.

Kenny Dalglish has, apparently, been told to spend another £5 million by Christmas. (Nice work if you can get it - ED)

He would be prepared to spend most of that on Forest's Roy Keane but, if Brian Clough refuses to sell, Dalglish may well take on Manchester City in the bidding for Wimbledon's Robbie Earle.

'There's only two Roy Races'

Roy of the Rovers has kicked his girlfriend into touch.

But before fans of the comic hero start panicking, it's the OTHER Roy Race, the 24-year-old who plays for Deltone in the Rotherham Sunday League, who's got love trouble.

He's banned his fiancee Katrina Stancill, and his sister Jackie, from going to watch him because he gets embarrassed when they chant his name. "I feel a right plonker," he says.

GETTING SHIRTY

More of those kits you could buy your worst enemy for Christmas.

THIS WEEK: SHREWSBURY

GOOD   **BAD**   **UGLY**

Wimbledon star John Fashanu knows exactly why The Dons are struggling this season - they've got too many pretty boys in defence.

Big Fash reckons: "What we're looking for is a big, strong ugly defender. We've got too many good looking guys at the back."

So who would you recommend Fash. "If we had Neil Ruddock we'd be alright." We're not sure Neil will be too happy with that.

So you think a footballer's life is all glitz and glamour, do you?

It might be for the likes of John Barnes and Ian Rush, but for Chesterfield's motley marauders, who held Liverpool to a 4-4 draw in the Coca-Cola Cup at Anfield last month, it's a different story.

Chesterfield's players are paid peanuts (£200 per week to be precise) compared to the Premier League big boys and, what's more they also have to:

* Pay £1 to park their cars near the ground

* Wear recycled sock tie-ups

* Have their boots repaired by a cobbler rather than replaced

* Travel to and from away games on the day of a match because the club can't afford overnight stays

* Take their own sandwiches on away trips

Tough at the bottom, innit?

SNAPSHOT

David Speedie arrives in court charged with assault. The verdict? In that tie? **GUILTY!**

Have you ever wondered what happened to Ipswich's 1978 FA Cup Final hero Roger Osborne? No, neither have we.

Everton boss Howard Kendall came up with a novel way of punishing Tony Cottee for slagging off his team-mates. He made Cottee take the rest of the squad out for a slap-up Chinese meal, so solving his discipline problem and boosting morale at the same time.

OTT

Well, they say everyone is famous for 15 minutes

It seems that the 'Hand of God' is back in action. Dirty Diego has been spotted palming crosses into the back of the net during training with his new club Sevilla. Let's hope no 'keeper accidently punches him.

KASEY GROANS

Millwall 'keeper Kasey Keller reckons that facing the cream of the First Division's strikers is a picnic compared to getting to work.

The big American (right) has received rave reviews for his displays this season but he still can't cope with London's traffic.

He says: "Over in the States, if you want to go somewhere you just drive, simple as that. Here, you have to go East to get West, and round half-a-dozen one-way systems to get anywhere. I can't believe it."

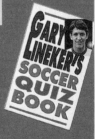

YOU'RE STILL THE G

JOHAN CRUYFF

'I admire Brian Clough more than most managers. His record is outstanding and he insists on playing football even when his team are up against it. His teams have been, and always will be, a joy to watch'

BOBBY ROBSON

'Cloughie has kept his sides playing the game the way it should be played for 27 years. He has never compromised and never given way to pressure, which is the mark of a great manager. I hope he gets away from the bottom of the League because he still has a lot to offer the game'

RON ATKINSON

'Cloughie has got to be the greatest manager of our time. He has won Championships with clubs you wouldn't exactly describe as 'big' or with great resources. That has to be a tremendous achievement. He will get Forest out of trouble this season and be around for a long time to come - probably long enough for another title success'

ALEX FERGUSON

'He's one of the all-time greats, rivalling men like Revie and Shankly. His domestic record speaks for itself and what he did in Europe with Forest was tremendous. He is a man who has stuck to his principles which is what I admire most about him. And he has STILL got what it takes to compete with the best'

PETER SHILTON

'There will never be another Brian Clough. He will go down in history as one of the best-ever managers, having established a reputation unmatched by his rivals. Most people still believe he should be manager of England and I'm sure he would have been as successful as he has been for Forest and Derby'

KENNY DALGLISH

'I think Brian will overcome Forest's poor start to the season and get them winning again. His single-mindedness has not made him the most popular of men, but it is his confidence in getting what he wants that will see him through. I wouldn't write him off just yet'

The knives are out for Brian Clough. For the first time in his glorious career as Forest boss, City Ground cries of *'Cloughie out'* have underlined the desperate situation Old Big Head and his young team find themselves in. But, while many people are wondering if Cloughie has finally *'shot it'*, some of the biggest names in management have leapt to his defence - and the message is clear...

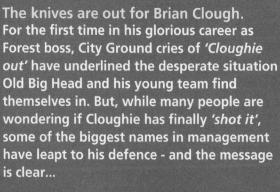

IT'S A FACT

Forest have already conceded as many League goals this season (24) as they did throughout the whole of the 1977-78 season - the last time they won the title.

And the great man himself says...

I'LL GET IT RIGHT

Our failure - my failure - to sign players has cost us dearly. I'm the first to admit that.

For a start we lost a player many believe to be one of the top defenders in the world. Desmond Walker wanted to taste life as a millionaire in Italy and good luck to the lad. I can't blame him for that.

I tried hard to keep hold of Darren Wassall, who would have stepped into Des's place, but he wanted to see if the grass was a bit greener down the A52 at Derby.

And yes, I let Teddy Sheringham go to Tottenham when I didn't have a quality striker ready to come in and replace him.

The fact of the matter was

14

CLOUGHIE: The record

A season-by-season guide to Cloughie's League record as Forest boss since he took over in January 1975:

Season	P	W	D	L	F	A	Final pos
1974-75	17	3	8	6	16	23	16th (Div 2)
1975-76	42	17	12	13	55	40	8th
1976-77	42	21	10	11	77	43	3rd
1977-78	42	25	14	3	69	24	1st (Div 1)
1978-79	42	21	18	3	61	26	2nd
1979-80	42	20	8	14	63	43	5th
1980-81	42	19	12	11	62	44	7th
1981-82	42	15	12	15	42	48	12th
1982-83	42	20	9	13	62	50	5th
1983-84	42	22	8	12	76	45	3rd
1984-85	42	19	7	16	56	48	9th
1985-86	42	19	11	12	69	53	8th
1986-87	42	18	11	13	64	51	8th
1987-88	40	20	13	7	67	39	3rd
1988-89	38	17	13	8	64	43	3rd
1989-90	38	15	9	14	55	47	9th
1990-91	38	14	12	12	65	50	8th
1991-92	42	16	11	15	60	58	8th
1992-93	15	2	4	9	11	24	???
TOTAL	732	323	202	207	1094	799	

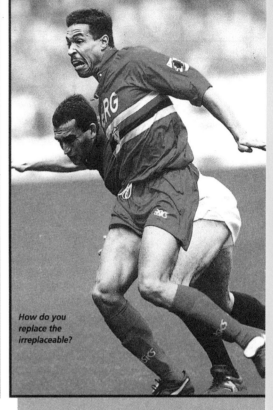

How do you replace the irreplaceable?

CLOUGHIE'S CUPS

League Championship	1978
European Cup	1979;1980
League Cup	1978;1979;1989;1990
European Super Cup	1980
Simod Cup	1989
ZDS Cup	1992

IT'S A FACT

Sheffield United's reincarnation last season offers Cloughie some hope. The Blades looked dead and buried at this stage but still managed to finish in the top half of the table.

IT'S CLOUGH AT THE BOTTOM

Forest have got a 50-50 chance of avoiding the drop this season. Over the last ten years, five of the clubs occupying bottom spot at this stage of the campaign have been relegated. So, as the saying goes, where there's life, there's hope - as our chart below shows:-

1982-83 Birmingham 17th

1983-84 Wolves 22nd

1984-85 Stoke 22nd

1985-86 West Brom 22nd

1986-87 Newcastle 17th

1987-88 Charlton 21st

1988-89 Newcastle 20th

1989-90 Sheff.Wed 18th

1990-91 Sheff.Utd 20th

1991-92 Sheff.Utd 9th

0   10   20
Final League Position

key: red: relegated   white: safe

that Teddy wanted to get back to London to be with his family and, once Spurs registered their interest, he would have walked down the M1.

It's easy to say I should have kept him but I have always maintained that, if a player's heart is not in the club, the sooner he goes the better. That's what happened to Teddy.

Of course, I have been looking for players - and still am - but I've been loathe to pay some of the daft prices that we have

been quoted in recent months.

I thought by now we would have had a change of luck but we'll stick at it until it does.

Being at the bottom of the League is a totally new experience for me and one I'm glad I've not been acquainted with before in management.

We'll pick ourselves up, dust ourselves down and get on with the job of winning a match or two. Things have got to change; I've just given the chairman a vote of confidence.

'Maybe it's because I'm a Londoner'

AIN'T NO STOPPING

Title-hungry Arsenal have got that Championship feeling again. George Graham's side are on course for their third title in five years... and it's all down to the Four Tops. Ian Wright, Kevin Campbell, Paul Merson and Alan Smith are the men who give The Gunners

'Alan Smith holds the ball up very well and is an excellent finisher'

Arsenal are back on the title trail. After a poor start - they won only three of their first nine League games - The Gunners have turned their season around. Here's how they've done it...

DATE	OPPONENTS	RESULT	SCORERS
Aug 15	Norwich (h)	L2-4	Bould, Campbell
Aug 18	Blackburn (a)	L0-1	
Aug 23	Liverpool (a)	W2-0	Limpar, Wright
Aug 26	Oldham (h)	W2-0	Winterburn, Wright
Aug 29	Sheff Wed (h)	W2-1	Parlour, Merson
Sep 2	QPR (a)	D0-0	
Sep 5	Wimbledon (a)	L2-3	Wright (2)
Sep 12	Blackburn (h)	L0-1	
Sep 19	Sheff Utd (a)	D1-1	Wright
Sep 28	Man City (h)	W1-0	Wright
Oct 3	Chelsea (h)	W2-1	Merson, Wright
Oct 17	Nottm Forest (a)	W1-0	Smith
Oct 24	Everton (h)	W2-0	Wright, Limpar
Nov 2	Crystal Palace (a)	W2-1	Merson, Wright
Nov 7	Coventry (h)	W3-0	Smith, Wright, Campbell

Sansom's verdict on...The Fab Four

George Graham reckons he's got the best strikers in the country, but are Arsenal's fab four really that good? We sought the neutral opinion of former Highbury favourite Kenny Sansom, who failed to stop them with Coventry earlier this month.

Alan Smith: Holds the ball up really well and is very good at bringing other players into the game. He's also an excellent finisher. Wasn't too confident at the start of the season and perhaps it was good for him to be left out, though I'm sure he wasn't happy. But now he knows he's going to get a run in the side, we'll see the best of him.

Ian Wright: The first time I saw him was when I played for QPR against Crystal Palace a few years ago and he made some great runs in that game, always looking to get into scoring positions. He's quick and skilful and has that bit of arrogance that sets him apart from other players. He always wants to be the best player on the pitch, and he often is.

Kevin Campbell: I played with him in Arsenal's reserves for a few months and knew then he was going to be special. He's big, powerful, good in the air, quick and has a good shot - everything a striker needs. Needs to keep listening and learning and he couldn't have three better players up front with him to learn from. He's going to be a real force in the game.

Paul Merson: Has always impressed me. Capable of doing the unexpected, but can also do the simple things as well, which is not always the case. So much skill and can do some incredible things on the ball. He's got a good touch, good vision and an excellent shot in either foot.

more firepower than any other team in the country.

And since the fab four were pitched together for the first time against Manchester City on September 28, Arsenal have put together a run of results which has sent them soaring to the top of the Premier League.

Alan Smith, out of the side until that 1-0 win, admits: "There's a real air of confidence about the place again and a strong feeling that we're back in business. We'll take some stopping, now.

"Our attacking formation has worked really well and is causing other teams problems.

"Although I'm still playing my usual role, Kevin, Ian and Paul have all adapted their game to drift wider or deeper, and opposing defenders don't know how to mark them all."

Yet not so long ago Smith wasn't even sure if he had much of a future at Highbury.

On the subs' bench while The Gunners put together an 18-game unbeaten run at the end of last season, the double SHOOT/adidas Golden Shoe winner knew he wouldn't be Graham's first choice striker when the Premier League kicked off.

That sparked all sorts of transfer rumours, with goal-shy Everton and Forest both showing an interest in the England international.

"I heard all the rumours and was feeling a little unsettled, but I had a chat with the Boss and he assured me I still had a future at Arsenal.

"It was simply a case of biding my time and fighting my way back into the side."

He's also back among the goals and now plans another Golden Shoe grab. "Wrighty's got a bit of a lead on me, so he's got to be favourite, but we really treasure that Golden Shoe at Arsenal and want to keep it here," he says.

And Smith pays tribute to the versatility of his three amigos which has made Arsenal's all-out attack such a success story.

"Paul's move back has probably helped him, because he loves running at defenders and his great close control is taking him into more central positions for a shot.

"He loves scoring spectacular goals from the edge of the box and is always trying to chip the 'keepers in training, which drives them mad.

"Ian has been a terrific signing. He's a real character and one of the most exciting players in the game.

"Because he plays off his instincts, nobody knows what he's going to do next. That doesn't cause any problems for me, though.

"Kevin has had to adjust his game more than anyone because he's really an out and out centre-forward. But he's taken the change in his stride and with his speed and strength there's no reason why he can't go on to play for England."

And though Smith refuses to commit himself to another Championship medal just yet, he does feel Arsenal's past experience will stand them in good stead.

"I'm not surprised Norwich and Blackburn are up at the top of the table right now because they've got some good players," he says.

"But when the jitters start to set in at Easter, we'll have been through it all before.

"This time last year we were all at a real low after going out of the European Cup to Benfica. That defeat cost us the title because it took us so long to get over it.

"Leeds are experiencing the same problems now and it's a lot harder to defend the Championship than to win it for the first time."

US NOW!

It was the shock transfer of the season and many people - most of them east of the Pennines - are still not over it. So just why did Eric Cantona swap his white rose for the red of Lancashire? SHOOT investigates.

Cantona made his United debut against Benfica

Eric Cantona hadn't even made a first team appearance for Manchester United before he was setting his sights on a unique Championship double.

Eric the Red helped Leeds to the title last season and within days of arriving at Old Trafford he announced: "I'm not here to play in the reserves; I'm here to play in the Premier League and win the Championship."

As Howard Wilkinson - and one or two managers before him - discovered, Cantona is not satisfied with playing a supporting role in any side.

He wants one of the two frontline places at Old Trafford and he says: "I will fight hard to win, and keep a place in the side. I have got a duty to score goals for Manchester United.

"I had a great year at Elland Road but I am sure I will enjoy myself even more with United."

Cantona has been angered by some reports of him kicking up a stink behind the scenes at Leeds and walking out on the club in protest at losing his first team place.

"I never had any problems with anyone at Leeds," he insists. "Everything was fine and if there hadn't been this offer from Manchester I would have stayed.

"Let's look at the facts. Apart from being rested

THE DIARY OF SECRET AGENT FERGIE

Alex Ferguson's under-cover coup to capture the gifted Frenchman was an operation MI5 would have been proud of.

Behind the scenes manoeuvres, cloak and dagger meetings between lawyers and chairmen...the Cantona deal had it all.

And these are the dramatic steps the United boss took to make sure the deal went through smoothly:-

OOH, AAH... MAN

between two European ties I played in all the matches. The only time I didn't play was against Arsenal when I was injured.

"Howard Wilkinson accuses me now but you only have to look at my performances for Leeds to be convinced I was worth my place. I was a hit with everyone.

"But my style of play will probably be better suited to Manchester United and I have been delighted with the reception given to me by the fans. Now it's up to me to prove to them what I can do."

CANTONA TRANSFER TALK

I have no doubts or fears about this player. It's well known that I only sign players who are keen to join my club and I was delighted that Eric did not hesitate nor wish to speak to anybody else. It's all made for him here. He tipped the title Leeds' way last season and has the ability to help us get the goals required to challenge for the Championship
ALEX FERGUSON

The signing represents a coup for Manchester United and their supporters. Eric has the style, skill and arrogance which will delight our fans. Sadly there are not too many names in English soccer that set the pulse racing as Eric does.
MARTIN EDWARDS

I have no hard feelings about Eric joining us. Football is all about challenges and competition and there will always be someone pushing you. But I'm not worried about losing my place because I am confident I can still do a good job for United. Cantona can increase our chances of winning the title and that has to be good for everyone at the club
BRIAN McCLAIR

When the news broke that Eric was going to Manchester there were so many people knocking on my door wanting to know if it was true and why it had happened. I could only tell them it was true. They were very upset and did not want to believe it
ISABELLE CANTONA

Eric the Red says 'make mine a double'

Wed. Nov.25...2.50pm:
Fergie makes a secret phone call to Leeds boss Howard Wilkinson to discuss the possibility of a straight cash deal for Cantona. Wilko plays ball and the deal is on.

Later the same day: United chairman Martin Edwards and Elland Road managing director Bill Fotherby are brought into the discussions and, within an hour, a fee of £1.2m is agreed.

Later that evening: The transfer talks hot up as Fergie discusses and agrees a contract with Cantona's lawyer Jacques Bertrand.

Thurs. Nov.26...11am:
Cantona knows the move is on and talks with both Bertrand and Ferguson. United and Leeds double check to make sure the deal is watertight.

Later the same day: Fergie meets Cantona and Bertrand at a secret rendezvous. A three-year deal is discussed and the French player agrees personal terms.

Fri. Nov.27...10am:
Cantona arrives from Leeds at Old Trafford. A contract is drawn up for signing and the player has extensive medical examinations and X-rays.

Later that morning: The transfer is settled and papers are rushed to the Premier League headquarters in London in the hope of registering Cantona in time to play Arsenal the following day.

Sat. Nov.28...10am:
Fergie realises the formalities haven't been completed in time for Cantona to make his debut, but the Frenchman flies to London to link up with his new team-mates.

Later in the evening: Cantona and the rest of the United squad fly out to Lisbon in readiness for his debut against Portuguese giants Benfica to celebrate Eusebio's 50th birthday.

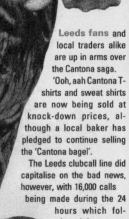

CHESTER!

He could be brilliant for United, he could be terrible. Who knows what may happen? One thing is for certain though, Cantona is an exceptionally gifted player who can turn a game with one flick of his boot. He is that good. Playing for a team like Manchester United could bring the very best out of him, but he is very much the master of his own destiny
MICHEL PLATINI

My interest is in the future of Leeds United while Eric Cantona's is with playing for Manchester United. He arrived as an exile from the French game with a far from flattering reputation yet I believe we have been good for each other. Eric walked out of this club happy, he wasn't pushed. This isn't the first time a popular player has departed and it won't be the last.
HOWARD WILKINSON

Eric's transfer was a complete surprise to the players. Time will tell if we will miss him, but the players are good enough to do well with or without him. The lads have proved they can win without Eric in the team
DAVID BATTY

Leeds fans and local traders alike are up in arms over the Cantona saga. 'Ooh, aah Cantona T-shirts and sweat shirts are now being sold at knock-down prices, although a local baker has pledged to continue selling the 'Cantona bagel'.

The Leeds clubcall line did capitalise on the bad news, however, with 16,000 calls being made during the 24 hours which followed the move.

Now the Manchester United promotion bandwagon expects to hit top gear with the club shop expecting a bumper Christmas turnover of Cantona goods.

SOUNESS FACTFILE

Born Edinburgh May 6, 1953.
Played for: Spurs, Middlesbrough, Liverpool, Sampdoria, Rangers, Scotland.
Managed: Rangers, Liverpool

Graeme took over at Liverpool on April 16, 1991, after they had won 5-4 win at Leeds. The team that day was: Hooper, Hysen, Burrows, Nicol, Ablett, Molby, Houghton, Beardsley, Rush, Speedie, Barnes.

The team that beat Crystal Palace 5-0 on November 28 1992 was: Hooper, Marsh, Burrows, Nicol, Piechnik, Hutchison, McManaman, Redknapp, Rosenthal, Barnes, Jones.

SOUNESS' SALES

Sold: Glenn Hysen, Gary Ablett, Ray Houghton, Peter Beardsley, David Speedie, Gary Gillespie, Steve Staunton, Jimmy Carter, Barry Venison, Steve McMahon, Kevin Lampkin, David Collins, Warren Godfrey.
Total: £9,025,000

Bought: Dean Saunders (since sold), Mark Wright, Mark Walters, Michael Thomas, Istvan Kozma, Paul Stewart, David James, Rob Jones , Torben Piechnik, Lee Jones, Scott Paterson.
Total: £12,575,000

It's impossible to escape talk this week of Kenny Dalglish's return to Anfield where he will cross managerial swords with Graeme Souness for the first time as Blackburn take on Liverpool in the Premier's battle of the big spenders.

*Left: The Old Pals Act will be forgotten on Saturday
Right: Mark Walters has followed Souness from Rangers to Liverpool*

SOUNESS

Battle of the

The best of friends but the keenest of rivals - that will be Graeme Souness and Kenny Dalglish this weekend.

Having come from similarly humble backgrounds in Glasgow and Edinburgh before playing together for Liverpool and Scotland, the two football giants have so much in common.

Both stepped into management at the top level as high profile player-bosses of Liverpool and Rangers - Britain's biggest clubs. And, having dominated their respective Leagues, both become victims of the pressures of management; with Kenny walking out on Liverpool to take a nine-month break and Graeme forced to undergo a triple, heart by-pass operation.

They are back in full swing now though, squaring up to their respective challenges - proving that money can buy success.

They have each spent millions rebuilding their teams, but it may surprise some people that Souness has spent almost £2 million more at Anfield than Dalglish at Blackburn.

One player who knows both men as well as anybody is Ian Rush, who has played with and under both of them during his glittering Anfield career.

The Welsh goal ace confirms: "Kenny and Graeme are great friends and used to room together, but once the match at Anfield kicks off they will be deadly enemies for 90 minutes."

Blackburn's success has surprised a lot of people, but not Rushie.

"Kenny is a tremendous maanger and has turned Rovers from a lowly Second Division side to genuine

RUSH on SOUNESS

Graeme is a completely different type of character to Kenny, yet they are similar in many ways, but Graeme is more flamboyant and shows his feelings more openly.

He is hard but fair as a manager, just as he was as a player. When you are winning, there is no better manager to play for.

He is just as ruthless as Kenny and not afraid to spend money, as he showed at Rangers. If things are not as he would like, he has no hesitation in going into the transfer market.

Like Kenny, Graeme tends to stand up in the dug-out, so when Blackburn come to Anfield, I'm sure we'll see both managers standing there shouting instructions'

DALGLISH'S DEALINGS

Sold: David Speedie, Scott Sellars, Mick Duxbury, Simon Garner, Lenny Johnrose, Craig Skinner, Keith Hill, Lee Richardson.
Total: £2,027,000

Bought: Alan Wright, Colin Hendry, Mike Newell, Gordon Cowans, Gary Tallon, Chris Price, Tim Sherwood, Roy Wegerle, Duncan Shearer (since sold), Matt Dickins, Alan Shearer, Stuart Ripley, Wayne Burnett, Lee Makel, Nicky Marker.
Total: £10,740,000

DALGLISH FACTFILE

Born Glasgow March 4, 1951
Played for: Celtic, Liverpool, Scotland.
Managed: Liverpool, Blackburn Rovers.

Kenny took over at Blackburn on October 12 1991, in time to watch them beat Plymouth 5-2. The team that day was: Mimms, Atkins, Moran, Duxbury, Hill, May, Irvine, Richardson, Reid, Garner, Speedie.

The team that beat QPR 1-0 recently to keep Blackburn among the Premier League leaders was: Mimms, Price, Wright, Sherwood, Hendry, Moran, Ripley, Cowans, Shearer, Newell, Wilcox.

DALGLISH

Alan Shearer will be the main threat to Liverpool

ig spenders

Championship challengers. He saw the job as a challenge and has thrived on it, and I think Ray Harford has helped him a lot."

While Rovers were getting off to a great start, Liverpool were in the rare position of struggling at the wrong end of the table. Now they are steadily moving up and Rush says: "The same people who were writing us off a few weeks ago are suddenly tipping us for the League, but it doesn't bother us.

"We've had a difficult start and know that two swallows don't make a summer, but now we are starting to gel, the young lads are starting to shine and we are all playing with loads more confidence.

"Also, we are getting back players such as John Barnes, who can win a match with one stroke of genius, and are back to the ideal situation of having everyone fighting for a place.

"If we are to make a serious challenge for the League, we cannot afford to lose our home games and must look to win more away games, so we'll be very disappointed if we don't beat Blackburn."

RUSH on DALGLISH

'Kenny is very quiet until you get to know him, and even then he likes to keep himself to himself. That's how he was on the field and how he is as a manager. But he was always very good to me.

He has a quiet determination, and knows exactly what he wants. He has spent a lot of money at Blackburn, but then he has had to in order to win promotion and challenge for honours. And it must be said that he has spent wisely.

Like Graeme, Kenny demands total commitment from his players, and if you give 100 per cent, you will be treated fairly'

GAZZA'S CHRISTMAS

The Prince of English football; the King of Rome - Paul Gascoigne is back in business as one of the most talked about players in world football. This time though, it's Gazza who's doing all the talking in another SHOOT exclusive (and we mean exclusive!).

After being out of the game for so long, what's it like to be a national hero all over again?
I'm not a 'national hero'. The England performances against Norway and Turkey were team efforts. That's why I handed back the flight tickets I was awarded as the man of the match against the Turks. Every goal needs a build-up and scoring twice doesn't entitle me to a knighthood. Not just yet, anyway.

How would you assess your first few months at Lazio?
Good for me but not so good for

the team. But we had a bit of luck against Pescara recently - when a last-minute goal gave us a valuable victory - so perhaps we've turned the corner after too many near misses and too many draws. Against Roma I felt one of our shots crossed the line but I suppose in a match like that nobody takes any chances - most of all the referee. I heard he has a wife and kids to support!

What was it like playing in your first Rome derby?
It was an incredible occasion, the biggest game I've played in - bigger even than the 1990 World Cup. I thought I knew all about pressure until then. The goal was very important for me, the team, the club and Dino Zoff as well. The Press asked who I wanted to dedicate it to and I jokingly said 'Sciosa's teddy bear' when perhaps I should have said Zoff.

How do you get on with Dino Zoff?
He's been very patient with me and is a nice, honest, hard-working man. We get on well, though I wish he'd give up smoking - it's ruining his chances of getting back into the national side! There are times when I feel a bit sorry for him because of the pressure from the fans and the media. I think he finds me a bit hard to understand...and not just because of my Geordie accent.

How would you describe your relationship with the Lazio fans?
They've been a bit hard on the team and the manager, but seem to appreciate I am doing my best for them - although my 'real best' is yet to come. When I scored the equaliser against Roma I just wanted to jump in among them and get swallowed up. Believe me, those tears were real - a mixture of joy and relief.

Can the intensity of the support be a bit frightening at times?
Sometimes, yes. They are very emotional people. There have been occasions when I'm with the team that they have tried to climb into my hotel bedroom. I was even assaulted by Roma supporting nuns when I went to visit my girlfriend's daughter in hospital the other week!

Are you able to go out in Rome without being pestered?
I'm finding it easier to go out in public, though wherever I go the fans want autographs and love to talk about football. Now that the first derby match of the season is over they are already talking about the next one...and the return against Milan. Even though we lost the first game against Van Basten and Co, it was still the best game I've played in all season.

What's your relationship with the Italian media like?
It's improving all the time. We had a bad start when they told some 'untruths' about me and I wouldn't talk to them for two weeks. Everybody said I wouldn't get away with that but I did and they've been much better since then. I don't get asked nearly as much about my personal life as I did in England.

Is it true you don't get on with Lazio's other 'foreigners', Riedle, Doll and Winter?
I get on well with everyone at the club, despite the fact the papers have said a few things about me and the Germans. I think Doll and Riedle are very good players and Winter is a real tough cookie.

Who's your best friend at the club?
The reserve team 'keeper Fernando Orsi - or 'Nando' as we tend to call him. He's a really good, experienced 'keeper who's dying to play in England. Because we don't have a reserve team he gets very few chances and the club wouldn't demand a big fee for him. So, if there's anybody out there looking for a 'keeper, you could do a lot worse than take my mate Nando on loan.

What's the best thing about living in Italy?
The Roman lifestyle and the pasta. I've gone crazy over Mozzarella cheese. I eat so much of it, it's not worth keeping it in the fridge.

Do you get regular supplies of anything sent from England?
The English newspapers, which is strange because I never read them when I was in England. I also get visitors to bring plenty of English tea and biscuits...and my copy of SHOOT, of course.

Who is the best player you've come up against in Italy?
My Lazio team-mate Signori is one of the best, but Marco Van Basten still takes some beating. There's a world of difference between the Serie A and the English Premier League, mainly because the game is slower over here and there are more players prepared to put their foot on the ball.

You're known as a practical joker, but have you been the victim of any pranks?
I've been the victim more than the villain just lately. The last time I was on England duty, someone cut my socks off at the bottom. Everybody said it was Carlton Palmer, but I suspect a Geordie hand at work. I'll let you work out the name of the prankster for yourselves.

Will you be coming home for Christmas?
There's a bit of a break in the season out here and I'm looking forward to getting back for Christmas if I can. I got back for my sister's wedding last month (when I took the blame for a fire alarm going off at 3am in the guests' hotel even though I was 300 miles away with the England squad) and it will be nice to see all the family again.

Have you changed since you moved to Italy?
I don't think so. I still like a laugh, I still find it hard to relax, and I still just live for football. But I don't react the way I used to in certain situations. If there's trouble on the field - or off it - I just walk away. One lesson I've learned is not to get involved.

Have you had to take much stick on the field?
All the warnings I was given about being a marked man have proved untrue. For the most part it has all been very sporting - though we do have our share of players in Italy who will be up for Oscars one day.

How close are we to seeing the 'real' Paul Gascoigne?
Scoring in consecutive games against Roma and Pescara didn't do me any harm at all - I was beginning to think the goals would never come. I'm getting fitter all the time and, when I'm 101 per cent fit, I'm sure it will all come together - goals AND performances.

Finally, do you have a message for all your fans in England?
I want to wish all the fans, both here in Italy and back home, a Merry Christmas and a Happy New Year - and thank them all for their support and belief during what has been a difficult period for me. I hope the coming 12 months brings them and the England team everything they want.
Ciao.

23

PREMIER LEAGUE: *WINNERS*

When Scotland's football historians dissect 1992, only one name will be worth talking about....RANGERS.

With only two defeats in the whole of the year, a clean sweep of the domestic honours and the defeat of English Champions Leeds for a place in the European Cup Champions League, Rangers are almost invincible.

It's a record that's on a par with Milan's dominance in Italy, and with their wealth, stadium and facilities leaving all the rest trailing it's fair to say Rangers are now the Milan of British football.

One man perfectly placed to assess that judgment is striker Mark Hateley, who wore the red and black of Milan in the 80s and is now spearheading the Cup Rangers reign.

SCOTTISH CUP: *WINNERS*

SKOL CUP: *WINNERS*

EUROPEAN CU

1992: THE YEAR OF THE TEDDY BEAR

The statistics prove just how comprehensive Rangers' dominance has been this year.

LEAGUE
P 37 W 28 D 7 L 2 F 85 A 23 Pts 63

SCOTTISH CUP
P 5 W 5 D 0 L 0 F 9 A 1

SKOL CUP
P 5 W 5 D 0 L 0 F 18 A 4

EUROPEAN CUP
P 5 W 4 D 1 L 0 F 9 A 4

TOTAL
Played 52 Won 42 Drawn 8 Lost 2
Goals For 121 Goals Against 32

Scorers:

Ally McCoist *50*

Mark Hateley *21*

Alexei Mikhailichenko *12*

John Brown *6*

Ian Durrant, Pieter Huistra *5*

Dale Gordon, Richard Gough, Stuart McCall *3*

Ian Ferguson, Davie McPherson, Gary McSwegan, Trevor Steven *2*

Scott Nisbet, Paul Rideout, Gary Stevens *1*

Own Goals *2*

THE IBROX INS & OUTS

Signed	From	Fee
Paul Rideout	Notts County	£500,000
David McPherson	Hearts	£1.3 million
Ally Maxwell	Motherwell	£300,000
Trevor Steven	Marseille	£2.4 million
	TOTAL	£4.5 million

Sold	To	Fee
John Spencer	Chelsea	£450,000
Paul Rideout	Everton	£500,000
Nigel Spackman	Chelsea	£485,000
	TOTAL	£1.435 million

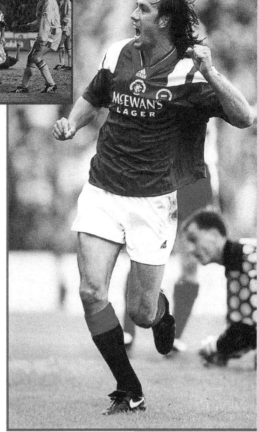

SHOOT: *What is the secret of Rangers' success?*
HATELEY: Consistency. We've never let our guard slip against smaller teams and keep grinding out comprehensive wins.

Like Milan, we have great depth in our squad. Rangers obviously don't have their array of big stars but both clubs are able to bring in top players as replacements when others get injured. In the last few weeks we've had Alexei Mikhailichenko and Dale Gordon on the bench and the club spent £3.5 million on them.

SHOOT: *Only Celtic, last March, and Dundee, back at the start of this season, have beaten Rangers in 1992. Can any other team in Scotland stop you?*
HATELEY: We're definitely the strongest team in Scotland. Others raise their game against us, but that only makes us try harder. Winning is one thing, but the secret is hanging on to that success. If you don't maintain that high standard you're on a slippery slope.

A lot of the credit is down to Walter Smith. He's getting a lot of publicity now, but a lot of people down south wondered why he was given the job when Graeme Souness left.

But you have to be a clever manager to be at the top and that's Walter. At Rangers we always get rid of two or three players at the end of every season and bring in two or three others. Walter sees our weaknesses and acts on them long before opponents get the chance to notice those weak spots.

The other similarity we have with Milan is the men who run the clubs. Milan have Silvio Berlusconi and we have David Murray. They are two chairmen who want the very best. That's what they have in their business lives and they use the same single-mindedness to achieve that goal in football.

ANGERS
THE MILAN OF BRITAIN

SHOOT: *So are Rangers now in the same European super-team bracket as Milan, Real Madrid and Barcelona?*
HATELEY: Absolutely. Off the park there's never been any doubt. Now we're getting there on the pitch, too. In fact, in many ways we have assets that even Milan can't match.

For instance, they don't own their own stadium, which is rented and shared with Inter. The San Siro looks impressive but because it's owned by the local council it can't compare with the restaurants, corporate entertainment facilities and all the trappings that Rangers have.

Ibrox is on show seven days a week and that is important in promoting the club. It's among the best four or five stadiums in Europe.

The only thing that lets us down is that we don't have our own training camp. Milan have a spectacular place in the hills called Milanello which is more like a country club.

SHOOT: *What have been the key areas of Rangers' dominance in 1992?*
HATELEY: The whole team - from one to eleven. I know Ally McCoist and I get a lot of publicity but we're not foolish enough to let that go to our heads. What we've achieved is because of a squad of 16 players and team work.

Our defence is very solid. Andy Goram fitted in superbly after taking over from Chris Woods and David Robertson's arrival strengthened things, too. Richard Gough showed for Scotland in Sweden what a great player he is and in the summer we added Dave McPherson. Now that Gary Stevens is back, that's an international back four. And don't forget John Brown, who has been superb.

There's some real class in midfield, too, and that department has also got stronger this year now that Ian Durrant is back and Trevor Steven has returned from France. Stuart McCall and Ian Ferguson provide the power.

Up front, me and Ally have obviously been clicking and Pieter Huistra has provided good service along with Dale. And then there's guys like Alexei...I could go on and on.

The season before I came we only conceded 17 goals and scored about 40 in the League. Now we concede about twice as many but score three times that at the other end. We're breaking scoring records all the time and I think the fans appreciate that.

SHOOT: *And what of your own contribution?*
HATELEY: I'm playing as well as I've ever done, which is down to being fit. I'm not getting as many injuries as I did at Milan and Monaco, which is amazing when you consider I'm playing twice the number of games. I scored 25 last season and am hopeful of doing that again this time. Important goals like those against Leeds and Marseille mean this is one of the best periods of my life.

SHOOT: *Can the Rangers domination of Scottish football continue?*
HATELEY: That's our aim. We've set our standards and we want to keep to them.

SHOOT: *Thanks very much. Happy Christmas.*
HATELEY: My pleasure.

GOLDEN GOALS

No.21 ALAN SHEARER
ENGLAND V TURKEY
WORLD CUP QUALIFIER 1992

Paul Gascoigne's superb flick sets Ian Wright free down the left flank. The Arsenal striker crosses to the near post and Alan Shearer dives to head England's second goal in their 4-0 World Cup win over Turkey at Wembley.

Mehmet

Hayrettin

Shearer

Gascoigne

Wright

Wright

SHOOT

HEY, HEY, ALRIGHT....

CALM DOWN!

He's cocky...he's gifted...and trouble seems to follow him around.

Sounds like the perfect description of Paul Gascoigne - but it also applies to Dundee United problem kid Duncan Ferguson.

Yet one man believes the Tannadice tear-away can still become Scotland's next superstar ...if he steers clear of bust-ups OFF the field.

Hibs striker Darren Jackson has partnered both Gazza and Fergie in his time and says: "There will only ever be one Gazza, but in terms of personality, Fergie comes close.

"They're both daft, with bags of self-confidence and great talent. They both have a great love of the game and put everything into it, but it's off the park they find trouble."

Punch-ups in his home town of Stirling - which earned him a £100 fine for breach of the peace - and allegations of a hotel prank in Switzerland with the Scotland side three months ago have cast a cloud over 20-year-old Fergie's rapid rise.

He's also due to appear in court soon on an assault charge.

And though the 6ft 2in beanpole was part of Scotland's European Championship squad in Sweden last summer, he's since been axed by Andy Roxburgh.

But Jackson, who left Dundee United for Hibs in the summer, believes Ferguson can still make the grade.

"He's not a trouble maker but he's got to learn that he's going to attract publicity and that it's best to keep out of the public eye," says Jackson.

"Just like Gazza, he now has a reputation and when he goes out other guys will try to wind him up.

"Gazza only ever wanted to be one of the lads when we were together at Newcastle and then in London with Spurs. But there comes a time when that is no longer possible.

"I feel sorry for Duncan in that respect. His height has a lot to do with his problems. When he walks into a bar he just towers over everyone.

"But if he can sort himself out, there's no doubt he can become a great player.

"I loved playing with him because he takes the pressure right of you. He's brilliant in the air when he puts his mind to it and has a great touch.

"I also think he's going to become a great goalscorer because he's learned how to use his strength and can keep defenders off the ball all day."

Problems off the park? Your boss at his wits end? Fear not. Your life is about to change with SHOOT's

TEN POINT PLAN FOR SOCCER SAINTLINESS

- Hang around with Trevor Brooking and Gary Lineker
- Put ice cubes down your underpants
- Drink more Horlicks
- Take elocution lessons
- Meet a nice girl, settle down and raise a family
- Do a lot of good work for charity
- Attend more bible study classes
- Go to bed with a good book just after Coronation Street
- Swap that flashy Italian sports car for a Reliant Robin
- Develop a hobby - butterfly collecting, ballroom dancing or philately perhaps

On second thoughts - who wants to hang around with a saint anyway? Stuff it, Fergie. We like you just the way you are.

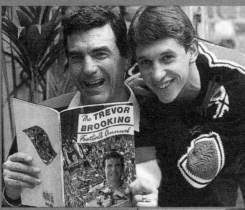

'So Trev, what do you think of Fergie?' 'Well Gary, I wouldn't really like to say.'

MY CALCIO KINGS

VLADIMIR JUGOVIC
(Sampdoria)

The former Red Star midfielder hasn't really been given the credit he deserves, mainly because he's been in the shadow of Italian star Roberto Mancini.

But the truth is that, whenever Mancini has been out injured or suspended, Jugovic has filled the role brilliantly and Sampdoria haven't missed the ace in their pack.

Anyone who can come in and replace a player like Mancini has to be something special.

Jugovic seems to have everything. He is quick, has great stamina...and scores goals. I love the way he runs at players and is always looking to attack.

MARCO VAN BASTEN
(AC Milan)

An obvious choice, perhaps, but you can't ignore a player who sets such high standards and then manages to top them year in, year out.

And it would be wrong to suggest that any striker worth his salt would score goals for a side like Milan. No matter how many chances a team creates, a player has still got to put the ball away and he does it with style.

Not just against second rate opposition either. His four-goal blast against Swedish Champions Gothenburg - not to mention his international record - confirms that he can do it at any level.

I'm sure he will come back from his injury set-back - an operation on a troublesome ankle - as good as ever.

PAUL GASCOIGNE (Lazio)
How could I leave my England buddy out of this illustrious group? He has done tremendously well and I'm full of admiration for the way he has handled all the pressure.

To come back from a long-term injury and set Italy - not just Rome - alight the way he has epitomises the character and personality of a special player.

They said he would struggle to come to terms with the Italian way of life, but he has proved them all wrong. He loves it out here - and the Italians love him.

Whether the publicity he gets is good or bad, he thrives on it and takes it all in his stride. He has taken hold of the Lazio side and is now their team leader.

TOTO SCHILLACI
(Inter Milan)

I've selected him because of the way he has bounced back after two torturous years with my current club Juventus.

After his heroic performances during the 1990 World Cup -

PLATT PRIZE OFFER

Thanks to our colleagues from Sondico we have got a host of David Platt goodies to give away in this magnificent competition.

Answer the two questions right and you could be in with a chance of winning the following:-

10 David Platt shinguards
10 David Platt footballs
10 David Platt posters

Sondico

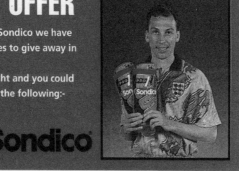

QUESTIONS
1. Against which country did David score England's only goal in the European Championship finals?
2. Which of David's fellow 'foreigners' at Juventus is sidelined with a broken leg this season?

Send your entries to: SHOOT/Platt competition (9/1) 25th Floor, King's Reach Tower, Stamford Street, London SE1 9LS.

STEFAN EFFENBERG
(Fiorentina)

Everyone raves about Michael Laudrup and the impact he has made at Fiorentina this season but his good mate Effenberg is the man who makes the team tick.

When he plays, Fiorentina are on song. Similarly, when he doesn't play, the team is not so effective. That's why he is in my magnificent seven.

He came to everyone's notice for Germany during the European Championship in Sweden and has been playing brilliantly ever since.

Fiorentina are a very attacking side and much of that is down to the fact that Effenberg, an all-round midfield player, loves to get forward in search of goals himself.

GIANLUCA VIALLI (Juventus)

I have nothing but the utmost respect and admiration for Vialli -and not just because he's my Juventus team-mate and next door neighbour.

He's one of the best professionals I've ever come across and, despite the superstar status he is rightly afforded, he is a brilliant bloke too.

Because he hasn't scored too many goals this season he has come in for a lot of criticism (not that it worries him). But that is totally unfair because the work he does for the rest of team is immense.

People talk about the goals of Baggio and Moller but they wouldn't be getting them if it wasn't for the efforts of Vialli. He is the fulcrum of virtually all our play.

when he finished as leading scorer with six goals - everyone expected him to reproduce that sort of form the next season.

But Schillaci has never been an 18/20 goals-a-season man. He just happened to hit a purple patch during Italia 90 and was thrust into the spotlight.

For two years he was under immense pressure and it is only now, since his move from Juve to Inter, that he has recaptured his best form. He deserves a lot of credit for that.

GIUSEPPE SIGNORI (Lazio)

He's really taken Serie A by storm this season and while he might be a new name to Channel 4 fans, I rated him as a player to watch when he was with Foggia last year.

He managed to score goals in a struggling side (11 I believe) and now that he's playing for a team

which creates chances galore I'm not surprised he's top of the charts.

In fact, now that Marco Van Basten has been sidelined by injury, he's got a great chance of finishing the season as Italy's most prolific striker.

He's a thin, waif-like figure but he's so quick and has a lethal left peg. He fully deserves his place in the Italian national side.

Manchester United keep up their Double bid with an FA Cup Fifth Round trip to Sheffield United this Sunday. But Old Trafford insiders are getting even more excited about the next generation of Red Devils ready to pull on the famous United shirt.

They're the best bunch of kids I've ever worked with

THE OLD TRAFFORD EIGHT
Meet the kids who've set the soccer world alight.

CHRIS CASPER (17)

Son of the former Burnley player and manager Frank Casper, Chris is regarded by the United coaching staff as having the potential to become one of the best centre-backs and sweepers in the modern game. His greatest strengths are his vision and ability to read the game with uncanny accuracy.

BEN THORNLEY (17)

A local hero from nearby Bury with two good feet and a great pair of lungs. A true flying machine who prefers to raid down the left but is able to switch flanks, and has more tricks up his sleeves than Paul Daniels. Has a great shot and, like Lee Sharpe and Ryan Giggs, loves taking on and tormenting defenders.

KEITH GILLESPIE (17)

A brilliant right-winger (right) from Ulster with exceptional speed and crossing ability - not to mention a keen eye for goal. He has already made his first team debut and scored in the FA Cup win over Bury as a more than adequate replacement for Old Trafford sensation Ryan Giggs.

NICKY BUTT (18)

Manchester-born midfield dynamo (above) with the engine of Bryan Robson and the scoring ability of David Platt. Building a reputation for strong tackling and running - and, even though he's had no League experience, several top European clubs have shown an interest.

PAUL SCHOLES (18)

An influential midfielder who, according to our sources inside Old Trafford, has been the most outstanding player in the youth team this season. A great passer of the ball who likes to control proceedings in the middle of the park where he has the vision to create goals out of nothing.

DAVID BECKHAM (17)

London-born midfielder but Red through and through. Creative and elegant but dangerous and uncompromising going forward. His playmaking skills are second to none . Came on as a second-half sub against Brighton in the Coca-Cola Cup in September.

JOHN O'KANE (18)

Powerful right-back from the Nottingham area who is strong in the tackle and capable of getting forward in support of the attack. Tall and well-built, he is comfortable on the ball and not afraid to take players on. His size makes him a handful in the box at set pieces.

30

FERGIE'S BRAT PACK

The capture of Eric Cantona may well prove to be the key which unlocks Manchester United's Championship treasure chest. But the Old Trafford insiders insist that even the flamboyant Frenchman won't be Alex Ferguson's best bit of transfer business this season.

Because Fergie, who has spent more than £19 million in his six years as United boss, has just secured the long-term futures of a crop of youngsters who could make that figure seem like peanuts in years to come.

For when they're not talking about that elusive title or this Sunday's FA Cup trip to Sheffield United, the talk at Old Trafford soon turns to the club's all-conquering youth team which has already been compared to the brilliant Busby Babes.

And the United chief, with unprecedented forward planning, has just signed up EIGHT of last season's FA Youth Cup winners on four-year contracts.

Teenage sensation Ryan Giggs and comeback king Lee Sharpe are the young men of the moment, but Fergie believes that future success for the club lies at the feet of his gifted pack of cost-nothing whizz kids.

They are all still young enough to play in the youth team but some are already knocking on the first team door and could be household names this time next season.

The fact that Fergie has signed them up on such long-term deals speaks volumes about the faith he has in them and the United boss says: "These boys are the best crop I have had in my management career.

"In fact, they could turn out to be the best the club has ever had. I don't have any doubt that they will reach the very top - that's how highly I regard them.

"To have them all come through like this is very rare and now it's just a matter of fitting them into the first team."

When the Busby Babes took the title in 1956 - finishing 11 points ahead of second placed Blackpool - the average age of the team was just 22.

Fergie's fledglings have an average age of 17 at the moment and the boss says: "With their potential and promise, who knows what they could go on to achieve in five years time."

The class of 89

This isn't the first time United have got all hot and bothered about their youngsters. Four years ago we had 'Fergie's Fledglings' when eight lads aged 20 and under bailed the club out of an injury crisis midway through the 1988-89 season. But what's happened to them since?
SHOOT reveals all...

Lee Martin: Scored the FA Cup Final winner in 1990 (above) but then suffered a serious back injury and is now battling back in the reserves.
Lee Sharpe: Shot to instant fame with club and country and, after beating illness and injury, is one of the few successes of the class of '89.

Russell Beardsmore: He's made only a dozen appearances for United since the 88-89 season and last year went on loan to Blackburn. Now back in the stiffs at Old Trafford.
Mark Robins: Nicknamed 'Rummenigge' for all the goals he scored in the reserves, he grew tired of waiting for his first team chance and his is now a hit at Norwich after his £800,000 summer move.
Tony Gill: Made ten appearances before injury forced him out of the game.

David Wilson: His only flirtation with first team stardom came during the 1988-89 season and he has since left United and drifted into non-League obscurity.
Giualano Maiorana: Burst onto the scene from sleepy Cambridgeshire and was hailed as 'the new George Best'. He's still at United, but only in the reserves.
Deniol Graham: Former Welsh Under-21 international who managed just two League games in four seasons at Old Trafford. Moved to Barnsley in 1991.

GARY NEVILLE (17)

Captain of the youth team and a rock solid central defender (below) who loves to get forward. He was a key figure in United's FA Youth Cup triumph last season and, like Gillespie, has already had a taste of first team action as a sub against Torpedo Moscow in the UEFA Cup.

RYAN GIGGS

THE WONDER YEARS

Man.United & Wales

Twice voted the Young Player of the Year, Manchester United's Ryan Giggs is set to become the star of the decade. SHOOT plots the amazing rise of the Welsh wizard tipped by Ian Rush to become 'the best player in the world'.

THE EARLY DAYS

Ryan was born in Cardiff on November 29, 1973 - during the season Manchester United were relegated to Division two for the first time in 37 years. His surname then was Wilson.

His Dad, Danny, was a Rugby League player and when he signed for Swinton in 1975, the family moved to Manchester.

It was during his time at Moorside High School in Swinton that his soccer skills developed and teachers recognised he was no ordinary pupil.

His former headmistress, Mrs Alison Banks, recalls: "He was a good pupil and he worked hard but it was his sporting talent which shone through.

"I'm not surprised to hear that he does not particularly enjoy the limelight as a soccer star. He was never the sort to stand up and give a speech in a school debate.

"The fact that he has gone on to achieve such a lot so quickly is a delight to all of us. We are very proud of him."

THE TEENAGE TRANSFORMATION

Before he became a Red Devil, Ryan was a boy in blue as a schoolboy star with Manchester City.

It was at that time he was made captain of the England schoolboys side, skippering the country nine times during the 1989-90 season.

ENTER GEORGE BEST MK II

Ryan kicked off his United career in the youth team but was soon staking a claim for promotion to 'the big time'.

And it wasn't long before his performances were bearing comparisons with former Old Trafford legend George Best.

Manager Alex Ferguson couldn't hide his delight. "He is definitely the best prospect I've ever had as a manager," enthused Fergie.

He made his first team debut on February 26, 1991 against Sheffield United, coming on for the last five minutes of the 2-1 defeat but it was the start of something very special...

...as he proved when he made his full debut in front of 40,000 at Old Trafford in the Manchester derby with rivals City. It was a fairytale start as United won 1-0 with Ryan scoring the winner.

Since then Giggs has gone from strength to strength, prompting AC Milan to bid for him and Fergie to say: "We have been delighted with his progress. He has remarkable balance, which is the final part in a great player."

THE INTERNATIONAL STAR

When Welsh manager Terry Yorath first saw Ryan play for the United youth team he knew he was watching a very special and rare talent.

"He was just 16 and head and shoulders above everyone else," Yorath remembers.

"I picked him for the Welsh youth team to find out a bit more about him. He hasn't looked back since.

"There was some talk of him playing for England but that was just a joke. He only played for England schoolboys because he was going to an English school.

"He was born in Cardiff of Welsh parents and he is Welsh through and through.

"Our fans think he is marvellous. He doesn't get ruffled by anything, he's quiet and very professional. There really is only one Ryan Giggs."

Yorath gave him his Under-21 debut against Poland on May 29, 1991 and his first full cap a few months later against Germany.

Since then he has become a hero.

Fellow international star Ian Rush even goes as far as to say: "He has the ability to become one of the greatest players in the world." Few people would argue with that.

England manager of the time Dave Bushell recalls: "Even then Ryan had a body swerve that was the best I had ever known."

Ryan hit four goals for England and set up quite a few for his partner...Nick Barmby.

The Spurs sensation remembers Giggs as 'something special' and says: "I'm not surprised he has achieved so much."

He switched to Old Trafford during a period of upheaval. His mother and father split and he took his mother's maiden name of Giggs.

He signed his first contract for United on December 1, 1990.

THAT'S LIFE

Vinnie Jones

With the help of the game's biggest names, we will give you a unique insight into the boy and the man behind the player through their very own family albums...it's another trend-setting feature from SHOOT - the soccer mag with all the best ideas!

This week we take a peek into Vinnie's very own scrapbook and trace the rise of his astonishing career from nowhere to Wembley wonderland.

Vinnie says: "I'm not a great one for keeping photos, but, with the help of my family, I hope these pictures give an insight into life with the Joneses.

"I hope you have as much fun as I did looking through these snaps. But it's the last time I'll be searching around my dusty loft for a while - the things those boys at SHOOT make you do for a story."

Young, bright-eyed and goofy. Check out the wicked hair style and snazzy school tie.

Back at Wembley. I took my chance to kiss the greatest Cup of all after helping Wimbledon to beat Liverpool in the 1988 FA Cup Final.

From hod-carrier to male model. Going through my photos, I even came across one of me posing as a page seven fella for a newspaper more used to printing the opposite sex on Page 3.

That's me on the left, the angelic one in the striped pyjamas, with assorted family members. My dad, Peter, is the one wearing the tie. There are nine in my dad's family - all younger than him!

That's me handing over a pennant before playing my first match against a Merseyside team - Burscough Dynamoes - when I was 13.

NEXT WEEK
We rifle through Spurs hot-shot Sheri's family album

Dealing out the cards on the coach to Wembley with Wealdstone for the 1985 FA Challenge Trophy. I can't remember if I won at cards, but we beat Boston United 2-1 to win the Cup.

Brotherly love. Dreaming about winning at Wembley with my sister, Ann. I'm very protective towards my family - they've all been a great help to me.

Here's me, at Wimbledon, protecting my ear from a member of the famous Vidal Sassoon hairdressing salon.

TRICK

Q: Do you think you stayed at Forest too long?
Roy: If Forest hadn't gone down I'd still be there now. I wouldn't have moved for another couple of years.

Q: Did you have a clause in your Forest contract which said you could move on if they went down?
Roy: It stated that if the club went down I would be allowed to leave for a certain amount of money.

Q: Were you worried because United left it so late to come and get you?
Roy: Yes, things did drag on for a bit but I was always patient and waited for the right club to make their move. Thankfully United did.

Q: Are you fed-up with ex-pros telling you how to live your life at Old Trafford off the pitch?
Roy: Yes I am. There are only a certain few people I listen to. I've had a lot of advice from players in the Irish squad like Kevin Moran and David O'Leary. Alex Ferguson has also been good.

Q: How do you feel about agents?
Roy: I spoken to hundreds of agents over the last few years but I basically didn't trust any of them until I spoke to the PFA. There is no 20 per cent of this or that, they just charge a reasonable fee.

Q: Do you get grumpy sometimes?
Roy: Yes. I've got a really bad temper and it shows when people annoy me. Sometimes straight after a game if we've had a bad result then I'm in a bad mood.

Q: How do you react when somebody annoys you?
Roy: Well you are always going to get one or two idiots who won't leave you alone and are ready to have a go and I'm afraid that does my head in. But now I'm here I've got to be more careful off the park.

Q: Do you think you let Forest down by getting into trouble off the pitch?
Roy: Without a doubt but we all make mistakes and I'm only 22. I'm sure I'll make a lot more but hopefully I've calmed down a bit.

Q: Why did you turn down Arsenal and Blackburn?
Roy: I agreed a deal with Rovers and got flack for going back on it, but I here to look after myself.

Q: How would you feel if you crash of the European Cup and don't make it to the World Cup finals?
Roy: I wouldn't like to bump into me afterwards either. It could change my whole career in the short term.

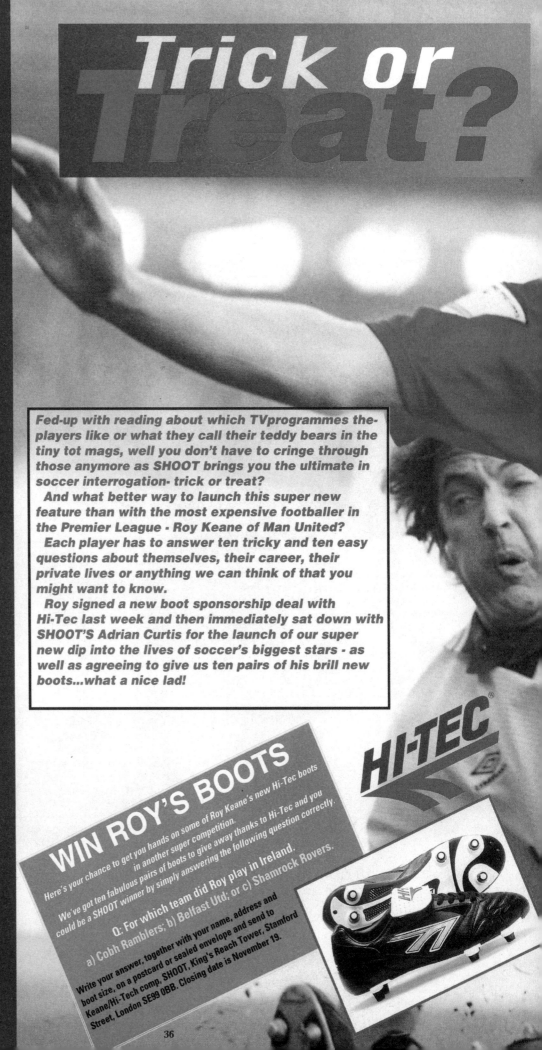

Trick or Treat?

Fed-up with reading about which TV programmes the players like or what they call their teddy bears in the tiny tot mags, well you don't have to cringe through those anymore as SHOOT brings you the ultimate in soccer interrogation- trick or treat?

And what better way to launch this super new feature than with the most expensive footballer in the Premier League - Roy Keane of Man United?

Each player has to answer ten tricky and ten easy questions about themselves, their career, their private lives or anything we can think of that you might want to know.

Roy signed a new boot sponsorship deal with Hi-Tec last week and then immediately sat down with SHOOT'S Adrian Curtis for the launch of our super new dip into the lives of soccer's biggest stars - as well as agreeing to give us ten pairs of his brill new boots...what a nice lad!

WIN ROY'S BOOTS

Here's your chance to get you hands on some of Roy Keane's new Hi-Tec boots in another super competition.

We've got ten fabulous pairs of boots to give away thanks to Hi-Tec and you could be a SHOOT winner by simply answering the following question correctly.

Q: For which team did Roy play in Ireland.
a) Cobh Ramblers; b) Belfast Utd; or c) Shamrock Rovers.

Write your answer, together with your name, address and boot size, on a postcard or sealed envelope and send to Keane/Hi-Tech comp, SHOOT, King's Reach Tower, Stamford Street, London SE99 0BB. Closing date is November 19.

HI-TEC

36

TREAT

Q: What has been your most embarrassing moment?
Roy: That's easy. It was my somersault after scoring against Norwich in the FA Cup a few years back. Brian Clough gave me a bit of a slating for it and said I should have been in the circus. I didn't even do a good one.

Q: Which part of your body would you change if you had the chance?
Roy: No part of it. I'm happy with the way it is so I wouldn't change the nose or the ears or anything. At least the women tell me they are quite happy with how I look.

Q: What is your most prized possession?
Roy: Right here goes. My international caps, my CD collection, my cars (two Mercedes and a Golf GTi), my family and my Scottish terrier called Ben.

Q: If you were given £1 million tomorrow, what would you spend it on?
Roy: I'd spend it on the lads. We'd have a good summer I'd make sure of that.

Q: Which past player would you most like to have in your team?
Roy: Easy, that one. George Best or current player Gazza. I played against Paul a number of times and he's a great character and brilliant player. I've never actually met George since being here. I met him when I was younger and he was opening a betting office in Cork.

Q: If you had a film made of your life, who would you choose to play the starring role?
Roy: Harrison Ford.

Q: Which group or record inspires you?
Roy: That's hard 'cos I've got so many CD's. My music tastes vary, I like a of mod-music as that was my era. So it would have to be that kind of music.

Q: If you could be in a pop group which one would it be or have been?
Roy: I would have loved to have been in Madness. I could have been Sugsy!

Q: What's the most exciting thing about playing for United?
Roy: We are always winning and that means plenty of win bonuses.

Q: What is the toughest thing about playing for United?
Roy: There's a lot of pressure of the pitch with functions and signing autographs. I have no private life. I don't mind that so much unless I'm in a bad mood.

Inter

Nuff respect!

Norwich boss Mike Walker is revelling in the limelight created by his team's stunning Euro success. Now he wants a bit of credit.

The man who was once sacked by Colchester after winning six games in a row believes a bit of praise is long overdue for his Norwich heroes.

"All last season people were saying the bubble would burst and that we wouldn't last the pace," he says. "The criticism was useful for us to use as a motivation for the players.

"But I don't enjoy it when people fail to recognise what an achievement it was for a club of our resources to qualify for Europe.

"I never said we would win the Championship last season, just as I'm not going to say we'll win the UEFA Cup this time. I just want recognition for trying to play the game the way I think is right.

"It's time people stopped treating us as though we have no right to be up here."

Bargain Boys

Next week's tie will be a real case of Princes v Paupers as Inter's mega-bucks superstars look to put Norwich's budget buys firmly in their place. In fact, the entire Canaries squad which drew with Bayern in their decisive Second Round match at Carrow Road cost less then HALF the £5 million Inter paid Ajax for Dennis Berkgamp in the summer. Here's the bargain basement boys who made such a mess of Munich...

Player	From	Fee
Bryan Gunn	Aberdeen	£150,000
John Polston	Spurs	£300,000
Ian Culverhouse	Spurs	£50,000
Ian Butterworth	Nottm Forest	£160,000
Mark Bowen	Spurs	£90,000
Rob Newman	Bristol City	£600,000
Ian Crook	Spurs	£80,000
Jeremy Goss	From youth team	
Ruel Fox	From youth team	
Chris Sutton	From youth team	
Darren Eadie	From youth team	
Scott Howie	Clyde	£250,000
Gary Megson	Man City	Free
Daryl Sutch	From youth team	
Ade Akinbiyi	From youth team	
Spencer Prior	Southend	£200,000
TOTAL COST: £1.88 million		

Inter Fear

The Inter Milan team which takes on Norwich next week reads like a Who's Who of soccer superstars. These are just a few of the men The Canaries will have to watch...

Dennis Bergkamp: Widely regarded as one of the world's best strikers. No-one in England should need reminding of his talents after the goals he scored for Holland in the World Cup qualifiers.

Ruben Sosa: Silky Uruguayan who is lethal from set-pieces. Bryan Gunn will have his work cut out if Norwich concede any free-kicks on the edge of the box.

Igor Shalimov: Became the most expensive Soviet of all-time when he joined Inter for £9.2 million from Foggia in May 1992. Gifted midfielder who can open up any defence in the world.

Walter Zenga: One of the world's top goalkeepers, he has played all his career at the highest level. Has won over 50 caps for Italy so will take this game in his stride.

Salvatore Schillaci: Shot to fame when he finished the 1990 World Cup finals as top scorer. Had a disappointing spell at Juve but is back to his best.

Norwich and Peterborough BUILDING SOCIETY

38

mission

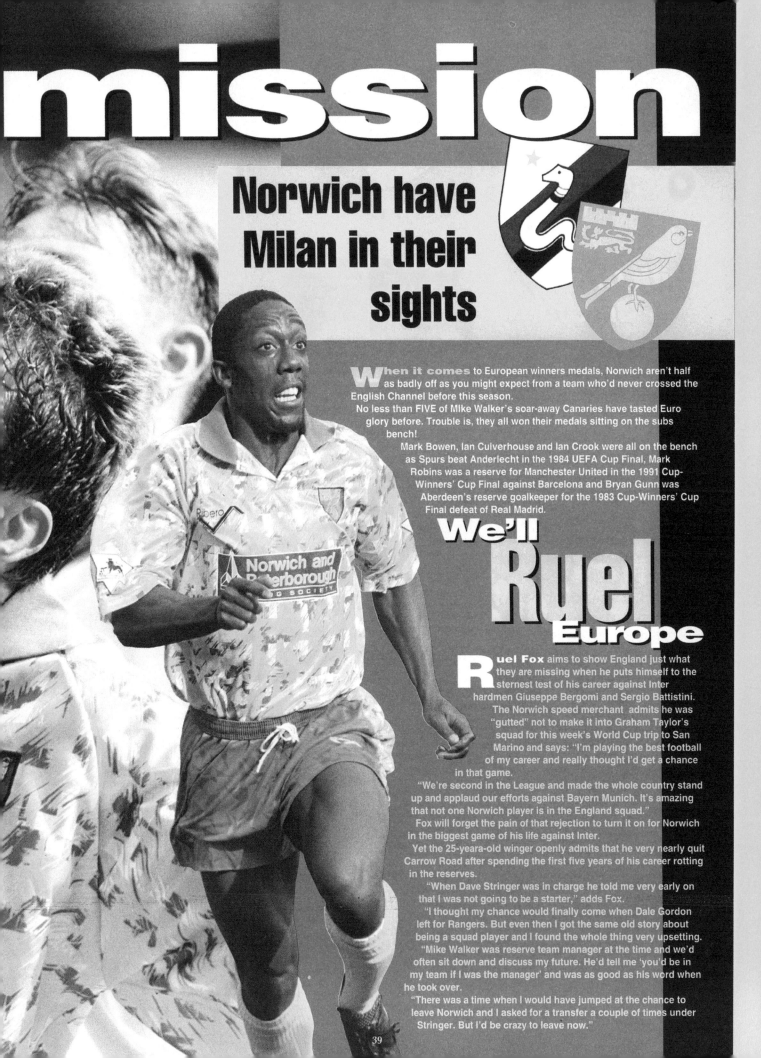

Norwich have Milan in their sights

When it comes to European winners medals, Norwich aren't half as badly off as you might expect from a team who'd never crossed the English Channel before this season.

No less than FIVE of Mike Walker's soar-away Canaries have tasted Euro glory before. Trouble is, they all won their medals sitting on the subs bench!

Mark Bowen, Ian Culverhouse and Ian Crook were all on the bench as Spurs beat Anderlecht in the 1984 UEFA Cup Final, Mark Robins was a reserve for Manchester United in the 1991 Cup-Winners' Cup Final against Barcelona and Bryan Gunn was Aberdeen's reserve goalkeeper for the 1983 Cup-Winners' Cup Final defeat of Real Madrid.

We'll Ruel Europe

Ruel Fox aims to show England just what they are missing when he puts himself to the sternest test of his career against Inter hardmen Giuseppe Bergomi and Sergio Battistini.

The Norwich speed merchant admits he was "gutted" not to make it into Graham Taylor's squad for this week's World Cup trip to San Marino and says: "I'm playing the best football of my career and really thought I'd get a chance in that game.

"We're second in the League and made the whole country stand up and applaud our efforts against Bayern Munich. It's amazing that not one Norwich player is in the England squad."

Fox will forget the pain of that rejection to turn it on for Norwich in the biggest game of his life against Inter.

Yet the 25-years-old winger openly admits that he very nearly quit Carrow Road after spending the first five years of his career rotting in the reserves.

"When Dave Stringer was in charge he told me very early on that I was not going to be a starter," adds Fox.

"I thought my chance would finally come when Dale Gordon left for Rangers. But even then I got the same old story about being a squad player and I found the whole thing very upsetting.

"Mike Walker was reserve team manager at the time and we'd often sit down and discuss my future. He'd tell me 'you'd be in my team if I was the manager' and was as good as his word when he took over.

"There was a time when I would have jumped at the chance to leave Norwich and I asked for a transfer a couple of times under Stringer. But I'd be crazy to leave now."

Why is Tim Flowers associated with a top TV soap character? Just what does David Batty do with hotel menus? What is all the fuss about Kenny Dalglish's jewellery and why does nobody ask Alan Shearer the time? SHOOT brings you all the answers and more revelations from the Rovers dressing-room in our hot new series You're Nicked - the feature that brings a smile to you and the players!

SPYMASTER

Code No: 0025 SHER 00004

Tim Sherwood

This week's Spymaster is a player who is in the best position of them all to give us the lowdown on the mickey-taking nicknames and laughs at Ewood Park - skipper Tim Sherwood. The former Norwich star put himself on the line with this rib-tickling rundown on his mates and the gaffer himself...

Tim Flowers
Sherwood's Snippets
"Tim is a lovely fella but he's known around Ewood as 'Arfur'. Not after Arthur Daley, but after Arthur Fowler from the BBC soap EastEnders because, like Arthur, Tim's got an allotment. We're not quite sure where it is yet but he's been known to spend a lot of time digging around."

David May
Sherwood's Snippets
"This is an easy one. You only have to take a look at his 'barnet' (that's hair to the rest of us) to understand why he gets crucified by the name of 'Syrup'. That's cockney slang for Syrup of Figs, meaning wigs. It's got to be a wig 'cos nobody at the club can believe it actually grows in the style he has it.

Graeme Le Saux
Sherwood's Snippets
"Graeme might be a nice bloke to talk to, but nobody at the club really knows. That's because whenever we are travelling to away games on the coach, he's always on his mobile phone. We can never get it away from his ear and it's just as well they don't allow them to be taken on the pitch. We are all going to get one to ring him for the ball!"

Kevin Moran
Sherwood's Snippets
"Kevin is a quiet kind of bloke who just gets on with things. He hasn't really got a nickname as such but he gets slaughtered a lot because of his age. Nobody really knows how old he is.

Stuart Ripley
Sherwood's Snippets
"A real academic and a bookworm. He's always got his head buried in a book when we are travelling but, when it comes to being streetwise, he's not so clever. We reckon he's read every book in the world...although he'll probably list the ones he hasn't now!"

Kevin Gallacher
Sherwood's Snippets
"He gets off quite lightly because he tends to pal around with Colin Hendry and Graeme Le Saux. They stick together like the Three Musketeers."

're KED

Alan Shearer
Sherwood's Snippets

"He's got quite a few nicknames but none that I can mention here. But he's getting a lot of stick at the moment because of the fact that he rolls his sleeve up so high on his arm. That's to show off his Rolex wristwatch to everyone. Nobody dare ask him the time now. Also, we reckon he's got blue blood in his veins because he's always talking about Blackburn Rovers. They are in almost every sentence!

David Batty
Sherwood's Snippets

"He's just mad. I mean that in a nice sense though. He seems so quiet to most people but really he's a livewire underneath. Has this habit of stealing breakfast menus off other players' hotel doors whenever we stay away and then rings them at three in the morning pretending to be reception trying to confirm the orders...nice guy! I know because he's done it to me!"

Colin Hendry
Sherwood's Snippets

"We can't quite believe he has so many friends in Blackburn. Every day at training he brings a shirt in for everyone to sign. We spend half our life signing shirts for him. A Mr. Blackburn if ever there was one."

Jason Wilcox
Sherwood's Snippets

"He's the club's impersonator. He does a great one of Tony Parkes, our coach, and Chris Eubank the boxer. But his current fad is to do Graham Taylor and Lawrie McMenemy from the Cutting Edge documentary. Lots of 'Do I not like that's,' are flying around at the moment.

Nicky Marker
Sherwood's Snippets

"Not a lot we know about Nicky apart from the fact he has a friend who seems to bite people's earholes off!" (What? - Ed)

Kenny Dalglish
Sherwood's Snippets

"The Gaffer has been slaughtered for wearing this bracelet his wife bought him. He never takes it off and even flashes it around while he's giving us our team talks. I think he thinks the worst is over now but, when he reads this, he'll know otherwise.

Tim Sherwood on himself

"I'm called Slippery. Don't ask me why though, the Gaffer gave me the nickname and I suppose it's because he can't trust me..(and after this who could blame him? - Ed).

Worm your way out of this one, Stuart!

41

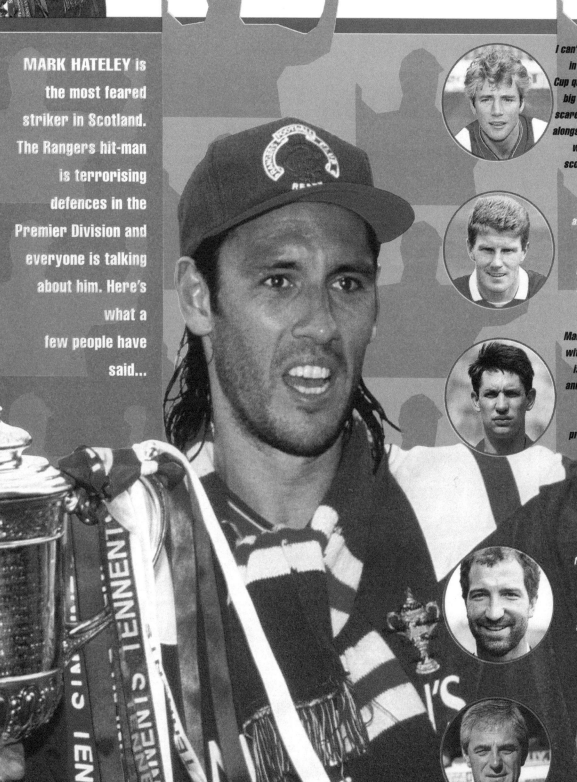

Mark Hateley

MARK HATELEY is the most feared striker in Scotland. The Rangers hit-man is terrorising defences in the Premier Division and everyone is talking about him. Here's what a few people have said...

I can't believe that big Mark was not in the England team for the World Cup qualifiers. He would have made a big difference. His pace and power scares teams to death. I love playing alongside him. He's a terrific partner who creates lots of chances and score goals himself. *ALLY McCOIST*

He is a master. I believe that, if anything, he has got better since coming to Scotland. He is certainly worth a place in the England side. I don't think I have played against a better striker. *DUNCAN SHEARER*

Mark is real class - a cool finisher with his head and with his feet. He is always a danger to opponents and a delight to have on your side. His positioning is great and his passing is perfect. He is a top professional who is a pleasure to watch. *GARY LINEKER*

When I bought him to Rangers from Monaco the fans didn't take to him at first because they thought he was there to replace Ally McCoist. But once they had seen him play a few times, Mark soon became their hero as well. *GRAEME SOUNESS*

I travel extensively throughout Britain and I haven't seen a better striker than Mark - and I have seen a lot of international forwards. He would be in the England squad if I was picking it. He is an exceptional player with so many qualities. *WALTER SMITH*

Back Chat

I've played against Mark in Old Firm matches and he often seems worth a goal start to Rangers. He is very difficult to subdue. When he and McCoist are together it can be a nightmare for the opposition to try to stop both of them. CHARLIE NICHOLAS

His importance could not be better summed up than by his consistent performances. He creates chances for others and is useful all over the pitch, as well as scoring some amazing goals. Give him a job - any job - and he can do it. RICHARD GOUGH

He is a superb player. He made all the difference when we played Rangers in the European Cup. He was excellent at Ibrox and scored a terrific goal in the return leg at Elland Road which was a real heartbreaker for us. HOWARD WILKINSON

He was sensational when we played Rangers. Mark holds the ball up well, distributes it brilliantly and is a great finisher both in the air and on the ground. He scored a brilliant goal against us at Elland Road and has proved time and time again that he is a winner. GARY SPEED

Mark is an essential part of Rangers' play. All our opponents fear him and change their tactics to try to keep him quiet. But he is so powerful that, whatever they do, they can't contain him. He can spend a whole game feeding everyone else or he can become the centre of attack and get among the goals. TREVOR STEVEN

THINGS can only get BETTER

Jimmy Greaves gives his England verdict

Before his team have even kicked a ball in anger, the new England boss has come up with a winning line-up with his choice of coaching staff.

Bryan Robson, Dave Sexton, Don Howe and Ray Wilkins are four guys who've been there and done it all before. They'll get the instant respect of the England players and that's something Graham Taylor's backroom boys never had.

Taylor and Lawrie McMenemy never played in the First Division, never mind at international level. They never gained managerial success with a big club, either.

Robson would be in anyone's all-time England XI, Wilkins has been a model pro, Howe is the best defensive organiser in the business and Sexton is the quiet man who has already won Under-21 Championships.

Together, they make an excellent, professional set-up. Now they've got to gang up and get rid of Director of Coaching, Charlie Hughes.

English football has got a new theme tune now that Terry Venables had taken over from Graham Taylor...Things Can Only Get Better.

For the last four years, England's best players have been weighed down by a huge burden of pressure, gloom and fear.

Now Terry can breathe new life into our national team by introducing a light-hearted, casual approach into the dressing-room and getting his men to actually enjoy playing for England again. No England manager has ever had such a glorious opportunity for success. Terry has got two years of pressure-free friendlies before his first serious game, we're already guaranteed our place in the European Championship finals and we'll be playing every game at home.

In fact, if the odds are good enough, I'll even risk a few quid on England winning the Championship.

It all confirms my suspicions that if Terry fell head first into a barrel load of horse manure - which is where he was three months ago - he'd still come up smelling of roses.

But anyone expecting to see a new line-up when he names his first side for the game against Denmark next Wednesday will be disappointed.

Graham Taylor took a hell of a lot of stick for his team selections, but the simple fact is that he picked all the best players whenever they were available.

What Terry will do is change the way they play. There will be a lot more lightness and freedom of expression about his team and less of the fear factor which was so evident in Taylor's reign.

I remember watching the England squad in their hotel during the European Championship two years ago and they all looked as if they were having the most miserable time of their lives.

And that misery was reflected on the pitch, where they played as though they were carrying a weighted rucksack on their backs.

Terry will lighten that load and give Gazza and the lads the freedom of expression they want but were always denied by Taylor.

He's not going to turn us into a nation of world beaters overnight, but when you inherit a team that has hit rock bottom you know that things can only improve. And they will.

Adams - top stopper

Gazza - the best

And that's no D:Ream for England!

Tel Stars

These boys will set the record straight

Platt - Mr Reliable

Paul Gascoigne

Terry has already made it clear that Gazza will be his first name down on the team sheet and I agree with him because he's the best player we've got. Because he's so excitable, Gascoigne will always be a man with problems and he'll always create trouble for himself and his manager. But nobody is better equipped than Terry to handle him and if anybody can bring the best out of Gazza, he can. And God knows we need it.

David Platt

Platty has very rarely let his country down and though he didn't play particularly well in his last couple of games for England, nobody else did either. A lot of critics reckon he's over-rated but since Gary Lineker retired from international football he's been the only reliable goalscorer we've had. His experience of Italian football and level-headed attitude are going to be invaluable.

Paul Ince

Picks himself. The best player in the country right now, he's doing an amazing job for Manchester United and is the nearest we've got to another Bryan Robson. Wins tackles, uses the ball intelligently, gets the other players going and terrifies the life out of the opposition.

Alan Shearer

Venables it spoilt for choice in the goalscorers department, but Shearer has to be his number one choice. Wright, Ferdinand, Cole, Sutton, Beardsley and Le Tissier are all fighting to partner this guy. Taylor was very unlucky to have Shearer injured for the major part of the World Cup qualifiers. I'm not saying we'd have got to America if he was fit but he would have made a difference.

Tony Adams

Every time I go up north I get into a row with Manchester United fans about Adams' inclusion in the England team. They all argue that Gary Pallister and Steve Bruce should be together because they form the best central defensive partnership in the country. But while I can see their argument, I still reckon Adams is the best stopper we've got and his record at Arsenal proves that. I'll be very surprised if Terry drops him.

24 WONDERS OF THE WORLD

No.11
Holland

While one Dutch superstar faces a fight to save his career, another carries the hopes of his nation on his slender shoulders.

AC Milan striker Marco Van Basten is undergoing intensive treatment on the ankle injury that has ruined his season and induced whispers that his career is over.

But while he faces an uphill battle to be fit for US 94, his countryman Dennis Bergkamp has emerged from his shadow to be hailed as the best striker in the world.

The Inter Milan golden boy played a vital role in helping the Dutch reach the finals, scoring in both games against England, and with the enforced absence of Van Basten, he is the key to Holland unlocking the door to their first World Cup triumph.

The experience of Ronald Koeman, Ruud Gullit and Jan Wouters is still very prominent in the side, but it's the younger men in orange that pose the biggest threat now.

Alongside Bergkamp is the silky Foggia winger Brian Roy, lightening quick Ajax star Marc Overmars and his club team-mate Ronald De Boer, twin brother of defender Frank.

But it's Dennis the Menace who the rest of the world fear.

He was the most wanted striker in Europe when he left Ajax for Inter last season in a bargain £5 million deal.

If he grabs the goals that give the Dutch glory in the summer, his transfer value will go through the roof.

Dennis the M

World Cup Record

1930 Did not enter
1934 First Round
1938 First Round
1950 Did not enter
1954 Did not enter
1958 Did not qualify
1962 Did not qualify
1966 Did not qualify
1970 Did not qualify
1974 Runners-up
1978 Runners-up
1982 Did not qualify
1986 Did not qualify
1990 Second Round

Defence
Attacking Power
Star Quality
Entertainment Value
Experience
Overall Chances

10 9 8 7 6 5 4 3 2 1 0

The Squad

Dick Advocaat is their manager and was appointed in July, 1990

Player	Club	Age	Caps/Goals
Keepers			
Ed de Goey	Feyenoord	27	8/0
Theo Snelders	Aberdeen	30	8/0
Edwin Van der Sar	Ajax	23	0/0
Defenders			
John De Wolf	Feyenoord	31	4/2
Danny Blind	Ajax	32	22/1
Frank De Boer	Ajax	24	19/1
Ronald Koeman	Barcelona	31	68/12
Midfield			
Wim Jonk	Inter Milan	27	9/3
Erwin Koeman	PSV Eindhoven	32	30/2
Arthur Numan	PSV Eindhoven	24	2/0
Frank Rijkaard	Ajax	31	64/6
Aron Winter	Lazio	27	32/2
Rob Witschge	Feyenoord	27	18/3
Jan Wouters	Bayern Munich	33	63/4
Forwards			
Bryan Roy	Foggia	24	16/2
Marc Overmars	Ajax	21	7/1
Ronald De Boer	Ajax	24	4/3
Ruud Gullit	Sampdoria	31	64/16
Dennis Bergkamp	Inter Milan	25	26/16
Marco Van Basten	AC Milan	28	58/28
Regi Blinker	Feyenoord	25	2/0
Johnny Bosman	Anderlecht	29	24/11

Menace

Bergkamp is the new Dutch destroyer

Former Oldham defender Denis Irwin opens the floodgates

Bryan Robson keeps up his impressive FA Cup Semi-Final strike rate

Ryan Giggs completes the scoring at Maine Road

Kanchelskis strikes with a Goal of the Season contender

Kan they do it?... yes they Kan!

Manchester United are back on course for the double...and how!

Alex Ferguson's rampant side ruthlessly swept aside Oldham in a pulsating Semi-Final replay at Maine Road.

All the swagger and style that has been missing in recent weeks was back and poor Oldham simply had no answer to it.

And two men in particular made it possible - Bryan Robson and Andrei Kanchelskis.

Robbo proved there is life in the old dog yet with a barnstorming performance which turned the clock back to his glory days in the the 1980s.

He was everywhere and capped a memorable display with a typical goal, charging in from a corner to force the ball over the line.

Manager Alex Ferguson says: "He defies age. His run for the second goal was typical Robbo of old. He was superb."

Robson now has the chance to become the first man in history to lift the FA Cup for the fourth time but even he had to play second fiddle to his team-mate, the flying Kanchelskis.

The speedy Russian was in sensational form and broke Oldham's hearts with a stunning goal and an overall display which had class stamped all over it.

Kanchelskis has always had frightening pace, but now he's added more control to his game and is yet another terrifying weapon in the United armoury.

And he's set to be rewarded with a new deal at Old Trafford. His contract expires in the summer and many people felt he would be leaving but Fergie insists: "We have an option on Andrei and we will be taking it up.

"Obviously we would talk to him and make sure the contract is right. He is such a good player."

Oldham Kan testify to that!

Red Review

* Bryan Robson has scored in all four FA Cup Semi-Finals in which he has played - 1983 v Arsenal, 1985 v Liverpool, 1990 v Oldham and 1994 v Oldham.

* Peter Schmeichel will play in a Wembley Final this season, after all. He missed United's Coca-Cola Cup defeat by Aston Villa through suspension.

* The FA Cup Final against Chelsea will be United's fifth Wembley Final in four years.

* United won't relish the prospect of facing Chelsea at Wembley on May 14. The two sides have met twice this season, and The Blues have won both games 1-0.

SHOOTIN STAR

Who has been the pride of Scotland this year? That's what we want you to decide.

We're searching for SHOOT's Most Exciting Players of the Year and this week we turn our attention to north of the border.

Last year's winner was Ally McCoist and Rangers will be hoping that either Mark Hateley or Gordon Durie can keep the trophy at Ibrox.

But the England international striker faces stiff competition from his Premier Division rivals.

Motherwell have been the surprise package in Scotland this term and we reckon Phil O'Donnell and Tommy Coyne are good bets for glory.

And then of course, there are Aberdeen aces Duncan Shearer and Eoin Jess, and Celtic star Pat McGinlay.

It's bound to be close and only you can decide who walks off with the Most Exciting Player of the Year award.

Scotland, it's over to you!

Vote for your Most Exciting Player

NEXT WEEK
Vote for your PREMIERSHIP PRINCES

Mark Hateley
Rangers
0891 889451

Duncan Shearer
Aberdeen
0891 889452

Keith Wright
Hibernian
0891 889453

Craig Brewster
Dundee United
0891 889454

Pat McGinlay
Celtic
0891 889457

Eoin Jess
Aberdeen
0891 889458

Phil O'Donnell
Motherwell
0891 889459

Gordon Durie
Rangers
0891 889460

Scots PREM

of the Year

How to vote

We SHOOT experts!!! have come up with 12 players we consider to be the best of the bunch this season. Study the Scottish hit parade and then select the Premier Division star you think has been the most exciting player this term. It's a tricky decision.

Then simply dial the number listed below your choice and your vote will be registered. Calls will cost approximately 10p.

If you don't agree with our selection and would like to vote for a player not shown in the gallery of stars, then phone **0891 889450** and leave the name of the player you think should win the award.

Calls for that line cost 39p per minute (cheap rate) and 49p at all other times.

Alan McLaren
Hearts
0891 889455

Roddie Grant
Partick
0891 889456

Billy McKinlay
Dundee United
0891 889461

Tommy Coyne
Motherwell
0891 889462

51

Red Rev

Take One: Eric Cantona sets up the double with United's opening goal

MANCHESTER UNITED finally got it right against Chelsea as they swept to FA Cup glory at Wembley.

The Blues were the only side to beat United twice in the League this season but they couldn't do it on the biggest stage of all.

Two goals from Eric Cantona and one each from Mark Hughes and Brian McClair ended Glenn Hoddle's dream of collecting the Cup in his first season at Stamford Bridge.

And now Fergie's United can take their place in the history books among the truly great sides.

They became only the fourth club this century - after Spurs, Arsenal and Liverpool -

Take Two: The Frenchman is on the spot again

Mark Hughes scored in each of his four games at Wembley this season

Brian McClair finishes off the scoring with United's fourth goal

to complete the League and Cup double and have earned the right to be talked about in the same breath as those magnificent teams.

Ferguson has built a side which plays the game with great style and no-one can say they didn't deserve their double success.

And yet again at Wembley, the man who set the ball rolling was Eric Cantona as United took sweet revenge on Chelsea.

The French star had been relatively quiet for the first hour but, when Denis Irwin was pulled down by Eddie Newton, he casually slotted the ball home from the penalty spot, and he did the same six minutes later after Andrei Kanchelskis was bundled over by Blues defender Frank Sinclair.

Perhaps it was fitting that, after all his negative publicity in the last couple of months, the Players' Player of the Year chose Wembley to remind the fans just how good he can be.

After his goals, Cantona was back to his arrogant best and the flicks and tricks were all there.

And when the pressure was really on, for the two spot-kicks, he kept his cool to fire United to victory.

Afterwards he said: "I keep calm because it's only a game. It is not a war out there."

Maybe not, but the rest of the Premiership are going to have a real battle stopping United from making it a hat-trick of titles next season.

Who said what at Wembley

I'm very proud of my players. We played 64 games this season and lost only six. That's tremendous consistency. **ALEX FERGUSON**

Now let's win the European Cup. It's wonderful to play for this team but now we must dominate like Liverpool did in the 80s. **ERIC CANTONA**

I have to pinch myself to believe that everything has happened to me in the last few years. When Eric Cantona is on a stage like Wembley he loves it. He could have scored those penalties all day. **STEVE BRUCE**

We've proved we're the best team in the country. It's the best day of my life. **ROY KEANE**

Our only regret is that Sir Matt Busby wasn't around to see this moment. But we're sure he's looking down on us and jumping for joy. Now we want the European Cup. It was a big disappointment this year and now we've got another chance to give the country what they missed. **PAUL INCE**

We won't be resting on our laurels. The boss wants another Championship next season and the European Cup. **PAUL PARKER**

I've watched the FA Cup Final on television for years and to win here is unbelievable. **PETER SCHMEICHEL**

It was a cruel result but I was proud of the way we played. We didn't stop battling. **GLENN HODDLE**

If my shot which hit the bar had gone in we would have won. We're disappointed with the scoreline because it flattered them. We were never four goals worse. But we'll learn from this and come back. **GAVIN PEACOCK**

I was very surprised the referee gave the second penalty. There was body contact but it wasn't a foul. It started a miserable ten minutes for me because the third goal came from my mistake. We're all gutted. **FRANK SINCLAIR**

What goes up, must come down - Newton's theory - United's penalty

SHOOT the best for Wembley action

Glad All Over

The Eagles have landed back in the big time

Crystal Palace have bounced back into the Premier League at the first and last opportunity.

Just 12 months ago the club was in turmoil as Oldham won their last three games to send Palace plummeting. Now, The Eagles are flying high again.

But manager Alan Smith, who masterminded Palace's triumph in his first year in charge, admits that if Palace hadn't won promotion this season, they may never have done.

"We had to go up first time around," says Smith. "If we hadn't we would have lost five or six players, the crowds would have dropped to under 10,000 and it would have taken us at least four or five years to get back to the top."

But go up they did and now Smith is full of optimism as he looks forward to pitting his wits against the country's best.

"We are a miles better side now than when we went down," he insists. "The players are a year older and we are a more solid and organised unit.

"It was very hard this year and it was difficult to cope with the expectations of people. But the players have done magnificently and I'm proud of them all."

But although it was the players who did the business on the pitch, Smith must take a large chunk of the credit for the work he did off it.

He persuaded players like Nigel Martyn, Andy Thorn, Chris Coleman and Chris Armstrong to stay at the club when they went down and then fostered the team spirit which has been paramount in their success.

Smith adds: "The players showed a lot of loyalty when we were relegated. It would have been easy for some of them to clear off but that common bond we had saw us through in the end."

And now Smith is hoping that camaraderie will do the job again in the top flight

"From day one I want to be up there and running. I want us to the near the top," he says. "Our aim has to be to follow what Newcastle did last year.

"It's a tall order but you have to set high targets. If you say before the season that you think you'll finish halfway, you'll probably end up two thirds of the way down the table. I have to give the players something to aim for."

Player	Games	Goals
Chris Armstrong	43	23
Bobby Bowry	17 (3)	0
Chris Coleman	46	3
Bruce Dyer	2 (9)	2
Dean Gordon	39 (5)	5
John Humphrey	32	1
Nigel Martyn	46	0
Stuart Massey	1	0
Damien Matthew	11 (1)	1
Ricky Newman	10	0
Martyn O'Connor	2	0
Simon Osborn	5 (1)	0
Simon Rodger	37 (4)	3
John Salako	34 (4)	8
Richard Shaw	30 (4)	2
Gareth Southgate	46	9
Paul Stewart	18	3
Andy Thorn	10	0
David Whyte	10 (5)	3
Paul Williams	21 (3)	7
Eric Young	46	5

Brackets denote substitute appearance

How they did it

P46 W27 D9 L10 F73 A46 Pts90

Biggest win: 5-1 v Portsmouth (h) Aug.28
Biggest defeat: 0-3 v Millwall (a) Jan.1
Biggest attendance: 28,749 v Watford May 8
Top scorer: Chris Armstrong 23
Hat-tricks: Chris Armstrong v Portsmouth (h) Aug.28
John Salako v Stoke (h) Oct.2
Clean sheets: 14

Div 1
Champions

Crystal Palace

SHOOT salutes the season's top dogs

SHOOT

the BIG story
with BIG Dippa

No Regrets!

Chris Waddle was on the verge of an England recall under Terry Venables when an achilles injury ruined last season and the start of this. Written off since, he is said to be on verge of quitting and wishing he'd gone back to Premiership leaders Newcastle when he had the chance. But in an exclusive interview with Big Dippa Curtis, Chris dismisses the rumours and reveals his feelings about Newcastle's rise to the top.

You could easily forgive Chris Waddle for being more than a little envious of Newcastle's return to greatness at the top of the Premiership.

After all, his former Tyneside playing pals Kevin Keegan and Peter Beardsley are pulling the strings and his former boss Arthur Cox is also back at St. James' Park.

Waddle had the chance to rejoin the Toon Army on his return to England from Marseille two seasons ago just prior to the start of the Newcastle revolution but opted for Sheffield Wednesday instead.

Waddle could so easily have been playing in the famous black and white strip he graced with such distinction for five years in the early half of the eighties, but the deal fell through because he couldn't wait for Newcastle to make up their minds.

Then Ossie Ardiles got the sack, Keegan was appointed, they escaped relegation from the old First Division and the rest, as they say, is history.

Now the Wednesday ace reveals for the first time that he doesn't regret a thing - even with Newcastle taking the soccer world by storm under his old pal's leadership.

Waddle told me: "I enjoyed my time at Newcastle and had five good years. To be really honest I thought I would be going back there when I left Marseille and came back to England. But Newcastle were not having the best of times and were nearly relegated.

"I spoke to them on my return to England but nothing was ever concrete between us. I was very interested in going back to St. James' Park but they never came up with a firm enough offer.

"Then they had a change and escaped relegation. But nobody knew which way the club was going to go and at the time I had to make a decision. I couldn't sit around any longer, so it never happened.

"People think that I turned down the chance to rejoin Newcastle but I wouldn't dream of that.

"I've no regrets about it at all. I've really enjoyed my time at Wednesday.

"I'm not surprised at what Kevin has done. The potential has always been there for Newcastle to be one of the great clubs again. The old board of directors were a bit set in their ways but since Sir John Hall took over it's all come together at the right time.

"Nothing surprises me about Kevin's success because he's very determined - and a winner.

"He knew what the Geordie fans wanted and he's given it to them.

"Up to now, he's not had a setback but I think he'll overcome it very quickly when he does have one.

"He's been England captain, he's played abroad, played at the top level for years, went away and had a rest and now he's come back and he's flying. But even though Newcastle are buzzing I don't wish I was there."

Out but not down

'I'm not sorry I missed out on Newcastle!'

'Don't Write Me Off!'

Chris Waddle has hit out at the critics who have written his career off.

The Wednesday ace's achilles injury has sidelined him since the back end of last season but he believes he's on the way back after undergoing American style rehabilitation.

Waddle is now building up his muscles with the help of swimming after an operation to drain fluid from his calf.

But in the interim, he has had to endure taunts that he's finished as he attempts to return to action and play out the last year-and-a-half of his Wednesday contract.

And it's the taunts that have got to him.

Waddle roars: "I would like to think I will be playing again by December, if not before. It's been tough for me because it's the first real injury I've had that's kept me out.

"The problem has worried me a great deal. I think when you get injuries with knees, ankles and achilles tendons, you doubt it more and more that it's going to go away.

"And when you haven't played for a while people begin to doubt whether you will come back. I never try to put a date on it because if I don't make it by the time I say, people start asking questions.

"I feel people have written me off already to a certain extent. I think some are just waiting for me to retire now.

"I've heard that I'm supposed to be thinking about quitting which is the biggest load of bull ever.

"If I've got to quit then I will but until an expert tells me that, then I'm going to give it every possible chance I can to come back.

But I'm not 23 anymore and when you get to 33 and get an injury like this, it does take longer to heal and people don't realise that.

"People think I've been out a long time but I didn't have the operation until the back end of April. I class the time I've been out as from when I had the op until now because basically I sat on my bum doing nothing and hoping that it would go away.

"It's disappointing to see that people are ready to write me off. The time to do that is when I've come back and I'm not right.

"The disturbing part about it is that I get people coming up to me who think I've packed up and that's really annoying."

"The disturbing part about it is that I get people coming up to me who think I've packed up and that's very annoying."

Roy 'Rocky' Race's first season as Melchester Rovers' number nine was characterised by fights with referees, with team-mates and a heroic eleventh hour escape from relegation. But this season has started like a dream. Rovers beat the champions in their first fixture thanks to goals from Rocky and Delroy. On the pitch things seem to be going well but off it, something stirs. Del is being unsettled by enquiries from top Italian club AC Versace. Neither player is keen to leave Rovers but after a secret meeting between their agent, Solly, and the Versace chairman, a story has appeared in the press on the eve of the Premiership game with bottom of the table Corby City...

ROY OF THE ROVERS

● Script by Stuart Green ● Art by Jim O'Ready ● Letters by Steve Potter

Y'COULD TELL FROM THE KICK-OFF IT WAS GONNA BE ONE OF THOSE DAYS...

CLARK'S BALL!

KARL'S!

IT'S DEAD HARD TO EXPLAIN WHY Y'DON'T PLAY WELL SOMETIMES.

WE'D HAD NO INJURIES OR - MIRACULOUSLY - SUSPENSIONS, SO WE WENT OUT WITH THE SAME ELEVEN WHO'D BEEN PLAYING SINCE AUGUST.

WE'D WON LAST WEEK WHICH LEFT US EQUAL THIRD, SO WE FELT GOOD ABOUT OURSELVES.

AND CORBY CITY WERE THE OPPOSITION - EVERYONE SAID WE'D BEAT THEM.

BUT THEY REALLY WANTED IT... AND WE DIDN'T.

IT WAS THAT STORY ABOUT ME AN' DEL LEAVING. NO ONE SAID ANYTHING, LIKE...

...THEY DIDN'T NEED TO.

DEXTER'S A NUTTER.

HE LIVES AND BREATHES ROVERS - EVEN WORSE THAN ME! SO SOMETIMES HE LOSES IT!

WE WAS ALL SICK AFTER THAT AND MERV HIT THE ROOF AT HALF-TIME...

WHAT THE 'ELL WAS THAT, EH? SOMETHING ELSE ON Y'MIND APART FROM THIS GAME?

BUT IT DIDN'T DO ANY GOOD. THINGS WENT FROM BAD TO WORSE.

WE JUST GOT NOWHERE IN THE SECOND HALF.

OUTBATTLED US EVERYWHERE.

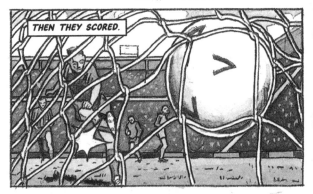

THEN THEY SCORED.

S'POSE WE HAD A BIT OF A GO AFTER THAT.

I EVEN GOT TO THE BYE-LINE...

SENT IT INTO MACCA...

IT WAS LIKE SOMEONE SAYING "SERVE YOU RIGHT".

KRAK

COULD'VE KNOWN THE SEASON WAS GOING TOO WELL.

ON SATURDAY IN ROY OF THE ROVERS MONTHLY DAMAGE LIMITATION!

Roy 'Rocky' Race's second season began like a dream. The promising youngster started to live up to his promise with a few goals, including a sensational hat-trick against Sloane Rangers. But this has sparked interest in the youngster and his strike partner Delroy from Serie A side, AC Versace. Versace have let the players know via their agent, Solly, that they will make the boys very rich if they will go to Italy. It is an offer Rovers say they cannot match. Meanwhile, Rovers sign the brilliant Brazilian, Malandro. He becomes the highest paid player in the country but his individualism means he is proving difficult to fit into the team. Merv brings a new assistant, ex-Rovers defender, Duncan McKay to discipline Malandro. Afterward, Rovers adopt a new 3-5-2 system to accomodate Malandro. The defence is weakened but the attack is brilliant. Now it's time for the FA Cup 3rd round draw...

• Script by Stuart Green • Art by Sean Longcroft • Letters by Steve Potter

BACK CHAT

The German scoring sensation has dive-bombed into English football and taken our game by storm. Many said that Tottenham's Jurgen Klinsmann wouldn't be able to handle the pressure and pace of the game over here - but he has proved all the doubters wrong...

 Jurgen is a character all of his own. He is not like anyone else I know. He is a great team-mate and scores some excellent goals. He is simply one of the best in the business.
RUDI VOLLER

 He is a tremendous player. His positioning is excellent, he is a constant worry to defenders and he is a great finisher with his feet or with his head. That's a world class player. **ALAN HANSEN**

 He gives everything to his team and yet he remains so much an individual. He sees the world through his own eyes. He will not compromise. It is very impressive.
BERTI VOGTS

He is the sort of player you always hope will be in your team. He is not only a world class player but a very nice guy with a lovely sense of humour.
GARY MABBUTT

A great player - a brilliant individual yet a terrific team player who never wastes a chance to pass a ball rather than take a half chance himself.
TEDDY SHERINGHAM

 Jurgen is a great player and it is a pleasure to see him at work. As a manager you know he is reliable and will always try his best. He has great skill and a great presence.
OSSIE ARDILES

Jurgen Klinsmann

Jurgen is simply a great international player. He has courage, skill, good temperament and is a team man, as well as an outstanding individual. He is a great example to the younger players.
GERRY FRANCIS

He is a real handful to play against. He came to England in the face of a lot of criticism, but he has proved beyond question that he is one of the best in the business. A real star.
STEVE BRUCE

Klinsmann is not only a superb player but a great ambassador for the game. A few other players would do well to follow his example.
IAN ST. JOHN

Klinsmann is another excellent foreign player who has adapted to English football very quickly. He has played in Germany, Italy, France and now England and has been a star in each of those countries. He is truly outstanding.
TREVOR FRANCIS

Jurgen is a super footballer with lots of energy and lots of skill. He has played and proved himself at the highest level and has great experience. He has been tremendous for his country and for every club he has played for.
LOTHAR MATTHAUS

Jurgen has a great reputation in Europe, but has fitted into English football brilliantly. You would think that he had always played in the Premiership rather than for just a few months.
DAVID PLATT

The Klinsmann Kareer

1980s

Birthplace/date: Geislingen/July 30, 1964

1981: Makes senior debut with German Second Division club Stuttgart Kickers

1984: Signed by Bundesliga club Stuttgart

1987: International debut for Germany in 1-1 draw against Brazil

1988: Finishes season at top scorer in the Bundesliga with 19 goals. Wins Olympic bronze medal with West Germany

1989: Last game for Stuttgart is UEFA Cup defeat by Diego Maradona's Napoli. Transferred to Inter Milan for £1.3 million

1990s

1990: World Cup winner with West Germany

1991: UEFA Cup winner with Inter Milan. They beat Roma 2-1 on aggregate.

1992: Moves to AS Monaco in France

1994: Scores five goals in five games in USA World Cup. Transferred to Spurs for £2 million.

1994-95 Record: Played 37 games, 23 goals

International Record: Played 74 games, 26 goals

* figures correct up to and including Saturday, March 12

Write to **Greavsie**, SHOOT, King's Reach Tower, Stamford St, London SE1 9LS

greavsie

Loyal supporters

I have supported Manchester United for seven years, but have never been to Manchester. I get a lot of stick for this at school, but do you really have to go to matches to be a true fan?
MARTIN HAWKINS, SOLIHULL

Yes. I don't believe my eyes when I walk around Essex and see people wearing United, Liverpool, Celtic and Rangers strips. I'm a firm believer that you should support your local club. My next door neighbour supports Arsenal and that's his problem, but at least he goes and sees them play every week. I find it incredible that the majority of football fans in Manchester support Manchester City, not United. As for you, you should be supporting Birmingham.

new balance ®

This week's Star Letter comes from Shane Matthews of Stanford-Le-Hope, Essex. He wins a pair of New Balance boots.

PICK OF THE POST

Blowing the whistle

Players and spectators do not have the right to abuse referees for making the odd bad decision. Referees are usually right and deserve our praise.

I agree. On the whole, referees do make the right decisions. We will never have a perfect world in which refs are always right and players don't complain, but I think some players are overstepping the mark. Players are far too aggressive when they complain these days. Obviously the close-up television cameras highlight this but certain players are guilty of going over the top. Players such as Bobby Charlton and Jimmy Hill always used to complain to the referee, but they did it in such a way that was so not so obvious to the crowd and without the aggression we see today. Refs do make mistakes, but not on purpose and no amount of moaning will make them change their minds.

What goes up

The First Division promotion race may be close and exciting, but could any of the top teams survive in the Premiership next season?
JUSTIN FISHER, EAST SHEEN

No, not as their teams stand at the moment. Of the promotion hopefuls I would like to see Wolves go up because I think they are the only side who have the potential to do well in the Premier. The Molineux board have built a great stadium and I'm sure they would back Graham Taylor in the transfer market if they won promotion. Tranmere and Reading do not have the players or resources to survive at a higher level, and even Middlesbrough may struggle to compete financially. Bolton have an excellent chance of going up but I fear they will also struggle because they face having to sell their best players. Even if they do go up, Bruce Rioch will find it hard to stop the likes of Stubbs and McAteer moving to bigger clubs.

Woods' woe

Chris Woods is too good a goalkeeper to be stuck in Sheffield Wednesday's reserves. He should ask for a transfer before it is too late for him.
NIGEL McCOMBIE, CUMBRIA

I think Chris Woods is better off in the reserves the way Wednesday's defence is playing these days. I wouldn't fancy being the last line for a team which lets in seven goals at home. In fact, if Woods does want a transfer he had better get in the queue because I think there will be a few players wanting to get away from Hillsborough if their results carry on as they have been in the Premiership over the last few months.

sack the board

The Sunderland board should have sacked themselves before they got rid of Mick Buxton. He didn't receive any support in the transfer market.
ANDY HUNT, SUNDERLAND

The Sunderland chairman, Bob Murray, has got nothing but the club's best interests at heart. I know that for a fact and it does not please me to see his club in such a dire situation. The relative success of Newcastle and Middlesbrough, and their comparative wealth, has not helped the Roker Park board, manager of players in what have been difficult times for the club. Sunderland's time will come again, but supporters should think twice before they start calling for the board to go. Just because someone is a club director, it does not mean they have Jack Walker's money to spend and I'm sure the Sunderland board would give way if they received an offer from a wealthy party.

Back Barnes

It doesn't matter how badly John Barnes plays for England, he does not deserve to be booed by the Wembley crowd.
LAURENCE LACEY, HERTFORDSHIRE
The verbal abuse of Barnes has become a cult and a very dangerous one in my opinion. It happens to players at club level too and has become a popular thing for sections of the crowd to join in with, but it should stop now. I don't necessarily think John Barnes is the right man for England, but if Terry Venables picks him he should not be booed. This is a worrying trend which has no place in the game.

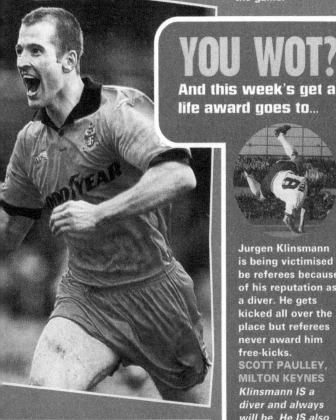

Lucky Jim

Jim Leighton has done well to return to international football, but it does not say much for the other Scottish goalkeepers.
JOHN LANGLEY, BRENTFORD
No, it does not. If Jim Leighton is playing for Scotland again, something must be very wrong with the rest of them. Most people know I have always given Scottish goalkeepers all the praise they deserve which is why I can only agree with this letter. The Russian strikers who failed to score against Scotland recently must be wondering if they are in the right profession.

YOU WOT?

And this week's get a life award goes to...

Jurgen Klinsmann is being victimised be referees because of his reputation as a diver. He gets kicked all over the place but referees never award him free-kicks.
SCOTT PAULLEY, MILTON KEYNES
Klinsmann IS a diver and always will be. He IS also an outstanding player, one of the best in the world, is a great ambassador for the game and has been a superb signing for Tottenham and the English game in general ...but he does fall over. Everybody gets kicked and players have to learn to handle that without flopping over all the time

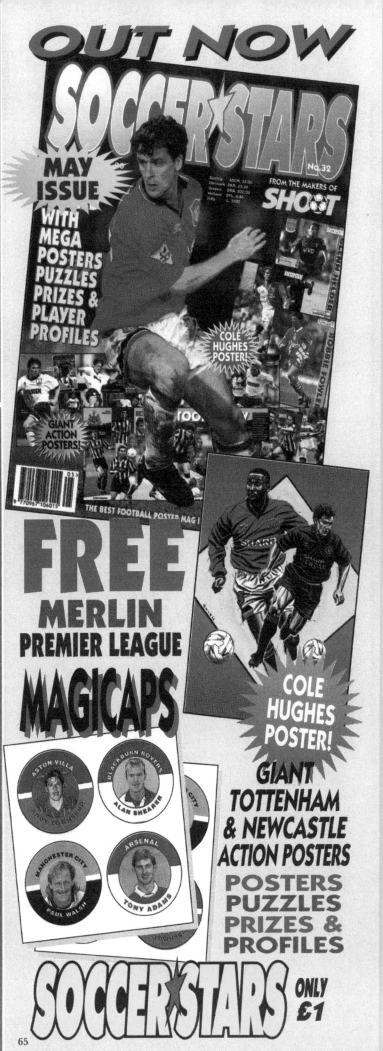

The England captain writes for SHOOT!

The England skipper teams up with SHOOT once more to bring you the latest news from Serie A - and his exclusive verdict on the key Sampdoria players he expects to gun down Arsenal in the Cup-Winners' Cup Semi-Ffinal.

My EURO Agony

But I hope it will end in triumph

Missing out on any Semi-Final is disappointing.

Missing out on a European Semi-Final against an English club is a nightmare...

...particularly as there were only two minutes left of the game which robbed me of the chance to take on Arsenal this week.

We were reaching the end of extra-time in the second-leg of our Quarter-Final clash in Porto when I committed a foul in the centre of the pitch.

Unfortunately, while I accept I was late with the tackle, the referee interpreted the challenge as a sending off offence.

The red card, the first of my career, means I have to sit out both legs of the Semi with Arsenal.

But the disappointment of my dismissal was thankfully overshadowed by our victory in Portugal...against all odds.

And now a victory over two legs against The Gunners will mean that I will be able to play in the Final in Paris on May 10.

With only four teams left in the competition, it is literally anyone's Cup. But I happen to think that we have been drawn against the toughest team of all....Arsenal.

Serie A's Sunday Specials

Time to run the rule over this weekend's top Italian clashes - including Sampdoria's home game with Cremonese.

LAZIO V REGGIANA

Perhaps not one of the most glamorous games of the weekend but arguably the most intriguing - if the stories about Gazza making a comeback are spot on.

This is the game the injury plagued star has earmarked for his return after such a lengthy absence from the game.

He's certainly looking good after losing an incredible three stone in weight in as many months. Now it's only his appetite for the game which is insatiable.

Nobody deserves a break more than Gazza, who is hoping to step back onto the international stage this summer. Everyone's fingers are crossed that his injury problems are finally behind him.

Even without Gazza, Lazio have been a bit tasty of late and it's hard to see Reggiana handling a Gazza-led onslaught.

PARMA v MILAN

This game is likely to produce the greatest entertainment because both teams have such good attacking talent.

Parma, of course, have been up

there all season and have provided the biggest threat to Juventus - but the Turin giants continue to hold the upper-hand in the title race. Milan, meanwhile, have been getting better all the time after a slow start and will give Parma a stern test of their character as much as their ability.

Defeat for Parma could signal the end of their title challenge - and the start of the Scudetto celebrations up in Turin.

SAMPDORIA V CREMONESE

Cremonese have been one of the surprise packages this season and have proved themselves worthy of a place among the Italian elite.

European commitments seem to have affected Samp's form, although they still have two routes open to Europe next season.

The key, as ever, is consistency.

● **LOOK out for the very best of the Serie A action in Saturday's GAZZETTA FOOT-BALL ITALIA (11am); Sunday's FOOTBALL ITALIA live match (1.15pm) and Tuesday night's MEZZANOTTE (12.30 am).**

SERIE A SNIPPETS

JUVENTUS will play the first-leg of their UEFA Cup Semi-Final against Borussia Dortmund this week at Milan's San Siro stadium - and not their home base in Turin. Juve asked to switch the match to another venue in an attempt to draw larger crowds after their previous Euro home ties had attracted modest gates.

LAZIO president Dino Zoff has denied reports that Croat striker Alen Boksic is to be sold to Barcelona, although the Spanish Champions are looking for a top striker to replace Hristo Stoichkov. "We are not in talks with Barcelona or any other team for the transfer of Boksic," insists Zoff.

INTER president Massimo Moratti has confirmed the club's interest in Manchester United's Eric Cantona. Although banned from football until next October, Cantona remains a top target for Europe's finest. "I have sent a fax to Manchester United to sound out whether they are prepared to sell the player," said the president. "I haven't made an offer yet, but that will be the next step."

My Samp STARS

Here's the inside info on the Sampdoria players I believe can blast The Gunners out of Europe...

WALTER ZENGA
He's been inspirational in Europe this season. He's the main reason why we're still in the competition because of his penalty save in Porto.

PIETRO VIERCHOWOD
He's nicknamed 'The Tsar' because of his Russian ancestry and we'll be looking to him to put the shackles on Ian Wright over the two legs. He's 35 but belies his age.

ROBERTO MANCINI
I've been fortunate to play with some great players but my team-mate and captain is the best of the lot. His vision is second to none and he gets as much enjoyment out of making a goal as he does scoring one.

VLADIMIR JUGOVIC
A young Yugoslav with a terrific eye for goal. Physically, he's very strong but has a great touch on the ball.

ATTILIO LOMBARDO
He's nicknamed 'Popeye' (can't understand why) and, in my book, our bald winger is one of the best players in the world. He's played 135 games on the trot and never seems to get injured.

SINISA MILHAILOVIC
He's got the best left foot I've ever seen. Any free-kicks within a distance of 40 yards and the goalkeeper's in trouble. David Seaman, you have been warned.

Arsenal have shown over the last couple of years that they are a very tough side to beat when the chips are down and I expect the first-leg at Highbury to be very close.

From Sampdoria's point of view, we want to take a good result back to Genoa for the return leg and I am confident the lads will be able to achieve that.

To do it we must keep a close watch on Ian Wright and his ability to score goals out of nothing.

We are also aware that Arsenal's recent European success has been built on a resilient attitude and a willingness to work until the final whistle.

We will be paying particular attention to their set plays as the height of Tony Adams and recent signing John Hartson could be very dangerous to us.

Shear Bliss

v Southampton (a) August 20, 1994 D1-1

It's always nice to start the season with a goal and this was our first game. I'd already missed a penalty in the first half but I managed to score one after the break to make amends for that. It was a vital goal because it gave us a 1-1 draw and meant we avoided defeat on the opening day.

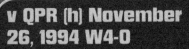

v Coventry (a) March 11, 1995 D1-1

This was in the last minute and it was another important one because it also earned us a 1-1 draw. We were chasing the game and decided to go direct. Graeme Le Saux hit a long ball and I just managed to beat the goalkeeper to it with my head. That won us a point and I said after the game that that point might be enough to win us the League and, as it turned out, we won the title by one point.

v QPR (h) November 26, 1994 W4-0

The third goal in a hat-trick and one of the best I've ever scored. I was about 25 yards out and just cracked it in off the underside of the crossbar. It was a great feeling. On another day I might have passed but we were winning the game comfortably and I was on a hat-trick so I decided to have a go. Luckily for me, it flew in.

Super Al picks his golden goals

Alan Shearer is THE number one striker in England at the moment. The Blackburn striker was named PFA Player of the Year by his fellow professionals and also picked up the SHOOT/Predator Golden Shoe as he helped Blackburn to win the Premiership title. His 34 League goals played a major part in that triumph, but which ones meant the most to him? Here, in another SHOOT exclusive, he picks his six of the best...

v Liverpool (a) May 14, 1995 L1-2

Although this goal meant nothing at the end of the day because we lost, it was great to score in such an important, high pressure game as this one. And it was one of my best because we under such a lot of pressure going into the match that it was important we started well and this goal gave us the lead. It's just a pity we couldn't hang on to it.

v Newcastle (h) May 8, 1995 W1-0

Another vital goal. We had to win this game for obvious reasons and my header gave us a 1-0 victory. Graeme Le Saux put over a great cross and I managed to get above John Beresford at the back post and head it in. As it turned out one was enough in that game because Tim Flowers made some brilliant saves to make sure we got all three points.

v Chelsea (h) March 18, 1995 W2-1

This was my 100th League goal and one I will never forget. Again it was Graeme Le Saux who created the opening with a great ball out of defence and I raced clear and just smashed my shot into the roof of the net. And apart from the fact that it was my 100th goal it also got us back into the game after we'd gone behind early on. And after that we took control and got the three points thanks to a goal from Tim Sherwood.

So, has the world gone mad or is a centre-forward really worth the best part of ten million quid? That sort of money seems to be the going rate

Cra[z]

This lot cost £40 million

these days as clubs fall over themselves to scribble out huge cheques. But is it good for the game? SHOOT investigates...

Sugar: It's Not Sweet

Tottenham chairman Alan Sugar has blasted the inflated transfer fees being paid by the top clubs in this country.

Since June 1, Premiership clubs have splashed out an astonishing £40,700,000 on recruiting new talent for next season.

AND THAT FIGURE WAS SPENT ON JUST 10 PLAYERS!

It was just 16 years ago that people blinked in disbelief when Brian Clough paid £1 million to take Trevor Francis to Nottingham Forest. These days, you can't buy a Second Division right-back for that!

And Sugar insists that it's got to stop.

"It's lunacy," he says. "We have got clubs going into the red to buy players to appease people and keep up with others. It's a sad, sorry world.

"It is becoming difficult to

compete in the transfer market when inflated prices are being paid that do not make sense with balance sheets.

"In any other business, you cannot trade when you are insolvent, but it seems in football you just get on with it. I'm concerned where this will stop. It has got to stop."

But what is the answer to the problem?

"It's down to the FA now," says Sugar. "We have to get back to normality, like £2.5 million deals.

"It's no good asking the Premiership chairmen to do something about it. We have meetings when they all say how ridiculous the game has got. Then they walk out and do the complete opposite.

"The transfer market has gone out of all proportion. It is total madness."

70

ZY!

The Dream Team

It's doubtful that even Jack Walker could afford to put together this little lot. We've picked the most expensive Premiership player [so far!] in each position and this is the costly line-up...

Tim Flowers
£2.3m

Warren Barton
£4m

Tony Dorigo
£2m

John Scales
£4m

Phil Babb
£3.6m

Roy Keane
£3.75m

David Batty
£2.7m

Paul Warhurst
£2.7m

Dennis Bergkamp
£7.5m

Stan Collymore
£8.5m

Andy Cole
£7m

The SHOOT Jury

There's been so much money flying around this summer that it's made the National Lottery look like a school raffle. But has the money been wisely spent? SHOOT takes a look at some of the big summer movers and gives our rating on the deal based on age, previous form and cost...

Stan Collymore
At £8.5 million he is now the most expensive player in the country and a lot will depend on how he handles that pressure. He needs a good start at Anfield and if he gets it, he'll go from strength to strength. If he doesn't, then it could be a very different story.
RATING [out of ten]: 8

Dennis Bergkamp
We reckon he's the best buy of the summer. OK, £7.5 million is a lot of money for a guy who was a flop in Italy, but he is still a world class player. If Bruce Rioch plays him behind Ian Wright and John Hartson, as we expect him to, Dennis the Menace will set Highbury alight.
RATING: 10

Chris Armstrong
Like Bergkamp, he needs a good start at Spurs after a disastrous first season in the Premiership with Crystal Palace. He scored only eight League goals last term - hardly the sort of form worthy of a £4.5 million striker. At that money, he must be a gamble for Gerry Francis.
RATING: 6

Les Ferdinand
When he is on song, there is no better striker in the Premiership, apart perhaps from Alan Shearer. Ferdinand has the lot - pace, power, a fierce shot and unrivalled aerial ability. They will love him on Tyneside and, like several famous number nines before him, he will become a legend.
RATING: 9

Savo Milosevic
He has a staggering record in his native Yugoslavia but he's still only 21 and the Premiership will be a big step up in class for him, especially as, for £3.5 million, the Villa fans will be expecting such big things from him. Could be a good buy, but it may take time.
RATING: 6

Gareth Southgate
Villa fans will also be looking for good things from Southgate but he's already proved himself at this level. He was the youngest captain in the Premiership last season and, although Palace went down, he emerged with great credit. At £2.5 million, he looks an excellent buy.
RATING: 8

Warren Barton
Now the country's most expensive defender, but don't be surprised to see him playing in midfield next season. Another product from the astonishing Wimbledon conveyor belt and expect him to be just as successful as most of his predecessors.
RATING: 8

Mark Hughes
He may be 31, but there's plenty left in Mark Hughes' tank. And if you ask most of the managers in the Premiership one player they'd like to have in their side, a lot would say Hughes. United could regret letting him join Chelsea, especially for just £1.5 million.
RATING: 9

Au Revoir

He was nicknamed 'Il Magnifique' in Paris and David Ginola is set to take Tyneside by storm. Newcastle's latest sensation reveals all in another exclusive interview with Adrian Curtis - including the reason he quit Paris and why he snubbed Barcelona to join Kevin Keegan's Geordie revolution...

Newcastle's £2.5 million superstar David Ginola quit Paris St. Germain because he could no longer work with club coach Luis Fernandez.

The French ace also turned his back on Barcelona in favour of Geordie giant Kevin Keegan and the chance to prove he can handle the rigours of the English game.

After winning every French honour possible with the Parisian club, the arrival of Fernandez last season was the turning point for the player.

Ginola claims that the new coach wanted to change the way the French international played and even hated him having a round of golf in his spare time.

The French ace couldn't stand the prospect of another year under that regime and decided to quit the club.

He reveals: "It was impossible for me to stay another year in Paris because I had a problem with manager Luis Fernandez. It was a problem of communication between us. He didn't like what I did on the field and was jealous of some of the things I did.

"He wanted to change my style completely. I said 'no I'm 28' and that he couldn't change the way I played. If I had been 20 then maybe it would have been different, but I'm not a young player.

"It became a big problem and that's why I left Paris. I said to the chairman of the club that there was no way I wanted to spend another year like I'd had last season.

"It would have been too hard for me. I want to play my best football and with Fernandez in charge it would have been impossible because he wanted to break me every day, every week, for the year.

"We had three years of success getting to the Semi-Final of the European Cup and winning the French Championship and Cup, but last season I didn't enjoy it.

"Fernandez came to Paris and told me not to do certain things. He didn't even want us to play golf it was that bad. He is a very strange person.

"The club had been successful for years, but he came in last year and wanted to change everything."

Ginola is full of praise for Keegan, though, and even the Newcastle boss reckons he has found a bargain in the Frenchman.

Ginola adds: "Kevin Keegan is really different. He is professional and he is sensible about football and life - about all the things that revolve around football.

"I like that. He wants to make sure I'm happy and I want to play my best for him and the club. He will let me have a free role in the side but when we lose the ball, I will come back to defend.

"This year Newcastle have a very strong side, especially up front. I'm very impressed by Peter Beardsley, who is like a youngster, even at 34.

"We must win something this year and we must qualify for Europe. It is very important for the fans, the players and the club that we do that."

SHOOT: Why did you decide to come to England?

DAVID: Because I like English football and I don't think it's that hard for a French player to come to play in England. The English people are not attracted by French football or its players and they don't know a lot about the French game, whereas they know a lot about Italian, German and Spanish football. I'm sure it will be no problem for me to adapt to the English game. It is more direct than in France, where it is a bit more vicious.

SHOOT: But why Newcastle?

DAVID: Why Newcastle? Because they made a proposition. At the beginning of June I spoke with Barcelona. They wanted me to sign for them but they had both Hagi and Stoichkov at the time and they had to sell one of those first so they asked me to wait. I said it was impossible for me to do that and when Newcastle came in for me I said yes.

SHOOT: Is it true you and Eric Cantona don't get on?

DAVID: No, I have no problem with Eric. I had words with him after the international game against Bulgaria but I never said any bad things about Eric. I never spoke to him before I decided to come to England.

72

Pet

I couldn't play for Fernandez any longer says Ginola

SHOOT: We're you surprised by his attack on a supporter at Crystal Palace last season?

DAVID: I want to remember all the best things from Eric, not the bad things. He has done more good things for English football than bad things. I was surprised by what he did but it is very hard. In France we have the same problem with the supporters. During the year you have the problem with the fans who say bad things about you for a number of games and in the end you say 'OK, stop now'. I try to tell them that we are like them. Before we became French footballers we were supporters and respected the players. Today the most important thing is we must try to have more respect in life for everybody. It is the most important thing, but it is not always the case in English football."

SHOOT: How will you cope with the physical side of English football?

DAVID: I want to learn the fighting spirit of the English game. The football here is harder physically. In France it is tough but it is not the same. I think it will be good for my football because the best points to my game are technique and, if I can add physical qualities to that, I will improve even more."

SHOOT: Is it a risk to come here when you could have stayed in Europe?

DAVID: People have said to me that English football is very different and that there are a lot of games to play every week, but I tell them that I will adapt to that. It is no risk for me to come over here. It was more of a risk to stay in Paris."

SHOOT: Will you feel a failure if it doesn't work out?

DAVID: I am confident about my situation here. I will do my best. If it doesn't work out, I will go back to France with my head held high. If I go back to France with no medals, I will at least be able to say I tried. I will not care. I have won cups and titles in France but I want to see how good I can be outside. If I had finished my career and never tried, I would have regretted it."

SHOOT: How do you rate France's chances of qualifying for the European Championship in England next year?

DAVID: We have a lot of young players but we must knit together. We found that cohesion against Slovakia - and beat them 4-0 - but we must do it more often. We play Poland this month and if we win we'll play in England next year. I feel we have a chance of winning if we qualify. But there will be a lot more pressure on England because they playing on home soil. If they lose it will very bad for them.

12 August 1995

Write to Greavsie, SHOOT, King's Reach Tower, Stamford St, London SE1 9LS

Barmy Bohinen

Lars Bohinen must be crazy to turn down the chance of an international cap because of a political point of principle.
JOHN CUNDALL, RETFORD, NOTTS

As you get older, things like caps are not quite so important, but clearly as a young man he has got principles. If he wants to stand by them, you have to respect that and it is wrong to criticise anyone who stands by their feelings. If that is what he wants to do, he has every right to do it. Most players wouldn't know what a point of principle is, but obviously Bohinen has strong opinions and is prepared to stand by them.

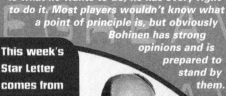

This week's Star Letter comes from Jim Forsyth, of Paisley. He wins a pair of New Balance boots.

PICK OF THE POST

Suspect Gazza

How long will it be before Gazza's suspect temperament lands him in big trouble in Scotland?

It seems that all is still not right in his mind. He is still going around swearing and kicking players when there is no need to. In Scottish football you only get three or four hard games a year, the rest are all patsy games really. He should show himself as Britain's best player because up there he will be able to juggle the ball and do whatever he wants because he is playing against a load of no-hopers. But we all know that what goes on inside him could let him down. I don't know how long he'll last up there, but none of us would be surprised if he is front page news within a few weeks.

Swede Dreams

Spurs are going to struggle in the Premiership if they can't even beat micky mouse Swedish teams.
PHIL LEVY, WEST BYFLEET

I wouldn't be too alarmed if I were a Tottenham fan because pre-season results always have a habit of being a bit wayward one way or another. Arsenal fans are getting lulled into a false sense of security, but thrashing a Swedish Third Division side 8-1 isn't that great a result. Getting beaten in Sweden is not that important for Spurs, but, like a lot of teams, they will need a good start if they are not going to get into trouble.

Corky the Catch

Terry Venables should put cricketer Dominic Cork in the England football team, because it seems he can do no wrong at the moment.
RICK NEVILLE, ASHTON-UNDER-LYNE

He has certainly done what no other Englishman has done under Terry Venables - got a hat-trick! Maybe Terry should pick him, because we need that sort of spirit. Ian Wright was the last man to score a hat-trick for England, against mighty San Marino after we had given them a goal start in ten seconds, so Corky might just be the man for the job!

Hughes a Clever Buy

Chelsea have got the bargain of the season in Mark Hughes.
COLM LAGAN, PIMLICO, LONDON

There is no question that Hughes has been the best buy of the summer. When you compare him with Bergkamp, Armstrong and Collymore, £1.5m for him was an absolute snip. He will be a great asset to Chelsea. United felt they needed to get rid of him because sometimes you can be at a club too long, so I don't blame them for selling him. But Glenn Hoddle should be congratulated for snapping him up.

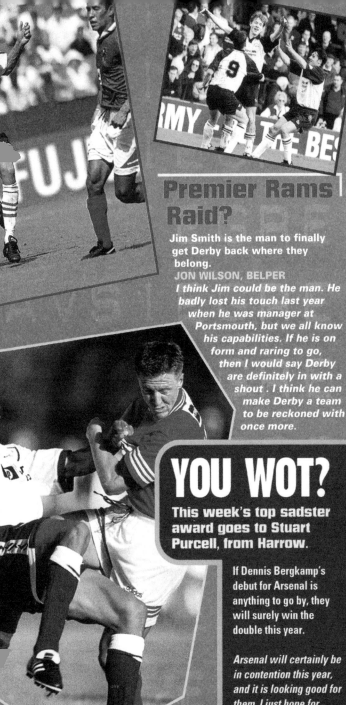

Premier Rams Raid?

Jim Smith is the man to finally get Derby back where they belong.
JON WILSON, BELPER

I think Jim could be the man. He badly lost his touch last year when he was manager at Portsmouth, but we all know his capabilities. If he is on form and raring to go, then I would say Derby are definitely in with a shout . I think he can make Derby a team to be reckoned with once more.

YOU WOT?

This week's top sadster award goes to Stuart Purcell, from Harrow.

If Dennis Bergkamp's debut for Arsenal is anything to go by, they will surely win the double this year.

Arsenal will certainly be in contention this year, and it is looking good for them. I just hope for Bergkamp's sake that he doesn't get saddled with the anticipation that he is going to do a Klinsmann. The German was a one-off, and he did better than even he believed he would do in his one season at Spurs. I think Arsenal supporters believe they have got another Jurgen Klinsmann on their hands, but they may not have. Scoring goals in pre-season is one thing, putting that into practice in the Premiership is very different. He's a good buy, and will do well, but Arsenal fans should not get carried away.

Rich Pickings

It is now official that the bigger clubs are getting richer at the expense of the smaller clubs. How long can this go on?
JANINE THORPE,
ALDERLEY EDGE, CHESHIRE

It will continue to go on, as there is nothing to stop it. Individual clubs are now building up to their own television contracts and you are going to get European Leagues in the near future. It is a fact that the big clubs are going to get more and more powerful, and it's going to get harder every season to join the elite band. But you can't hark back to the old days and say it was better then - we live in the modern world, and things are different.

Andy Cole may have made a quiet start to the season but it's only a matter of time before the Cole fire starts to burn. And when it does, the message from the man himself is that defenders had better watch out cos he's in the mood for goals...

COLE'S GOAL

I want to break my record says Andy

Andy Cole has not had the best of starts to season 1995-96.

He had to sit out the opening few games of the season with a calf injury, when he did get back he was missing his mate Eric Cantona, and to cap it all United got spanked by York and Rotor Volgograd.

Hardly the stuff of optimism, but to hear Cole talking you could be forgiven for thinking that everything in the garden is rosy.

And if the Newcastle striker has his way, both he and United will come up smelling of the sweet stuff.

Despite his faltering start to the season - at the time of writing Cole had scored just one goal - he still believes that he is on course for a hatful, and predicts that he may even better his own Premiership record.

Two seasons ago, Cole rattled in 34 goals - a total matched last season by Alan Shearer - and he reckons it's time that record was broken.

And who will break it? Well, don't rule out Andy Cole. He insists: "I'm still capable of beating the record."

Certainly Alex Ferguson will be hoping that the goals start to flow because, so far at least, his dream ticket pairing of Cole and Eric Cantona is firing blanks.

But his lack of success in front of the posts hasn't dampened Cole's enthusiasm or dented his confidence.

"I will score goals this season," he adds defiantly. "It's been a frustrating period but hopefully I'm over the worst. "The record is going to go and I think there is a chance I could be top scorer again. If I can stay free from injury I know I will be back as the player I was before."

Treble Trouble

Andy Cole is facing a triple threat as he bids to become the Premiership's top dog.

The Old Trafford hero is desperate to regain his place as the king of England's goalscorers, but he knows that he faces a real fight to grab back his crown.

And he believes there are three men who stand between him and his moment of glory - Les Ferdinand, Tony Yeboah and Alan Shearer.

They are the men Cole will be watching out for as he looks to get his season off the ground after a stuttering start.

Cole admits: "They are the three players to watch for and all three are capable of beating the Premiership record and finishing as top scorer."

Here's Andy's run-down on his three rivals...

Cole on: FERDINAND
He's doing my old job at Newcastle and could be the one to beat the record. He's got off to a great start and looks like he's going to go from strength to strength at St James' Park. It has obviously been a good move for him and, if he can stay free from injury, he'll take some stopping.

Cole on: YEBOAH
I'm a big fan of Yeboah. He's an excellent player to watch because most of his goals are screamers - he doesn't seem to score many tap-ins. There's a good chance he will get more than 30 this season. Leeds looks like they mean business so it could be Yeboah's year.

Cole on: SHEARER
Shearer is finding it tough at the moment, with Blackburn struggling, and he's also hit a bit of a sticky patch with England. But he will score goals and I won't be surprised if he breaks the 30-mark. He's got a great eye for goal and the fact that he's at the top of the scoring charts even though things haven't been going too well for Blackburn proves what a great striker he is.

Cashing In

LATEST PREMIERSHIP ODDS
ANDY COLE 10/1
ALAN SHEARER 3/1
LES FERDINAND 11/2

Kids up and down the country will be cheering on Andy Cole this season. The Manchester United star stands to earn a fortune for children's charity Barnados if he finishes as the Premiership's top scorer. Cole's sponsors, Reebok, have placed a £500 bet at odds of 10-1 on Cole to finish top of the file and they will donate the £5,000 to Barnados if he does it.

"I will be pulling out all the stops to make sure I win the bet," says Cole. "I'll give it my best shot."

Reebok

WIN!

Andy Cole's Reebok kit and boots

Yes, that's right, thanks to our good mates at Reebok, one of you is going to be strutting his stuff in this great gear.

You can win a pair of Jacquard shorts and a drill top - as worn by Andy in our picture - from Reebok's latest sports training collection which is available in the shops now.

But that's not all. Oh, no.

Because we've also got a pair of Supreme Cole RS boots (adults £39.99, children £32.99) to give away to help you score like the United star, plus an Andy Cole Reebok ball and a pair of Andy Cole Reebok Shinguards.

It's a brilliant prize package and a must for all football fans.

To stand a chance of winning, just answer the simple question below and send your entry on a postcard, to: Andy Cole Comp, SHOOT, King's Reach Tower, Stamford Street, London SE99 0BB.

QUESTION: **How many League goals did Andy Cole score in season 1993-94?**

...IT IS NOW!

QUIZ ANSWERS
Old Heads: 1. Leeds. 2. Ally McCoist. 3. Paul Rideout. 4. Testimonial. 5. Ipswich. 6. Motherwell. 7. £1.5 million. 8. Barnsley. 9. Centre-half. 10. Steve Bruce. **New Faces:** 1. Wimbledon. 2. True. 3. Leeds. 4. Paris St Germain. 5. Germany. 6. Scott Taylor. 7. Bolton. 8. Midfield. 9. David Beckham. 10. Liechtenstein.

CROSSWORD ANSWERS
Across: 1. Gerry Creaney. 7 and 14 Down. Paul Walsh. 8. Reading. 10. Bruce. 12 and 21 Across. Local Derby. 16. Kiev. 17. Kamara. 20. Sugar. **Down:** 1. Guppy. 2. Reuter. 3. Currie. 4 and 13 Down. Efan Ekoku. 5 and 14 Across. Neil Warnock. 6. Yugoslavia. 9. York. 11. Cooper. 15. Rough. 18. Mee. 19. Rob

Published by IPC Magazines Ltd, a member of the Reed Elsevier plc group. SHOOT incorporating GOAL must not be sold at more than the recommended selling price shown on the cover. Sole Agents: Australia and New Zealand, Gordon and Gotch Ltd : South Africa, Central News Agency Ltd. All rights reserved and reproduction without permission strictly forbidden. Distribution by Marketforce (UK) Ltd, 247 Tottenham Court Road, London W1P 0AU. Typeset and colour origination by Litho Origination, London. Printed by St. Ives Plc. ISSN 0306-5216. 12 month subscription rates: UK £50. Eire/rest of Europe, surface £66, airmail £70, rest of world, surface £65, airmail £100 includes contribution to postage. For American subscription queries please contact: Subscriptions Dept, PO Box 272, Oakfield House, 35 Perrymount Road, Haywards Heath, W. Sussex, UK, RH16 3FS.

Distribution by Marketforce. ©
IPC Magazines 1995

Double

SHOOT's secret seven with a Goldeneye for goal

Tomas Brolin/ Tony Yeboah

A bit of an unknown quantity so far, but this pairing looks made in heaven. With Brolin's silky Swedish skills and Yeboah's 'Thunderball' finishing, they will frighten 'The Living Daylights' out of the Premiership when they get going.

James Bond fever is gripping the nation as Goldeneye fills cinemas across the country. But who are football's Goalden Guys? SHOOT takes a look at 007 of the Premiership's striking partnerships which are licensed to thrill...

Alan Shearer/ Mike Newell

Tried and trusted pairing, who's attitude to Chris Sutton appears to be 'Live and Let Die'. Despite his much heralded arrival at Ewood Park last season, Sutton has slipped into the background this time around and the original Roving duo are back to together proving that 'Diamonds Are Forever', and these two are real gems.

Les Ferdinand/ Peter Beardsley

He's done it with Gary Lineker, he's done it with Andy Cole, now he's supplying passes to Les Ferdinand marked 'For Your Eyes Only'. And with the new Toon hero granted a 'Licence To Kill' on Tyneside, these two could turn out to be the pick of the bunch.

Andy Cole/ Eric Cantona

After avoiding a spell 'On Her Majesty's Secret Service' Cantona appears to be getting back to his best and that will be welcome news for Cole. The former Newcastle star has been struggling in front of goal lately, but with the Frenchman supplying the ammunition, 'Goldeneye' will soon be back at the top of the scoring charts.

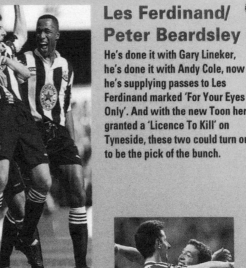

Robbie Fowler/ Ian Rush

Ian Rush has been sending bullets past goalkeepers 'From Rushy With Love' for years now and now Fowler is following suit. The young England Under-21 international has already been dubbed Rushie Mark II, proof that 'You Only Live Twice'.

Trouble

Teddy Sheringham/ Chris Armstrong

Many people felt that Spurs boss Gerry Francis was gambling in the 'Casino Royale' when he paid £4.5m for Armstrong, but the ex-Crystal Palace man has proved his critics wrong. And after a patchy start to the relationship, Sheri is now the 'Guy Who Loved Me' as far as Armstrong is concerned as their partnership continues to blossom.

Ian Wright/ Dennis Bergkamp

Those people who said Bergkamp would never settle in England have been well and truly silenced and you can be sure they will 'Never Say Never Again'. The Dutchman is a delight alongside Wright, who has a real 'View To A Kill' when in front of goal and they complement each other perfectly.

Brolin: The Baby Faced Assassin

He might look angelic, but defenders around the world will tell you that Tomas Brolin is anything but an angel of mercy. He is lethal in and around the box and seems certain to be a massive hit at Elland Road. Here, just for you, are a few things you may not know about the super Swede...

● Brolin was born in Huiksvall on November 29, 1969. His father, Rune, played for a Swedish Second Division side. His home debut for Leeds, against Blackburn last week, was on his 26th birthday.

● He began his career with local club Naskivens and made his debut at 17 in a victory over Elfsborg.

● He spent three years with Naskivens before moving on to Norrkoping. Shortly after switching clubs he made his debut for the national team, in a friendly against Wales, and scored twice in a 4-2 win.

● After his displays in the 1990 World Cup finals, Norrkoping were flooded with enquiries and Brolin moved to Italy, where he signed for Parma.

● He won the Italian Cup and the European Cup-Winners' Cup with Parma but, after injury wrecked his season last year, he was ready for a new challenge and Leeds have provided it.

● He is an excellent ice hockey player and could have made a career in the sport. He also enjoys playing handball and table tennis.

● When he was a part-time player, he worked in a corner shop selling sweets and lottery tickets.

Give me a month to get my full fitness back, and to adapt to playing in England, and then I will show people what I can really do. I believe I can help Leeds win the Championship again.
TOMAS BROLIN

He is a class player and I believe he will prove to be an excellent buy for Leeds. I am sure he is going to be an excellent partner for Tony Yeboah.
HOWARD WILKINSON

I am sure Tomas and I are going to work well together. He is truly world class. He can weigh in with goals of his own, and link up with the other good players in the side. We are going to be very difficult to defend against.
TONY YEBOAH

It's been a long and hard learning process for Liverpool goalkeeper David James. He's had his problems and been honest enough to reveal them and brave enough to deal with them. So how is life for DJ at Anfield now? ADRIAN CURTIS went along to Melwood's training ground to find out...

QUESTIONS Q&A ANSWERS

SHOOT: You seem to be on top of your game right at the moment, is that right?

DJ: I'm not happy with any performance I give. We played Rochdale in the FA Cup and won 7-0 and my contribution was minimal, but I still wasn't happy with my kicking. There's not a game this season when I've done everything right and I've said to myself 'I can't get any better'. Although I'm confident of getting picked for the next game, I would never say 'I'll be in the team in May'.

SHOOT: But surely there have been no horrendous clangers?

DJ: Yes there has. I dropped a clanger against Vladikavkaz in Europe. The guy took a free-kick and I don't know what happened but the ball went in somehow. To say it wasn't a clanger would be wrong, because it was. Fortunately we won 2-1, but every 'keeper makes mistakes.

Hey Mr D

James is pumping up the party at Anfield

SHOOT: What do you think about 'that' Tony Yeboah volley?

DJ: It winds me up every time I see it because I think I could have saved it. I can still remember the feeling I had going for the ball and although it doesn't give me nightmares, I was only millimetres away from it. If the same situation happens again, I want to be a few more millimetres further than I needed to be the first time. But, and I know I sound like Bruce Lee here, I strive for perfection.

SHOOT: Both yourself and Liverpool had a bit of a rocky start when you first joined - why was that?

DJ: It was down to people like myself who didn't do the right things at the right times, i.e. not conducting oneself professionally. If my form slips in the first team then the team's does as well.

SHOOT: What are your thoughts on England?

DJ: I had the call up to last season's training session and the Umbro Cup, and I haven't had a look-in since then. But if I never play for England in my life, then something hasn't gone right. If that is the case then hopefully it will be because someone overlooked me, as opposed to me not being good enough.

SHOOT: How is the drinking situation now?

DJ: I've cut down on it, but I still get bladdered every now and then. I gave up completely for a time when I was out of the side. I needed to stop it and say to myself 'get your head together and get back in the team'. But rather than getting drunk rather badly on a Wednesday knowing I can't handle it on a Saturday, I don't drink on Wednesday. Now I know when to drink and when not to.

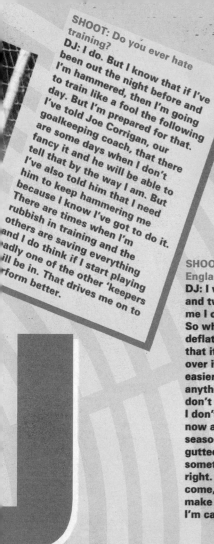

SHOOT: Do you ever hate training?

DJ: I do. But I know that if I've been out the night before and I'm hammered, then I'm going to train like a fool the following day. But I'm prepared for that. I've told Joe Corrigan, our goalkeeping coach, that there are some days when I don't fancy it and he will be able to tell that by the way I am. But I've also told him that I need him to keep hammering me because I know I've got to do it. There are times when I'm rubbish in training and the others are saving everything and I do think if I start playing badly one of the other 'keepers will be in. That drives me on to form better.

SHOOT: Does missing out on England concern you much?

DJ: I was building myself up and two or three people told me I could be in the squad. So when I wasn't I felt so deflated. I was down so badly that it took me a week to get over it. It would have been easier if no-one had said anything to me. Now, if I don't get picked, that's life. If I don't get picked between now and the end of the season I'm not going to get gutted about it because something's obviously not right. If my chance does come, then hopefully I'll make the most of it. I think I'm capable of handling it.

SHOOT: Do you expect to be in the England squads when they are named?

DJ: I do look at every squad and there are times when I feel I've done enough to get in and it gets me down when I'm not included. At the beginning of the season I felt on top of my form but then the Yeboah goal was scored, which again, was out of this world. I was just hoping to be in the shadow squad and have my name linked with England. But I wasn't and I just went into one then.

SHOOT: Can Liverpool win the title?

DJ: Nightmare November is when it all started going wrong for us. It was one of the worst months I've had at the club. But it showed us you can't be slapping everyone. We beat Manchester City convincingly twice in a matter of days and then had a bad run which tends to point towards a lapse of concentration somewhere along the line. But now we've hit a good run and things have completely turned round. We are capable of being up there at the finish.

WHO WOULD YOU BE IF...

...you could be any other sporting hero in the world?

No.1
DWIGHT YORKE

Dwight Yorke has Brian to thank for being the goal hero of Villa Park. But this Brian is little, not Little.

It was West Indies cricket legend Brian Lara who stopped Dwight from fleeing back to Trinidad & Tobago with the homesickness that threatened to bring his Villa career to an end in 1994.

Dwight has always been a cricket lover. As a kid he played cricket and football in Tobago with Brian and they watched the great Windies side take on the world. And the pair have been mates ever since.

So it was perfect timing when Lara arrived in Birmingham for that record-smashing summer of cricket with Warwickshire.

While Dwight recovered from injury, he cheered himself up watching Brian's amazing feats.

"I was finding it hard to keep my head up but I took encouragement from what Brian was doing," recalls the Villa ace.

"It was sensational stuff and he made me realise that I had a lot of work to do to make something of my career.

"Brian and I meet up as often as we can and if he is home during the summer, we always spend time together. He's a great mate and great fun."

Ruud Gullit is one of the game's deepest thinkers

What Do You Think About...

Your move to Chelsea?
For once, I let my heart speak. The first impression is usually right, and my first impression of Chelsea was very sharp. I needed a new challenge. I have to admit though, than when I saw Stamford Bridge for the first time before the start of the season, the place was in a mess. I did begin to wonder, but as soon as I played there I knew everything would be OK.

Your decision now?
Every day I'm very happy to be a Chelsea player because I'm having fun. My motives for playing in the Premiership are probably different from those of, say, Dennis Bergkamp or David Ginola. My concern is not to win a whole lot of Cups, but just to do something different and face a new challenge.

Leaving Italy?
I loved many aspects of playing in Italy, and could have stayed for another couple of years, but you have to know when enough is enough. I'd won everything with Milan and Sampdoria, but I needed to go.

Glenn Hoddle?
In Holland we couldn't believe how little England played him. If he'd been Dutch or Italian, he would have won a 100 caps. When I first came to talk to Chelsea I knew Glenn's intentions from the start, otherwise I wouldn't be here now. He told me 'this is the way we're going to play', and that was the challenge.

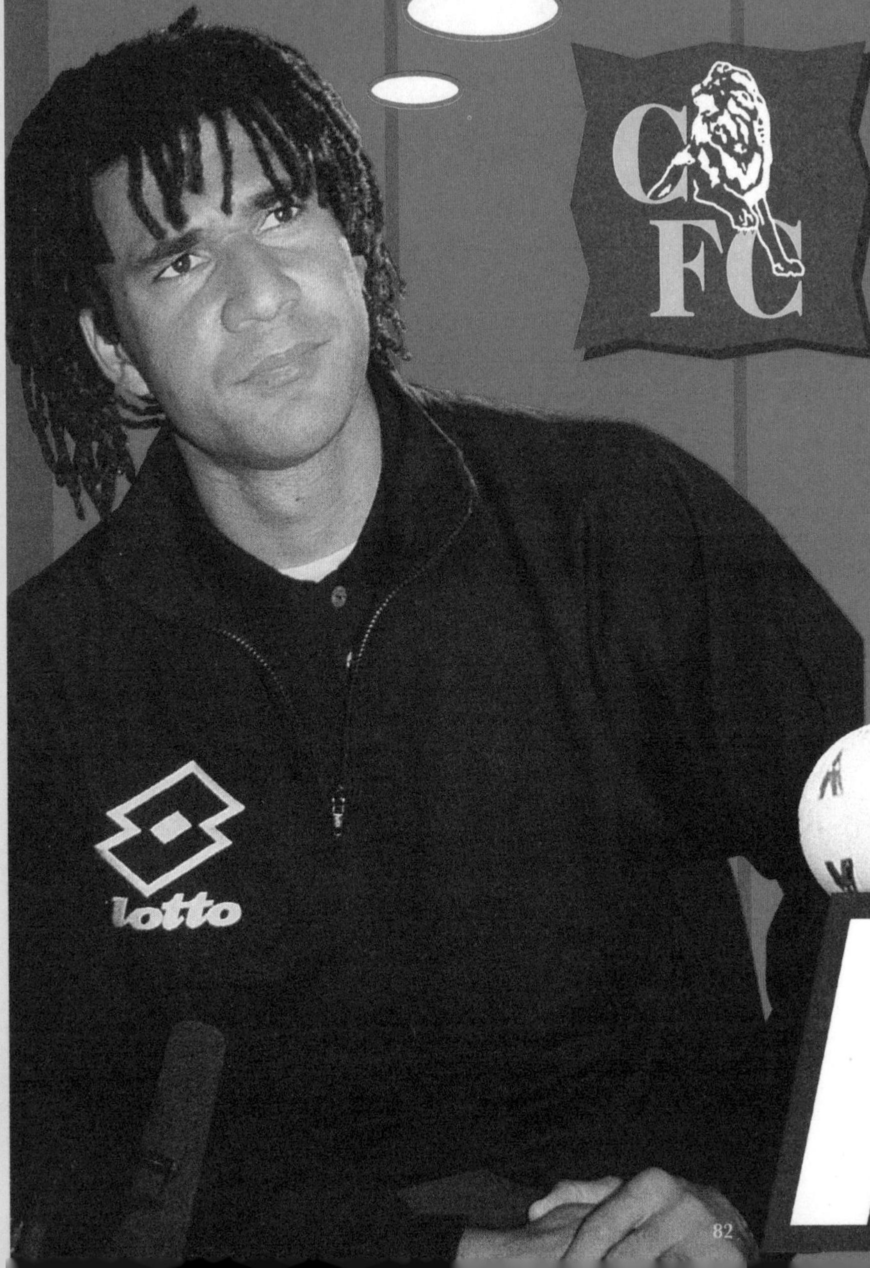

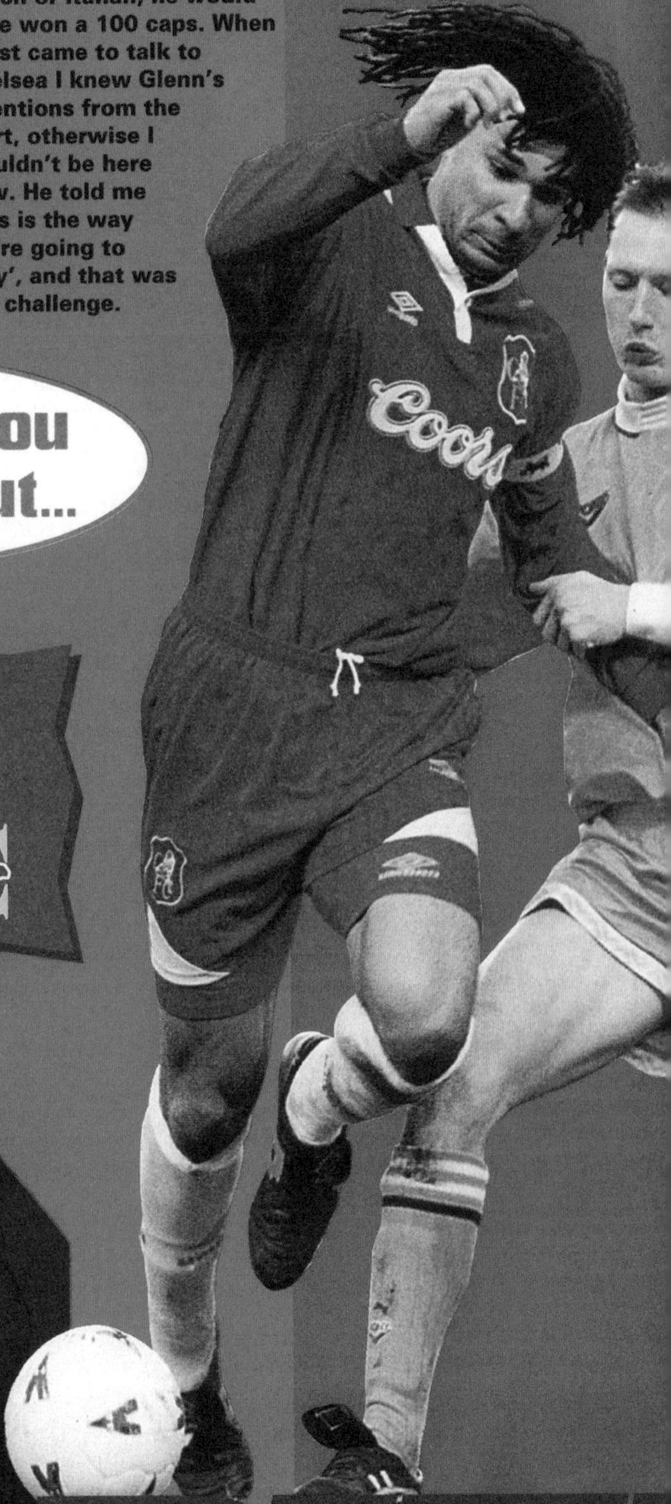

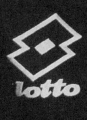

RUU

The foundations have been laid at Chelsea and success will definitely follow

The differences between Italy and England?

In Italy, it is so different. If you are playing on a Saturday, after a Wednesday game you go home and prepare for the weekend. Here, you go out for a few drinks. You can't do it in Italy. You have to be professional, go home, sleep and focus on the next game. The Italians wouldn't believe the players here on match day talking about tickets and using their mobile phones.

Your teammates?

They all know me well by now and they poke fun at me, but I enjoy their company. To start with, it was a bit like the first round of a boxing match. I could see that the players were all sizing me up and seeing what I was like. But as soon as they realized I was one of them they were OK. I play a lot of golf with them and I sometimes go out to the pub with them. It all provides the freedom I get out of playing my football in England. I feel so free over here, living in London, going to gigs and the cinema and just having fun.

The future for Chelsea?

The Foundations have been laid and success will definitely follow. But it will take some time yet. You can see on the faces of the Chelsea players that they are doing something now that gives them so much pleasure. They know they're better now than a few months ago, and they understand there is much more to the game than just kicking the ball into the box and hoping somebody might score.

I could have stayed in Italy for another couple of years, but I'd won everything and needed to go

The future for Ruud Gullit?

I don't know what I will do because I'm enjoying myself too much at the moment to think about it.

I feel so free in London, going to gigs and the cinema and just having fun

D GULLIT

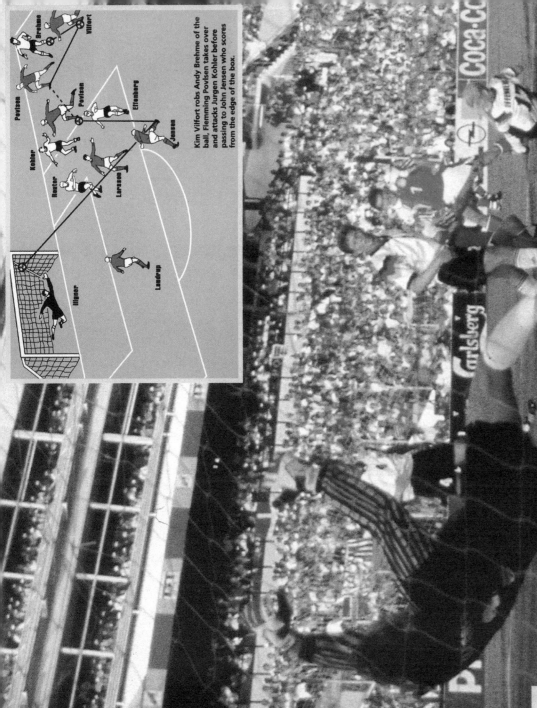

Kim Vilfort robs Andy Brehme of the ball. Flemming Povlsen takes over and attacks Jurgen Kohler before passing to John Jensen who scores from the edge of the box.

GOLDEN GOALS
No.22 John Jensen
DENMARK v GERMANY
EURO CHAMPIONSHIP FINAL 1992

SHOOT

Shooting to the top
Fowler

Robbie Fowler is the man with the golden shooting boots, and he's hoping they will shoot him all the way to the top this season with Liverpool and England...

How much pressure is on you to win something this season?

I wouldn't say it was pressure, but it would be nice to win something. I think we've got the makings of good side and if we become more consistent, there's a good chance we can win something. Last season, we weren't consistent and we've got to get that right.

How hard is it having different strike partners since Ian Rush left?

It's not ideal. Obviously I'd like to have a settled partner but as long as I'm playing, that's the main thing. There's so much competition for places here, no-one's guaranteed a place. There are a lot of good lads on the bench. I've played with Patrik Berger, Stan and Macca, and they all differ, but I'm learning to work with them all the time. It helps me in the long run because it improves my own all-round game. It makes me more of a team player.

What's it like playing with Patrik Berger?

He's superb. He works so hard and he's not scared to put a foot in. He's quick and he's scored a few goals which is good because we're spreading the goals around at the moment with me, Macca and Patrik getting some each.

Having such a great record, are you under pressure to score every game?

There is a bit, but I try not to let it bother me. But if I go a few games without scoring, you can sense the anxiety in the crowd. It's my own fault, though, through what I did when I first came into the side. Scoring so many goals then, I've put pressure on myself!

Is everything natural to you now?

No matter how old you are or how many games you've played, you always have to think. But at Liverpool, it's drummed into you to make near post runs, far post runs, get in front of the defender etc. But I think that happens naturally now with me. When I first came in, I'd think 'Where shall I go now? Oh, I've got to go near post'. You play for two or three years and your runs automatically take you there.

Do you ever switch off in a game?

Yeah. I've been like that a few times. But it's not through not trying. I'm learning all the time and I've got to get it out of my game. In the Premier, you've got to be alert all the time. And there have been times this season when I've been docile on the pitch.

Who are your toughest opponents?

Over the years it would have to be Man United. They're such a good side and they've won the title three times in four years and that doesn't happen very often. The two individuals I rate very highly are Gary Pallister and Tony Adams. I've played with Tony for England and as a leader on the pitch he was superb. He's got everything a captain should have.

How far behind the great Liverpool sides is this one?

I don't know, to be honest. It's always hard to compare us with the Liverpool teams of the past - it was so long ago now. We'll never be them and we don't want to be. We want to win the League and, in 20 years time, hope people will be talking about the 90s Liverpool.

You've got a great chance of winning the European Cup-Winners' Cup now, though?

There are a few good teams left in it so I'm pleased we've got this far. I'm not saying we shouldn't have got this far, but it's nice to do well in Europe - for a change.

How frustrated have you been by your lack of England chances?

To be honest, I've not been frustrated. I'd like to be more involved but I'm glad to be in the squad. You can hardly complain when you've got Alan Shearer or Les Ferdinand in front of you, can ya? Alan's first class. I know it'll be hard to get them out of those places. I'm unfortunate because I'm trying to get in when there are so many class strikers about.

What are your weaknesses?

I like to think I can work on everything and improve on every part of my game. One of my mates gave me a bit of stick saying I never score any headers, but I've got quite a few recently. That should shut him up for a bit!

What's Roy Evans like in the dressing room?

He's relaxed and calm but when he needs to be tough, he is. He doesn't hold back. If there's something to be said, he says it. He's not soft: you can't be if you're managing a great club like this.

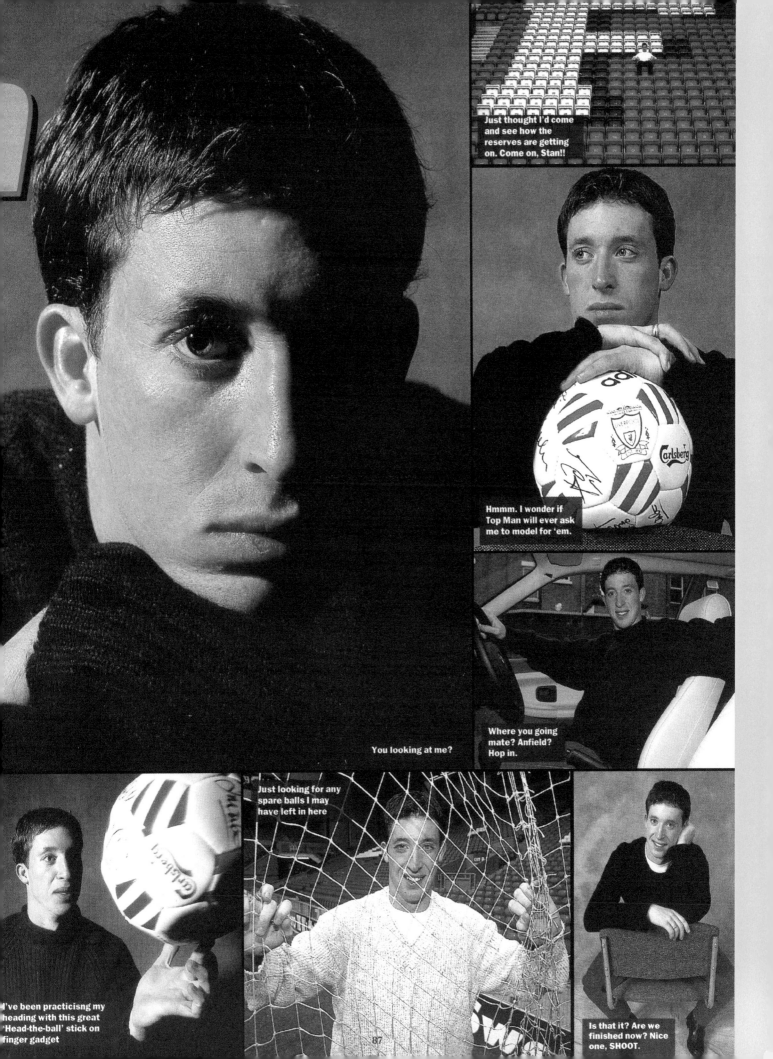

EURO 96

Wembley had never seen anything like it - singing, dancing, celebrating - and England putting four goals past the Dutch. Euro 96 was just one big party for England fans until the Germans went and ruined it all as usual by beating our boys and winning the thing. It was the tournament that announced England's return to the forefront of the international game, the year when football came home. Here's a reminder of those golden days of summer....

Never Forget

These are the moments all England fans will remember forever...

Shearer's Stunner

ENGLAND 1 SWITZERLAND 1

The look on Alan Shearer's face when he ended his 13-game international goal drought said it all. He latched onto Paul Ince's clever pass to hit a screamer into the roof of the Swiss net. Oh yes!!!!

Champagne Sheri

ENGLAND 4 HOLLAND 1

England's best performance since the 1990 Semi-Final - at least. There were so many wonderful memories from the time Ince tricked Blind into giving away a penalty, to Teddy Sheringham sliding in England's fourth to send everyone mental.

When Football Came Home

The End of a Dream

ENGLAND 1 GERMANY 1

What a way to go. It was just like 1990 when England should have won but didn't. Shearer was magnificent, so were the others, but they just couldn't finish the Germans off. And when Gareth Southgate shot straight at Andreas Kopke, the tears began to flow around Wembley.

Glorious Gazza

ENGLAND 2 SCOTLAND 0

Terry Venables' boys did t...but only just. Until Gazza's magic 12 minutes from time, England were iving on the edge. Dave Seaman's penalty save from Gary McAllister was vital: Gazza's strike seconds later was pure genius.

England's Main Men

DAVID SEAMAN
Proved himself Europe's top 'keeper

GARETH SOUTHGATE
Apart from penalty miss, he had a stormer

STEVE McMANAMAN
Rampaging runs caused havoc

PAUL INCE
A steel door in front of the back three

ALAN SHEARER
Best striker in Europe, maybe the world

Able Seaman

ENGLAND 0 SPAIN 0

Just when England needed some uck, they got it. Spain matched he hosts all the way and robably should have won but, when it went to penalties, ngland had THE man. Dave 'the ave' Seaman leapt to his left to unch away Nadal's spot-kick and ut England in the Semis. Wicked!

Do Eu remember these stormin' scenes from Euro 96?

Magic Moments

▲ Croatian Davor Suker's attempt to chip Peter Schmeichel from just inside Denmark's half.

▲ Karel Poborsky's amazing scoop over the Portugal 'keeper in the Quarter-Finals.

▶ Gianfranco Zola taking the ball off a Russian defender, flicking it over him and gliding past another on the other side. Genius.

▶ Ally McCoist's thunderous strike for Scotland against the Swiss took them to the brink of the Quarter-Finals.

18 January 1997

Meet
the boys from
FC SHOOT
Inside
your fave happenin' mag...

EiFFEL SEZ MAG 1 is

...home to ze kool kats, ze Crazy Gang, Higgy of ze Boro, ze Goalie on ze merry-go-round, Merse on 'ez loverley life, and ze young Engerland...not as good as me France boys, no!

ZiPPY SEZ MAG 2 is

...Final Score, where we go down my local chippy to get served by Wrexham's cup star, see what's going on wit'dose Scots, and youse lot can check your scores out in Dream Machine 2.

BUTTSY SEZ MAG 3 is

...Poster City, Arizona! Who d'ya want? Petrescu, Huckerby, Russell, Jan Aage, and monster double-sdied jobbies of our Jamie and Becks? Well, you got 'em!

in the net

I love it! Love it! Love it! LOVE IT!

BIRD OR BLOKE

RADIO ONE'S Mark 'n' Lard want to know...is it a bird or is it a bloke? You tell us and we'll tell them...

Tick one box or t'other	BIRD	BLOKE
CERI HUGHES		
NICKY SUMMERBEE		
JAMIE REDKNAPP		
CHRIS WOODS		
TONY ADAMS		
ANDREA SILENZI		

ANSWERS ON PAGE 4

Queen's Marc Ranger

Pushing for Europe on all three fronts and one of the Premierships top strikers — you'd have thought Wimbledon's Marcus Gayle would be happy.

But he'd rather be playing for his beloved QPR!

"I used to dream of playing for QPR," says Gayley. "I used to watch them and I played on a pitch right next door to the ground. But nobody ever noticed me. I was pretty upset 'cos I thought that was my only chance of pro football. I couldn't believe they weren't interested."

It's okay, Marky boy — at least one London club loves ya!

90

Hair Today...

Naughty Spanish defender Borja Aguirretxu has come up with a quality excuse for why he failed a dope test recently. The Celta Vigo bad boy claims the steroids were in tablets he took to stop himself going bald! And that's his defence to the FA!! Rumours that Steve Stone binned his pills when he saw the FA doctors coming and decided to settle for the Grant Mitchell look instead, are very untrue.

Fantasy Footballer

WONDERFUL WINONA RYDER is such a lovely lass that several Premiership teams have been trying to sign her up as a fan.

Well, what better way to inspire your players to win the title or beat the drop than by making sure a top Hollywood actress is in the crowd to watch their every move?

And, amazingly, it seems that Southampton are the club who've pulled off this major transfer coup!

Now Graeme Souness can rely on at least one Win at the Dell between now and the end of the season.

"Don't get in a strop, SHOP!"

TV Dale offers to help end Wrighty and Schmikey row

ITN's Showbiz correspondent reports

IN AN AMAZING turn of events, ITN has received reports that Dale Winton, host of top TV show, 'Supermarket Sweep', may help to settle the big row between Ian Wright and Peter Schmeichel.

WOULD PETE LOOK LIKE THIS BUYING IAN A SHIRT ???

IS THIS ⟨H⟩OW IAN WOULD ⟨L⟩OOK BUYING ⟨P⟩ETE A BOOK ???

These unreliable sources claim it is Dale's plan to take them on a secret shopping trip and that they will be encouraged to buy each other a nice present.

'Dishy' Dale has allegedly told close friends: "Everyone loves shopping and I truly believe this bold move could ease the bad feeling between them!"

Remarkably, Ian, Pete and the FA could not confirm any of this.

COMING SOON
to a cinema near you...

LARS ATTACKS

THE MOVING TALE of a quite talented alien midfielder who gets forward and scores...

WANNABEES

It's not been the happiest of times at Goodison Park this season. So Everton strikers **DUNCAN FERGUSON** and **NICK BARMBY** want to make it clear that they still like a laugh. Yep, they wannabee Shooting Stars again, just like...

reeves & mortimer

$+ - \times \div + - \times \div + - \times \div + - \times \div + - \times \div$

MATHS OF THE DAY

$$\text{IVERSEN } 18 \div \text{EMERSON } 6 + \text{BLACKWELL } 5 =$$

Ex-Leeds striker who's not exactly turned grey skies blue for the Sky Blues this season!

ANSWER OVERLEAF

Cup or Mug?

If you're ever feeling down, just be glad you're not the bloke who went into a bookies with £10,000 in cash hours before Leeds v Portsmouth and put it all on Leeds to win the FA Cup. By teatime they were out! Serves the dodgy bloke right.

Beckham

The Wonder Stuff

David Beckham is having his own private Goal of the Season competition this year. And here, in his own words, he tells us about six of the best...

Everyone knows about David Beckham's Golden Goal against Wimbledon on the opening day of the season, but the United ace has got a few other crackers as well. And it doesn't look as though the supply line is drying up!

He admits: "Everything I hit at the moment seems to go in, or at least go pretty close. It gives you self-belief but I know that all good runs come to an end.

"I don't like to think about though. Hard work and practice always works in the end."

And if you are lucky enough to win our great competition below, you could be practising your skills in your very own pair of Predator Traction boots - the same ones that David wears!

WIN! Signed Beckham boots

DAVID BECKHAM has scored all his great goals this season wearing adidas Predator boots. And we've got a pair of signed Predator Traction boots to give away.

All you have to do is pick your three favourite Beckham goals, put them in 1,2,3 order, and if your choice matches David's fave three you'll win a pair of boots. Send your entry to: BECKHAM'S GOLDEN GOALS, SHOOT, King's Reach Tower, Stamford Street, London SE99 0BB. The first correct answer out of the bag will win. Closing date is January 25.

Yeah well, he ain't bad I suppose...for a beginner like. But I'm the Bizz aren't I girls...girls...oi, come back, where are you all going?

92

Six appeal

◀ THAT shot from the halfway line

No.1 v Wimbledon

"I didn't give it a second thought and just hit it. I spotted the goalkeeper off his line and thought I might as well have a go. I was fortunate that I struck it well and it dipped at the right moment. Afterwards Neil Sullivan, the Wimbledon goalkeeper, congratulated me on a great goal which was a nice gesture. I have tried shots like that in reserve and youth games, but for it to come off in the Premiership was brilliant."

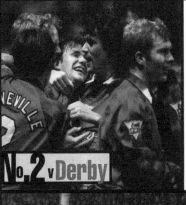

◀ A run from the halfway line topped off with a bullet shot into the top corner

No.2 v Derby

"You have to be ready to have a go at any time. If you see a half chance you have to deal with it. If I think there is something on I'll give it a try. As I was on the run I saw the chance for a shot and took it. I was delighted to see the ball fly into the top corner."

No.3 v Southampton

A superb 20-yard free-kick into the top corner ▲

"We had a bad day at Southampton so there was not really too much pleasure in scoring, but looking back on it I would sooner have scored than missed and it is another one to my credit. I don't work things like that out - if I think there is a chance from a free-kick I'll try to take it."

No.4 v West Ham

A glorious chip from the edge of the box ▲

"It went in off the post and it was a bit special for me because it was at West Ham, not far from where I was born. I saw the chance and chipped it in from about 20 yards. It was a sweet moment and when you score goals like that it is a reward for all the hard work you put into training."

No.5 v Nottm Forest

A delicate chip across goal and into the far corner △

"I latched onto a misplaced pass and had a quick look up at goal. There was a chance so I took it and was delighted to see it go into the net. The confidence to have a go comes from those around you. Everyone in United's team is prepared to go for goal, and it inspires you to join them."

A blistering curling free-kick from 25 yards ▶

No.6 v Spurs

"I practice those in training. It was a typical dead-ball situation and was just asking for a shot. It was great to see it curl into the corner of the net. I think it made the boss happy."

The Keegan Years

Feb 92 Ossie Ardiles is sacked from his post as Newcastle manager and Keegan becomes their 15th post-war appointment, taking a three-month contract in a bid to save them from relegation to Division Three. Terry McDermott joins him as assistant manager, Keegan so sure of his appointment that he offers to pay him out of his own salary. Newcastle are 23rd in the Second Division and win their first game under his charge, 3-0 against Bristol City.

May 92 They finish the season 20th, narrowly avoiding relegation after a win at Leicester. Keegan walks out of the club, believing his job to be done. He returns after being offered a three-year contract and an assurance that money would be made available for transfers.

Aug 92 Newcastle win their first 11 League games of the season to head the First Division.

Mar 93 He signs Andy Cole for £1.75 million from Bristol City.

May 93 Newcastle finish the season eight points clear of West Ham to win promotion to the Premiership.

Feb 94 Keegan threatens to leave the club after his 'keeper Mike Hooper receives threatening mail and phone calls from fans.

May 94 They finish the season third behind Man United and Blackburn, so qualifying for Europe. Cole ends the season as the League's top scorer with 34 goals. Keegan commits his future to the club, signing a ten-year contract reportedly worth £10 million and promising that Newcastle will become the biggest club in the world.

Aug 94 Newcastle go 11 games without defeat at the start of the season, scoring 29 goals. Keegan cites Cole as the most exciting player in the country.

Jan 95 Keegan sells Andy Cole to rivals Man United for £7 million.

May 95 They finish the season sixth, out of European qualification.

July 95 Keegan splashes out £12.5 million on Les Ferdinand, French winger David Ginola and Warren Barton.

Jan 96 Newcastle are labelled the most exciting team in the country as they lead the Premiership by 12 points.

Feb 96 Keegan buys Faustino Asprilla for £6.7 million and David Batty for £3.75 million.

Mar 96 Eric Cantona scores Man United's winner at St James' Park and the title race is back on.

Apr 96 The game of the decade ends with Newcastle losing 4-3 at Anfield. The Geordies' charge to the title is stalling and Keegan is showing signs of pressure, hitting out verbally at Alex Ferguson on TV.

May 96 The Toon Army are in tears as Man United beat Middlesbrough 3-0 to win the title and leave Newcastle in the runners-up spot.

July 96 Keegan signs Alan Shearer from Blackburn for a world record £15 million.

Aug 96 Man United beat Newcastle 4-0 at Wembley to win the Charity Shield.

Oct 96 Newcastle get revenge over United with a crushing 5-0 win at St James' Park.

Dec 96 Keegan offers his resignation after Newcastle lose at Blackburn on Boxing Day but is talked out of it by the directors.

Jan 97 Bye bye Kev.

Thanks

'What Keegan has done for Newcastle will never be forgotten'

Only Kevin Keegan could have got away with selling Newcastle's most prized asset to the club's biggest rivals and still have the fans hailing him as a hero.

That was the sign of the enormous respect the Geordie fans had for their leader - for Keegan was 'God' on Tyneside.

That's why they accepted the £7 million transfer of their beloved Andy Cole to Man United, that's why they accepted his decision to change a winning line-up and bring in controversial striker Faustino Asprilla and that's why they accepted, albeit tearfully, Newcastle's failure to win the Premier League title last season.

But one man who couldn't accept that failure was Keegan himself and the pictures of Steve Bruce lifting the Premiership trophy for Man United must have driven a dagger into his heart.

King Kev offered his resignation at the end of the campaign as the disappointment of seeing a 12 point lead at the top of table slip from his grasp sunk deep.

The club talked him out of it, Shearer arrived in a record £15 million deal, the goals flowed after an initial poor start and last season became a distant memory.

But not for Kev. The pressure to succeed grew more intense, the hair grew greyer and the doubts in his own mind that all the aggro was worth it reached mega proportions. In the end, he decided it wasn't.

Ironically, exactly two years to the day that he stood on the steps of St James' Park and defended his decision to sell Cole to United, Keegan bowed out of Newcastle.

"I feel that I have taken the club as far as I could and that it would be in the best interests of everyone if I resigned," he says.

"It was my decision and my decision alone to go. The board talked me out of resigning at the end of last season but this time there was no going back."

But while Keegan may have gone - he will never be forgotten on Tyneside.

"What Kevin has done for this club and the people of Newcastle is incredible," says Terry McDermott, his assistant during the glory days.

"For the first time in his career, he has put himself before anyone else and I respect him for that. He has given everything to this club and now we want to win a trophy this season and dedicate it to him."

Kev

They say

The managers, players and fans have their say on King Kev.

What Kevin Keegan has done for this club and the people of Tyneside will never be forgotten. I am only just coming to terms with his decision but I can understand his reasons for leaving and would like to put on record my thanks to him for the last five years we have spent together.
TERRY McDERMOTT

I'm obviously very disappointed that Kevin has left. It is only just beginning to sink in and, as you can imagine, it was a very sad day for everyone at Newcastle when he announced he was leaving. **LES FERDINAND**

Basically we are all to blame. With the pressure all of us fans have put on him it just became too much. He has been a messiah and he has made Newcastle the nation's team. We have no enemies like Man United and everyone loves them.
JOHN McCRIRICK (TV pundit and Newcastle fan)

Nobody has ever done more for Newcastle than Kevin Keegan. Thank you Kev.
BRENDAN FOSTER (Former Olympic athlete and big Newcastle fan)

Kevin Keegan took over at this club when we were destined for the Second Division and scaled the heights of the Premier League with a style of football never before seen at St James' Park. The squad of players he has built up in that time is one of the strongest in Europe.
DOUGLAS HALL, Newcastle director.

For the record

This was Newcastle's League record under Keegan after he took over in February 1992

Season	Div	P	W	D	L	F	A	Pts	Pos
1991-92	1	16	7	2	7	22	25	23	20
1992-93	1	46	29	9	8	85	37	96	1
1993-94	Prem	42	23	8	11	82	41	77	3
1994-95	Prem	42	20	12	10	67	47	72	7
1995-96	Prem	38	24	6	8	66	37	78	2
1996-97	Prem	21	11	4	6	38	22	37	4
Total		205	114	41	50	360	209	383	

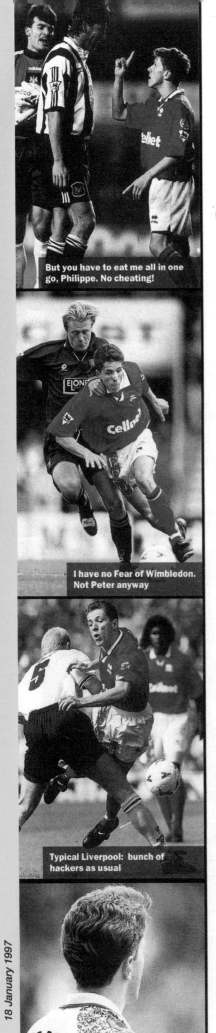

But you have to eat me all in one go, Philippe. No cheating!

I have no Fear of Wimbledon. Not Peter anyway

Typical Liverpool: bunch of hackers as usual

Since his arrival on Teesside in October 1995, Brazilian star Juninho has won the hearts of every Middlesbrough fan. And, as he tells SHOOT, no matter what the papers say, he has no intention of leaving...

Dive? Us foreigners? You must be joking.

 There have been stories about you moving to Italy, and recently you were linked with Real Madrid. What is your position at Boro?

I've been very annoyed with the speculation in the Press because I'm very happy with Middlesbrough. I have never spoken to any journalists in this country, or in Italy, about leaving. I have 18 months left of my contract with Boro and I intend to see it through.

 Have you and your family found it hard to cope with the weather in the North East?

The climate has not been a problem for me or my family. Obviously when we first arrived it was difficult, but we soon became used to it. Anyway, it is better to be playing football in cooler temperatures rather than in intense heat. Also the weather in Middlesbrough is no different to the rest of England. Take the day we played at Arsenal - it was colder in London than on Teesside.

 Does Boro's poor current form worry you?

It is very important to me that our form begins to improve. I said when I arrived in England that I had come to be successful with Middlesbrough and that is what I aim to do. I know we have had some bad results, but when everyone is fit, and we can put our best team out, I am sure we will begin to show the form we showed in the first month of the season. And then we will climb the table once again.

 How have you found English football in general?

The pace that the game is played at in this country makes it so enjoyable to play in, and it is also beautiful to watch. I think I have learned many things already and I hope to continue doing so in the future. The supporters in this country are the best in the world, and Middlesbrough's fans in particular are very special. They create an absolutely fantastic atmosphere inside the Riverside Stadium - I don't think I've ever come across a set of supporters who love their club so much. It is certainly time we gave them the success they deserve.

ZE LICKLE BORO BOY IS STAYING, YEAH?

'It's time to deliver

od, no-one else in this
to make me look tiny

Any chance of having
my shirt back, mate?

No? Well I'll just have
to have that blue one

Hey, look Robbo.
Emerson's over there

How do you get on with your team-mates at Boro?

The dressing room atmosphere is great. We have an excellent team spirit and that is vital. Even though the results have not been going for us, it is important that you have humour in the dressing room. As a team, we all socialise by going for a drink together, and sometimes with our families. It really helps to pull everybody together.

You've already scored a lot more goals than you did last season. Is there any particular reason why?

I'm playing further forward this season. With people like Emerson and Robbie Mustoe in midfield it allows me to push up more and I'm certainly enjoying it.

Which English players have caught your eye?

Steve McManaman is a very exciting player. He plays with a Brazilian style and has a lot of skill. John Barnes is another excellent player, but Paul Gascoigne is the best English player. He could play in the Brazil team. He is very skilful, has lots of vision and can pass well. He is also a very good marker. Remember the goal he scored against Scotland in Euro 96? That's where you see an outstanding player - calm and cold blooded at decisive moments.

Brazil will be defending the World Cup next year. Is this something you are particularly looking forward to?

I am very excited at the prospect of going to France to play in the World Cup next year and that is why it is so important for Boro's form to improve. There are many players coming through who will be available for the World Cup and I need to be playing well at club level to maintain my status in the international team.

Did Ju KnoW?

Since his arrival at the Riverside Stadium, Middlesbrough have failed to win a SINGLE League game that he has missed. In eight attempts, they have drawn two and lost six. He's missed a total of 17 games, in both League and Cups, and Boro have won only once - and that was against Hereford!

Did Ju Know?

When he arrived from Brazil, he brought his parents and his sister over here with him to help him settle in his new environment. Now why didn't Emerson think of that?

Did Ju Know?

He is rated as one of the best players in Brazil and wears the coveted number 10 shirt - made famous by the one and only Pele - when he turns out for the national side.

Did Ju Know?

The last time England played Brazil - at Wembley in June 1995 - Juninho scored his country's first goal in a 3-1 win. Typically, it was a brilliant curling free-kick.

WaNNabeeſ

And this week, Steffan Iversen, Darren Anderton and Teddy Sheringham wannabee...

the baYwatcH babeſ

IN THE WRONG

with IAN WRIGHT

Some people think bein' a bad lad's a right laugh. But it ain't always easy thinkin' up new ways to cheek the ref, annoy other players and wind up the crowd. Nah, man, it's well 'ard! Still, no-one's sussed that I scored some-a those 200 league goals by stickin' an extra ball up me shirt – safe!

Who Ate All The Hot Dogs?

SHOOT has discovered just who ate all the pies – or rather the hot dogs – at the last World Cup.

US '94 squads have had their vital statistics issued by FIFA and the results are fascinating. Graham Taylor was right when he said that Scandanavians were bigger than us, but whether that's due to all their outdoor pursuits is debatable. A certain rolly-polly Hand of God merchant made tipped the scales in favour of Argentina being the fattest team. Here's the final table:

USA '94 Honours Board

Lardie Gits

Winners: ARGENTINA
Runners-up: SPAIN

Skinny Ribs

Winners: BULGARIA
Runners-up: NORWAY

Lanky Planks

Winners: NORWAY
Runners-up: SWEDEN

Heavyweights

Winners: SWEDEN
Runners-up: HOLLAND

Flyweights

Winners: COLOMBIA
Runners-up: MEXICO

THE UMPIRE STRIKES BACK

We've all got our own opinions on referees, but what do the men in black think about the stick they keep getting? ITN's red card correspondent spoke to a few...

> I'm having a crap game, and nothing you will say will alter it!

IAN BORRETT, to former Palace boss **ALAN SMITH** during a game

More NEWS from

'CHECK-OUT' SCOOPS THE REST AGA

Kevin Keegan has quit Newcastle because he is fed-up of Terry McDermott spiking his shampoo. "Tegs keeps putting Go Grey in my bottle and now I look like him. I've had enough of this," says a livid KK.

Spurs boss Gerry Francis admits he messed up ove signing Ramon Vega. "I believed that Ramon was an Italian cousin of singe Suzanne Vega. I thought he could toughen up our defence." No, Gez, that's Lazio's Roman Centurion

98

And somewhere, somehow, sometime in a far distant

PARALLEL UNIVERSE

DAVID BECKHAM is a high-flying soft-ware wizard who owns a chain of incredibly trendy cyber-cafes.

I was twenty-five yards out, right, and still bent it round the wall and internet!

HAYES TREMENDOUS

Watch out for a big black lad scoring glorious 30 yard screamers and going on to play for England. The name will be JASON ROBERTS. He's Cyrille Regis' 18-year-old nephew and he's attracting scouts by the busload to Vauxhall Conference side Hayes....the former club of big Cyrille and a certain Les Ferdinand!

> "The day I had to book Gazza for celebrating for scoring a goal was the last straw. We're being programmed like robots with a list of instructions"
>
> **JIM McGILVRAY,** Scottish official who gave himself the red card

> "I always enjoy refereeing Man United matches... especially at Old Trafford. The players, fans and the management are so understanding"
>
> **IDENTITY UNKNOWN**

Chants of a Life-time

Here's a late Christmas carol courtesy of Southampton fans

> "Eyal, Eyal, Born is the King of Israel"
>
> (to the tune of The First Noel)

In The Net AND AGAIN...

And finally, Michael Atherton has revealed how he is terrified of being struck down by Plattyiatis. "It is a lethal disease that affects England captains of all sports," says Mike. "Once you start having a bad run, there is no way back. Your career is over." Oh, dear.

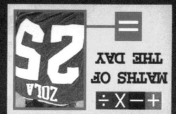

MATHS OF THE DAY

ZOLA + − × ÷ = £25

In the Net GLOVE STORY mega-spesh

Come here! It is now my turn to wear zem!

Brrr, ze soft Italian leather is stylish, yes- but maybe not so warm!

Hey, someone 'as stolen ze fingers!

I would give my right 'and to be warm

Mine cost me ten pence each – and they're still balanced on top!

Yeah, alright, we are soft down south!

Next winter you see me wear zem Nationwide

Issa great at Boro - I never once getta to wear zem at 'ome!

M

Wha

Arsenal's season so far?

➡ So far it's been brilliant. I've really enjoyed it, but losing to Man United and Arsenal at home in four days could ruin our season. We'd been really consistent until then. We'd had a couple of bad results before but

Arsene Wenger?

➡ He has been brilliant. I can't speak highly enough of him. He's got no favourites and everyone is treated the same, which is the best thing about him. Everything has changed under Wenger. From the warm-ups, to training, to the food we eat, everything has changed for the better. He's brought the whole continental approach into the club

erse

do you think about...

Your own future?

I'm really determined to make the most of the rest of my career. I want to enjoy myself and win things again. I wasn't really aware of the good times last time around, so it would be nice to go through it all again with a clear head. I want to end my career here. I'd sign my career away at Arsenal tomorrow. I don't ever want to leave this club.

bounced back and we've got to do it again. That's the name of the game if you want to win the League. It's all about who bounces back the quickest.

and it's really good. The whole team is playing with a smile on its face and things couldn't really have worked out any better. I'm enjoying my football more than ever before.

Your own form?

This is my best season ever, easily, on a consistent basis. It's pleasing that I've been getting nice reviews, but it's more important that the team keeps on doing well and keeps on winning. I'd rather have a couple of bad games and we win the League, but it has been good. I feel fit and my confidence is sky

high. And when you're feeling confident, that's when your football blossoms and that's what's been happening.

Playing up front?

It was good. I've been pushed back again now but I enjoyed it. It's nice to be able to play in a couple of different positions where you can just jump backwards or forwards. I've been playing left midfield this season and I've really enjoyed it, but in a free role, not just stuck out on the wing. In the past I've just been out wide and that's not me. Over the last four or five years people have been asking, 'Where's his best position?' because I've played all over the place. So, this season, it's been nice to have a settled position and for everyone to know what it is.

The Premiership?

I think it's probably the best league in the world, certainly entertainment

Winning the title again?

I think winning the League with Arsenal now would be a greater achievement than winning the first two. Football gets harder. We won the League one year losing only one game and that will never be done again. There are too many good teams these days. A few years ago, when we won it, there were a couple of easy games when you could say that's six points, and that's six more, but no more. There are no easy games. None of the sides in the Premiership are easy to beat. Winning another League title with Arsenal would easily be the greatest achievement of my career.

wise. And it can only get better with the foreign stars coming over. People moan that they shouldn't be here but you've only got to look at our young players. They're getting better playing with people like Dennis Bergkamp. The League's getting harder but that's the way it should be. This year, five teams can win it, and that's better than before when one team has run away with it. I think that's great for football.

The future at Arsenal?

There are going to be exciting times and big things to come. This is the place to be. Hopefully, this season we can get into the European Cup, or certainly into the UEFA Cup. We got knocked out early on this season by a not very good side in Moenchengladbach and that was disappointing. A big club like Arsenal needs to be in Europe playing against the best.

THERE'S ONLY ONE... Leeds

Continuing our series on the country's great clubs. This week we turn our attention to those Yorkshire giants - Leeds.

Having built a solid foundation to work from, George Graham will be expected to add some flair to Leeds' defensive solidity this season. And his team have already shown glimpses of it.

Jimmy Floyd Hasselbaink represents the new face of Leeds, with skills that will have the fans off their seats rather than fighting to stay awake. With the likes of David Hopkin, Lee Bowyer and Alf-Inge Haaland in support, they might even score some goals at Elland Road this year.

Not that any George Graham side will entertain for the sake of it. As any Arsenal fan will tell you, there's nothing he likes more than a flukey, dour 1-0 victory.

If he can win a trophy for Leeds doing that, the Elland Road fans may just come around to it too...

Stadium stats

Name: Elland Road
Address: Leeds, LS11 0ES
Ticket and match info: 0891 121680
Capacity: 40,000
Record Crowd: 57, 892 v Sunderland, FA Cup 5th Round replay. 15th March 1967

The Spion Kop at Elland Road was named after the huge hill in South Africa on which 322 British soldiers lost their lives in the Boer War.

THE GREATEST TEAM OF THE LAST 10 YEARS

John Lukic
Gary Kelly — Chris Fairclough — Chris Whyte — Tony Dorigo
Gordon Strachan — Gary McAllister — David Batty — Gary Speed
Eric Cantona — Tony Yeboah

TEN-YEAR LEAGUE RECORD

It's been a mixed decade in the League for Leeds, with the high of winning the final Division One Championship in 1992, alongside their three years in the old Second Division in the late 1980s. George Graham will be expected to improve on last season's 11th place this time around.

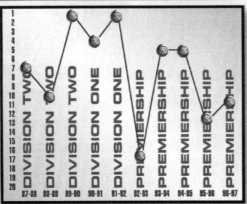

FA CUP

LEAGUE CUP

TOP LEAGUE GOALSCORERS OF THE LAST TEN YEARS

Despite the headline grabbing form of Tony Yeboah when he was on song, it is Lee Chapman that has been the main goalscoring talent for Leeds over the last decade. But special mention must go to Brian Deane and Lee Sharpe, who managed the amazing total of five League goals each last year to become the club's top scorers. Stop laughing at the back!

HOT SHOTS

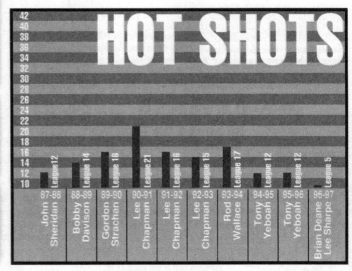

87-88	John Sheridan	League 12
88-89	Bobby Davison	League 14
89-90	Gordon Strachan	League 16
90-91	Lee Chapman	League 21
91-92	Lee Chapman	League 16
92-93	Lee Chapman	League 15
93-94	Rod Wallace	League 17
94-95	Tony Yeboah	League 12
95-96	Tony Yeboah	League 12
96-97	Brian Deane / Lee Sharpe	League 5

Leeds – did you know?

- The club used to be known as Leeds City FC but had to reform after 'irregular practices'. Strange George Graham ended up there, eh?
- Leeds were once sponsored by high street clobber shop Top Man!
- In 1970, Leeds took on Chelsea in the FA Cup Final and this became the first Wembley Final to require a replay.

- In 1990, they beat rivals Sheffield United to the Division Two title on goal difference.
- Last season, Leeds scored just 28 League goals, the lowest total by any top flight club that avoided relegation.
- Former Leeds boss Howard Wilkinson described Tony Yeboah as "a manager's dream". Wilko purred: "He comes in, trains, listens, contributes, practices, goes home, turns up for matches and does the business." Wonder if George Graham would agree?
- One frustrated Leeds fan went to see his heroes six times last year and didn't see them score once! No wonder their chant became: 'We'll score again, don't know where, don't know when!'

STAR SPOTTING

HARRY KEWELL

The Australian midfielder led the Leeds Youth team to FA Cup glory last year and is now looking to break in George Graham's first-team plans. Keep and eye out for him, he can turn it on Home & Away!

blast from the past

JACK CHALTON 1952-1972

Former Republic of Ireland manager and 1966 World Cup legend. Turned out for Leeds over two decades between 1952 and 1972. Now? Well Big Jack's happy mulling over the old memories and fishing. And why not?

STAR PLAYERS

Nigel Martyn
Has become one of the gme's most consistent 'keepers and cannot be ignored by Glenn Hoddle for much longer.

Gary Kelly
Pacy full-back who helps to keep it tight at the back and adds some much needed creativity with his crosses.

David Hopkin
Got Palace up last season. Now with Leeds, he's died his hair ginger and been made club captain.

Lee Bowyer
Bowyer's enthusiasm in the middle of the park took him to the fringes of the England set-up last season.

Jimmy Floyd Hasselbaink
The Dutchman is already earning praise for his determined displays up front for George Graham's men.

Allez Les Roug

Highbury hails their French Connection

Arsenal manager Arsene Wenger has brought a French touch to Highbury. Arsene's French Revolution has even caused the Highbury scoreboard to flash up 'Allez Les Rouges' – French for 'Come on you reds!' SHOOT met up with three of The Gunners' French collection to find out what they thought about English football – and quizzed Highbury's homegrown boys to see what English football thinks about them!

What first attracted you to come and play in England, lads?

PETIT: I've always been attracted to English football and when I was young I used to read magazines and comics with stories about English football. I had posters of Kevin Keegan and other strikers on my bedroom wall. I had the opportunity to go to other countries but it was an easy choice as Mr Wenger was here and there's the added attraction of living in London.

GRIMANDI: The crowds and the stadium and the whole atmosphere of English football attracted me here. When I had the chance to come to a club of Arsenal's size, it didn't take me long to make up my mind to join.

PETIT: I knew Spurs had been after me for two seasons and I'd spoken to them on a number of occasions. They were very good to me and acted correctly. But players like Patrick Vieira and Ian Wright, and the presence of Arsene Wenger made my mind up to come here. I see exciting things happening here and I see moving here as a good way of getting back into the French national side.

How easy are you finding it to settle in?

PETIT: Very easily, the players here make us feel at home. I like Ian Wright's personality, his outlook on life. He's the one we all look too. But it is also important that we learn the language.

GRIMANDI: There's been a very healthy reaction to us here from the English players. When we were at Monaco, we welcomed the foreign players and it's the same here. The language is just a short-term problem and it hasn't stopped us enjoying all the dressing-room jokes.

VIEIRA: As far as football was concerned, I felt completely at home here straight away when I

Don't cry, mate!

"When I was a boy in France, I often dreamt of playing Coventry"

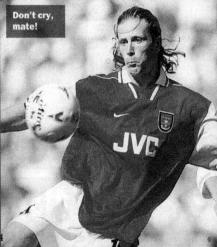

ALLEZ LES ROUGES

joined last year. There was no down side for me. The players play with the right attitude in the team sense and that makes their behaviour different and the rest follows on from that. For instance, the players here seem to be more respectful of referees and there's no-one trying to con them like they do abroad. I've felt part of things from day one and I love English football.

 **What do you think of the technical ability of English players?**

VIEIRA: I was impressed playing England during the summer at Le Tournoi. Everyone in France was impressed by their new style and technical ability. Hoddle's team wanted to play and get the ball on the ground which was good.

WENGER SAYS

I rated Gilles very highly when I coached him at Monaco. He can play as a defender or in midfield. He has the talent for both positions.

Patrick is a quiet lad but is a bundle of energy on the pitch who always gives total commitment to the game. He is a young man with a great future.

Emmanuel is a very adaptable player, he can play anywhere on the left side. He used to be a central defender but technically he had more to offer as a midfielder and that's why I bought him and used him in that position.

WHAT THE BRITS THINK

The French players have all proved to be great additions to the squad. I think that if a manager like Arsene Wenger has faith enough to sign a player then he has to be. IAN WRIGHT

We're all here for Arsenal, not for ourselves, and the French players that have come in have shown the right spirit for the game and for the club. NIGEL WINTERBURN

You can't look at any of the new French players and say they have not added extra class to the squad. Players like Grim, Manu and Patrick are top guys and are here because of that, not their nationality. MARTIN KEOWN

Arsene is no fool, he doesn't buy people because of what language they speak. You can take any of the French players he has signed and if they were available they would soon he snapped up by other Premiership clubs because they're quality players! TONY ADAMS

SHOOT'S 12 FAVE FRENCH THINGS

French and Saunders	French stick	David Ginola (in Keegan's days)
Eric Cantona	**French Fancies**	**Zinedine Zidane**
French Fries	Papa and Nicole	French cricket
France 98	**France** Beckenbauer	**Gerry France-is**

HE'S DONE IT!

OK, we know Wrighty isn't French, but congrats to him for coming up with that hat-trick against Bolton, which took his tally to 180 goals and beat Cliff Bastin's Arsenal goalscoring record.

SHOOT salutes Ian Wright of Arsenal and England – the deadliest striker in the game and The Gunners' greatest ever goalscorer. Here's how he did it:-

SEASON	LEAGUE	CUP*	EUROPE	TOTAL
1991/92	24	2		26
1992/93	15	15		30
1993/94	22	8	4	34
1994/95	19	3	9	31
1995/96	15	8		23
1996/97	23	5	2	30
1997/98 (so far)	6			6
Total:	124	41	15	180

* Including Charity Shield

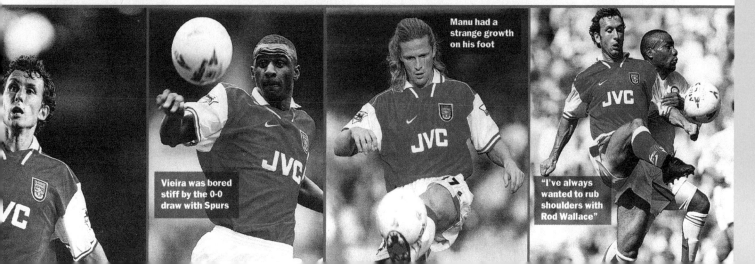

Vieira was bored stiff by the 0-0 draw with Spurs

Manu had a strange growth on his foot

"I've always wanted to rub shoulders with Rod Wallace"

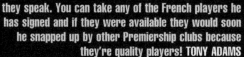

Rio Fer

What do you think about…

Becoming famous?

It's happened very quickly and from other people's point of view my life has probably changed but it hasn't changed me. I enjoy doing something well and if people keep recognising me and coming up for my autograph then I must be doing things right on the football pitch.

Going away with international squads?

It breaks things up nicely but it depends how your club's doing. Last season, to be honest, I was glad to be in any England squad, just to get away from West Ham and the threat of relegation. I'd come away and I was on a downer because results were going so badly. But once I joined up with the lads from other clubs, they cheered me up. They'd be buzzing and give me a lift. So when I went back, I'd have a new burst of life in me. West Ham are doing reasonably well this season but it's still nice to get away because it's a new challenge.

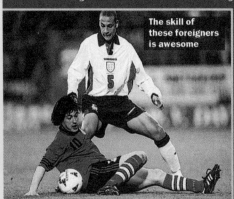

The skill of these foreigners is awesome

Training with England Under-21s?

It's a different set of lads so the whole scene is different, there's a different kind of banter. We concentrate more on technique. Peter Taylor tries to get into the lads what he wants us to do and how to react under pressure. It's more intense because they have less time to work with us. They try to get as much through as possible in the short amount of time. It's good and enjoyable. We've had some good games and good laughs. Peter wants us to pass positively and get the ball forward all the time.

Being dropped by England?

I've been over it, told my point of view and it's been well documented. Now I've got to put the whole incident to the back of my mind. It dirtied the slate and now I've got to clean it up. If I do well on the pitch, hopefully it will be forgotten a bit. I stayed on with the England squad after it happened which kept me out of the spotlight and I was grateful for that. But once I was on the football pitch, that wasn't in my head. That's what's good about football - it's like a breath of fresh air: you think about the game and forget everything else. I know I've got to prove myself to people again and show that I'm over it and what I'm capable of.

Bergkamp - come back here!

Playing against European strikers?

It makes a change because teams like the Italians and Georgians approach the game a lot differently to the English players. It's interesting and always good to be up against the best - that's what I enjoy doing and it's the way to improve. The foreign strikers I've marked all seem very intelligent. Don't get me wrong - English players are intelligent too, but the foreigners are very hard to pick up. Players like Bergkamp and Zola are world class players and the way they go about things is superb. Bergkamp is unbelievable at the moment - everyone's finding it hard to stop him. It's nice to see foreigners do so well over here and hopefully more English players can do the same abroad and follow Paul Ince in making such a good impression on the continent.

Getting thrashed 4-0 at Arsenal?

It didn't bring me down to earth because I don't think I'm big-headed. I don't go round thinking I'm a class player. I've got to improve every aspect of my game because I'm only just starting in football really. But a defeat like 4-0 at Arsenal really gets me down for the next day or two. Sometimes it makes you think to yourself 'Maybe I'm a bad player, maybe I shouldn't be in the team'. You put question marks over your ability. But that's part and parcel of football. If you're always criticising yourself and seeing what you can improve on, you're only going to benefit. I analyse my game all the time - that's just the way I'm inclined and I think it's very good for me.

Are you watching Wrighty? Oh, there you are!

25 October 1997

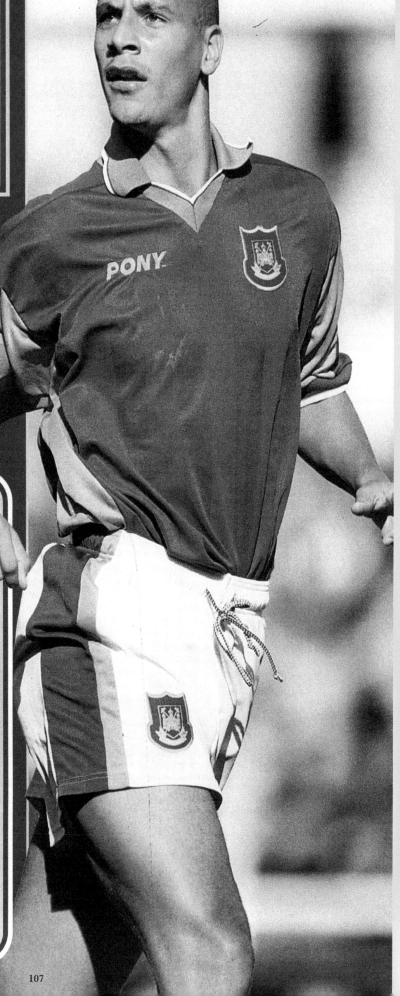

West Ham
nand

Having played so many games at 18?

I don't really look at ages. Once you're a first team player, age doesn't matter. It's experience that counts. A lot of us are from the same era so we are doing the same things. Some have girlfriends, some don't. There's not much difference between 18 and 23. Even in the Under-21s, you get a player like John Curtis who's older than me but hasn't played a League game. But people see his ability and John's speaks for itself. He's captained every England team he's played for. But at a club like Man United, you can't just walk into the first team. He's just biding his time but when he gets the chance, I know he will take it.

RIO

Glenn Hoddle's men did the nation proud with that heroic 0-0 draw in Rome but the night before Rio was in Peter Taylor's Under-21 team that went one better, beating Italy 1-0... with ten men!! Ben Thatcher's sending-off couldn't stop the Young Lions and Ipswich wonderkid Kieron Dyer capped a superb performance with the only goal. England topped their group and now must wait for other results to see if they've qualified for the European Under-21 Championship finals next year. Here are some of the lads who got England to the top:

GOALKEEPER

RICHARD WRIGHT *Ipswich:* Still only 19, the Ipswich star showed why he's worth millions, letting in only one goal in four qualifiers!

Richard Wright

DEFENDERS

RICCARDO SCIMECA *Aston Villa:* Captain Ricky can't get in the Villa side but has been a rock for the Under-21s. Set to partner Gareth Southgate for years to come.

BEN THATCHER *Wimbledon:* Frustrated by injury at Wimbledon, Ben's tenacious displays helped England to a goals against record of one goal in eight games!

Ben Thatcher

MIDFIELDERS

STEPHEN HUGHES *Arsenal:* A veteran of six Under-21 games, Hughesy has learned enough from these matches to force his way into Arsenal's international midfield.

JAMIE CARRAGHER *Liverpool:* Suddenly a regular in Roy Evans' side, Jamie has still played more Under-21 games - six - than League games!

Stephen Hughes

FORWARDS

EMILE HESKEY *Leicester:* The Foxes hero is one of the most experienced in the squad but he's still 19 - scary!

DARREN EADIE *Norwich:* The Flying Canary has provided a deadly supply of crosses for Heskey and goal machine Bruce Dyer.

Emile Heskey

Out on his Owen!

KID MICHAEL COULD BE THE BEST OF THE LOT

Liverpool's Michael Owen is being hailed as the best young talent in the game. But for now, the teenage wonder kid is happy to battle for a place in the Reds first team, as he tells SHOOT...

How did it feel when you were recently left out of the team, Michael?

It was hard, but I've got to get used to it because the manager's going to rotate the team around all year. Sometimes I'll start, sometimes I'll be sub, other times I'll have to watch the whole thing. I wasn't told in advance that I'd be left out, but I had an idea I'd be dropped sometime during the year. Obviously, Robbie's injury was helpful for me, but it was a longer run than I expected. It was just nice to get such a long run in the team from the start of the season and I'm looking to have another one soon.

Were you nervous before making your Anfield debut for Liverpool?

Obviously. I suffer from nerves slightly, but it doesn't really affect my game in any way. I've been nervous before all the biggest occasions in my career so far, from playing against Brazil at Wembley for England boys right up to playing for the Liverpool first team, but I've coped with it all OK. I tend not to get too tense before games, because I really look forward to them, but I do get excited about every match.

Pick that out!
with Michael Owen

The goal against Blackburn was really my favourite because of the timing. We were desperate for a point, so it was more of a relief. It was my best goal for the first team because I ran the length of the pitch to score.

"I got the ball inside my own half and there was no-one against me."

108

ar in the making

Top boy, top read

On target v Celtic

These boots were made for goals

Owen's having a ball!

Have you been working on any weaknesses?

Every player's got something they've got to improve on. We've all got weaknesses in our game. I've got to look at the defensive side of mine, and defend from the front, line. I'm working hard in training at that and I've also got to improve my shooting with my left foot. I can strike a good ball with that but I've got to do even better. Robbie and Ian Rush are prime examples of what Liverpool forwards are like. They're not just strikers, they're defenders when the opposition have got the ball and I'm trying to follow in the same path as them.

Most strikers have to wait a while for their first goal but you got yours after ten minutes. How did that feel?

It was a great achievement for me personally to score that goal on my debut against Wimbledon last season. But it was bad for the team that the game ended in defeat, and it was on that night that we

lost the Championship so everyone was really down.

Have there been any Premiership games when you thought 'I'd rather be banging hat-tricks in for the youth team'?

Not at all. I've always wanted to play in the first team and now the chance has arrived I want to take it. It's a great experience every time I play, so I'm not looking back now. I've played below my expectations in a few games, but I don't think I've really had a bad game yet.

Who's been the biggest influence on you so far?

Robbie Fowler and Steve McManaman. Watching them going through the ranks and showing the young lads that we can do it ourselves has given all the young lads hope and that was the biggest influence at Liverpool. We knew if we were good enough we'd be given a chance. Steve Heighway's been great to me too. He signed me with the School of Excellence, but since I've moved into the first team he's still looked after me and had a word in my ear every now and then.

What would you say has been the best moment in your career?

I don't think I could pick out one specific day but this period in the first team has easily been the most exciting I've gone through. I'm in and around the first team and just hoping to secure my starting-place again.

How are you coping with all the screaming fans?

I've always wanted to be a footballer and geared myself to being one, with all the fame and fans that comes with the job. A lot of people say it's an easy life, and that's fair enough, but there are other sides to the job that you've got to do that you might not enjoy so much. If people want your autograph, you've got to be prepared to give them your time – it comes with the job. I enjoy football but it is a profession and a serious business. The club rises and falls by our results and people's livelihoods are at stake.

"And then I could celebrate! It was a great relief to see the ball go in the net!"

"I've always done the same thing in front of goal, I just try to keep my head."

"So I hit a low shot under the Rovers 'keeper John Filan"

ere were people sing me but I was e to outpace them."

"I tried to forget that there were 30,000 people watching me."

* From PNE's Never Walk Alone - Liverpool 1997-98 video diary, out now.

shoot

What the stars say

Gazza's move back to England has been the transfer of the season so far. He may not have the fitness or show the skills he had when he last played in the top-flight with Tottenham, but he's still a football superstar. We asked the stars for their opinions on his long-awaited return.

BRYAN ROBSON
"On his day I know I have signed the best midfielder in the county. He's mixed in with the lads alright and helping us get promoted will not only be good for Middlesbrough but for England as well. He can prove his fitness with us and show Glenn Hoddle he's ready to push for an England place for the World Cup. It's all there for Paul to achieve."

PAUL MERSON
"Gazza will make the difference between us getting promotion or not. He will change things overnight because he is still the most outstanding player in England. Going to an away game with Paul will also be something else. The rest of the lads won't know what has hit them and all I'm going to say about him is do not give him your room number. He won't be getting mine!"

GLENN HODDLE
"I think it's a great move for him. It's interesting that Johan Cruyff made a point of saying that 30 minutes of Gazza is worth 90 of most other players. No player dictates for 90 minutes. Even the best players can dictate for only 20 minutes. Paul can do it whether he starts a game and plays for 60 minutes and you take him off or whether you start him on the bench but I'm confident he'll get his fitness back playing for Boro."

ROBERTO DI MATTEO
"I know what Gazza can do from our time together at Lazio and there are few better technical players anywhere. I think it's important that he plays Premiership football next season with Middlesbrough otherwise it could hinder his progress and rehabilitation."

JOHN HENDRIE
"The spotlight will be on Gazza because everyone is looking at him as the final part of the jigsaw to help Boro go up. There's a lot of responsibility on him but if he can get himself fit, there's no reason why he can't succeed."

WALTER SMITH
"We were all sorry to see him go and wish Paul all the best in the future. He was very popular with the fans and the other players here and certainly made an impact at Rangers. Some of the football he played in his first year at the club was superb and he had a big say in the club winning the title. We won't forget him."

shoot

Paul Ga

LOSING THE COCA-COLA CUP FINAL ON YOUR DEBUT?

"It was a massive disappointment for the club and I really felt for the fans and all the players who had got us to Wembley. It was a little bit embarrassing making my debut on such a big stage, especially when players like Craig Hignett missed out for me. That's the reason I gave him my runners-up medal. It was the least he deserves. I had not played in any of the games and Higgy deserves it much more than me. He helped Boro get to Wembley and that medal is his, not mine."

What do you think about…

LEAVING RANGERS BEHIND?
"I was very unhappy at leaving Rangers, especially the way it all happened. I had a great time there and I really enjoyed it. I have come away from Scotland with four medals and I really hope they do the job and win the title again. I was very close to the players and the staff, and I never really had a chance to say goodbye to all the lads at the club."

THE SCOTTISH PREMIER LEAGUE?
"People say it's a weak League but I found the competition very, very tough. It wasn't that long ago that Rangers had about six England players in the squad and I always used to give Terry Butcher stick but he said 'never give stick 'til you have tried it'. It's so true because when you're playing for Rangers you need to be winning at half-time, even more at full-time, otherwise you are going to get slaughtered by the press. That's pressure. The club has to win every League game, the Champions

League and if they were in the World Cup, they'd have to win that as well!"

PLAYING FOR BRYAN ROBSON?
"It took me just 24 hours after speaking to him to know where I was heading. I am coming to play for one of the people who was my favourite player as a kid. Anyone who knows Bryan Robson knows what a quality player he was. I am just pleased to be a part of his plans for the next three years. Bryan is willing to spend and take the club where it belongs. I have come a long way to help him do that and as soon as I get 100 per cent fit you will see the best of

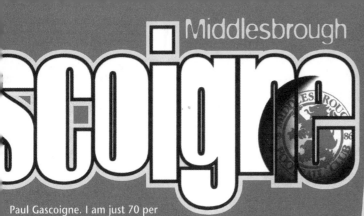

Middlesbrough
Gascoigne

Paul Gascoigne. I am just 70 per cent at the moment."

THE GAZZA FAN CLUB?

"The Rangers fans were fantastic to me, that's why it's hard to leave a place when you are wanted like that. But I'm now at a club where there's hopefully 30-35,000 fans on my side. The reaction I had at Wembley and when I signed for Boro was brilliant. The fans on the street, the letters and the faxes have been amazing. I've been lucky that whoever I sign for, I am a fans' favourite."

WINNING PROMOTION THIS SEASON?

"I can't see why we won't go up and hold our own. Boro have played against the best in Cup matches over the past couple of years and done well. There's no doubt that when we go up into the Premiership the gaffer will spend more and that's always the best way because everybody will be fighting for places. We're going to need a big squad otherwise we'll get punished."

RETURNING TO ENGLAND?

"A lot has changed since I last played in England with Tottenham. But I've also played with world class players in Italy's Serie A with Lazio and in Scotland with Rangers, so I know what it's all about. In fact I'm relishing facing up to the likes of Liverpool, Arsenal and Man United again, but we must get into the Premiership first. Winning this division is going to be hard enough, especially with Forest and Sunderland doing so well at the moment, but if we put our heads down, we know we have the quality to do it."

PLAYING IN THE WORLD CUP?

"If you take the last couple of games that I played in, versus Moldova and Italy, I was probably the best thing since sliced bread, well at least that's what the press wrote. So going on those couple of games and when the injuries are sorted out, I think my chances are good. I'm quietly confident of a place in the final 22 man squad."

Fowler

We've got what it takes for the title

Robbie Fowler believes Liverpool have finally assembled a squad to win the Premiership. But the strength of that squad could also cost him his place in the team.

With the added striking power of European Cup winner Karlheinz Riedle and the emerging talents of teenage sensation Michael Owen, keeping a place in the Liverpool front line is going to be a tough job this season.

A fact that England striker Fowler is very aware.

"If you're having a bad game, there'll always be some people who can come in and do a job," says the 22-year-old Anfield ace.

"So that means you have to work that little bit harder during the game and concentrate for the full 90 minutes."

Robbie also feels the disappointment of missing out on the Champions League by the length of Steve Stone's hair is inspiration enough for Liverpool to raise their game and finally end Man United's domination of the Carling Premiership.

"We let ourselves down by losing it last year but now we have players capable of coming in and doing a good job," continues the England striker.

"Realistically we would have liked to have gone into the Champions League because as far as club football goes it's the ultimate. That's our aim this year – to get into the Champions League – and hopefully we can do it as Champs and not as runners-up."

Many pundits complained Liverpool lacked strength in the middle of the park but that problem seems to have been solved with the signings of Paul Ince, Oyvind Leonhardsen and Danny Murphy.

Fowler admits that his new team-mates will make the side stronger but doesn't agree with the criticism about their weakness last season.

"People criticised us for having no steel in the midfield last year but I think that is unfair to the lads who were playing," he replies.

"They were good players as well as good tacklers – it was just that no one else was seeing that.

"We've bought a lot of good players over the summer which has served to strengthen the squad. That can only make us a better side in the long run."

ROBBIE ON...

... Ince

Paul Ince is a very good player and I've played with him before with England. I think he's going to add that little bit of extra toughness to the side but when people talk about Paul Ince, you think he's just a tackler but he's also such a good ball player and makes some brilliant runs. He's just a great all-round player and one that will benefit the squad immensely.

... Barnes

He has been brilliant for Liverpool and I personally have learned a lot from him. He will do well for Newcastle just as he has done well at Anfield. I know the fans will be sorry to see him go but football is like that, players move on. I'm sure he'll get a great reception if he comes back wearing a Newcastle shirt. The fans don't forget the sort of service he has given the club and I will be delighted to see him. But we have a new Liverpool now and we are all confident of bringing success to this club.

Owen & Riedle

Michael Owen's done superb. He came in when we were not having the best of times at the end of last season and he played really well. He scored a goal on his debut and he didn't look out of place. And he's come in again in the pre-season games and he's played brilliantly, scoring goals and that can only be a good thing for Liverpool Football Club. As for Karlheinz – he's been about and done everything. He's got a European Cup winners medal, a World Cup winners medal – he's got all the experience you need in a player. I think the three of us will all compliment each other given a chance.

'Our game against Newcastle last season was great to watch for the fans but a nightmare for the managers'

TURN OVER FOR MORE FOWLER ACTION ▶

..growing up in the limelight

you go out and you're doing stupid things there are always going to be people who want to put you down and it will be in the paper the next day. You've got to be very careful about what you do, where you go and that sort of thing. I'm only 22 and I'd like to be doing what every other 22-year-old does – you know, go out and have a good laugh but I'm in the position now where I can't. I did feel the pressure at first because I wasn't used to talking to people or having cameras pointed at me. But I'm quite comfortable with that now.

..his favourite game

wouldn't really know because there are that many that stick out. People might say the game last season against Newcastle which was great to watch for the fans. But we were 3-0 up and for them to get it back to 3-3 was very unprofessional from our point of view.

...replacing Shearer for England

Some people have said I'm the one to come in for Alan but the amount of good strikers today in the Premiership is frightening. So Alan Shearer being out of the team doesn't automatically mean that I'm going to play. There are a lot of people out there who can fill his boots. But if called upon I don't think I'll let anyone down and playing for England means a hell of a lot to me. It's the highlight of any player's career.

...missing the Tournoi

I was being told one thing and then another but I had to go with what the club said and that was to have the operation. .It was unfortunate to miss out on the tournament in France because I love playing for England – it's the best feeling in the world. It was very disappointing but I had to get on with it.

...wacky goal celebrations!

It's a bit like how I score my goals – it's just a natural instinct. The most stupid one I've done was against Tottenham a few years ago – it was me, Jamie and Stevie Mac and we all did a three amigos. It was awful!

Captain Chickenpox goes all spotty

Brian waves to his Aunt Edith in the guest seats

When they said I'd be in black and white stripes I thought I was moving to Juventus!

We thought you were on your way out of Ibrox in the summer, Brian.

There were a few clubs interested in signing me but I never said I wanted to leave Rangers. All I wanted to do was give the chairman the option of selling me so the club could make some money. Rangers have been so good to me for the past three years that I wanted to try and repay them for everything. But the chairman insisted he would rather have my company than £5 million in the bank. You can't ask for a bigger compliment than that.

Did you really want to quit the club after falling out with Gazza?

No! That's just not true. At the end of last season I said that Paul should concentrate more on football and everyone said I was having a go at him. But I said the things I did to help him and when we spoke personally after the summer break he knew what I meant.

So what do you think about Gazza then?

He is a smashing lad and a fantastic footballer and, although we will never be best buddies, we are good team-mates. Gazza is still such an important player for Rangers and has such a great influence on the team. I have a good understanding with him on and off the pitch and we both want the best for Rangers.

How do you feel about being named as the new Rangers skipper?

It was great honour to be asked in the first place. The manager, Walter Smith, spoke to me about it just after the end of last season and it didn't take much consideration. I've been captain of the Danish national team seven times and it's always a great thrill to lead any team onto the pitch.

What sort of captain are you?

Well, I'm not the kind of captain who will shout and bawl at players. Hopefully I can lead the team by example. My only concern is that when I was skipper for a few games last season we never won a match. Hopefully my luck has changed!

Have all the new signings taken the pressure of you and Gazza?

The English Premiership is attracting some very big names because of the money

Obviously having so many quality players at the club will benefit Rangers, especially in Europe. People will now look to other players to do well and not just Gazza and myself.

But are you REALLY good enough to do well in Europe at last?

The club has spent so much money in the summer that we will not be happy to simply to make up the numbers. We have been really unlucky in the past few seasons against Ajax and Auxerre so hopefully this season will be different. It looks like we could go out of the Champions Cup but the UEFA Cup is almost as tough a competition - if we win that it would easily make up for the nightmare in Gothenburg.

What about the League title, is it just Celtic who can stop you making it ten in a row?

Celtic are not the only team capable of producing a challenge to us although obviously they will be very determined to stop us reaching that record of ten titles in a row. Dundee United impressed me quite a bit last season and I expect them to do well now that their foreigners have had time to settle. Aberdeen have also made a few signings along with Hearts, so there are a number of teams with big ambitions this season. But we have set the standards and we have to live up to them.

All the British clubs are bringing in foreign talent. Is that good for the game over here?

Britain is the place to be at the moment. The Premiership is attracting some very big names because of the money and excitement which goes with the game. But Scottish clubs are attracting names too and the atmosphere here is fantastic.

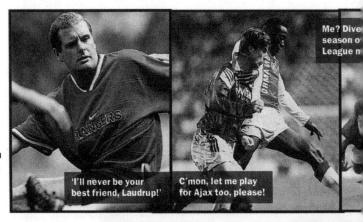

'I'll never be your best friend, Laudrup!'

C'mon, let me play for Ajax too, please!

Me? Dive season o' League n

Walter Works

Rangers have dominated Scottish football for the last nine years and this is what they've won under Walter Smith's management, since he took over from Graeme Souness in 1991.

League Champions Premier Division

1991-92, 1992-93, 1993-94, 1994-95, 1995-96, 1996-97

Scottish Cup Winners

1992, 1993, 1996

League Cup Winners

1992-93, 1993-94, 1996-97

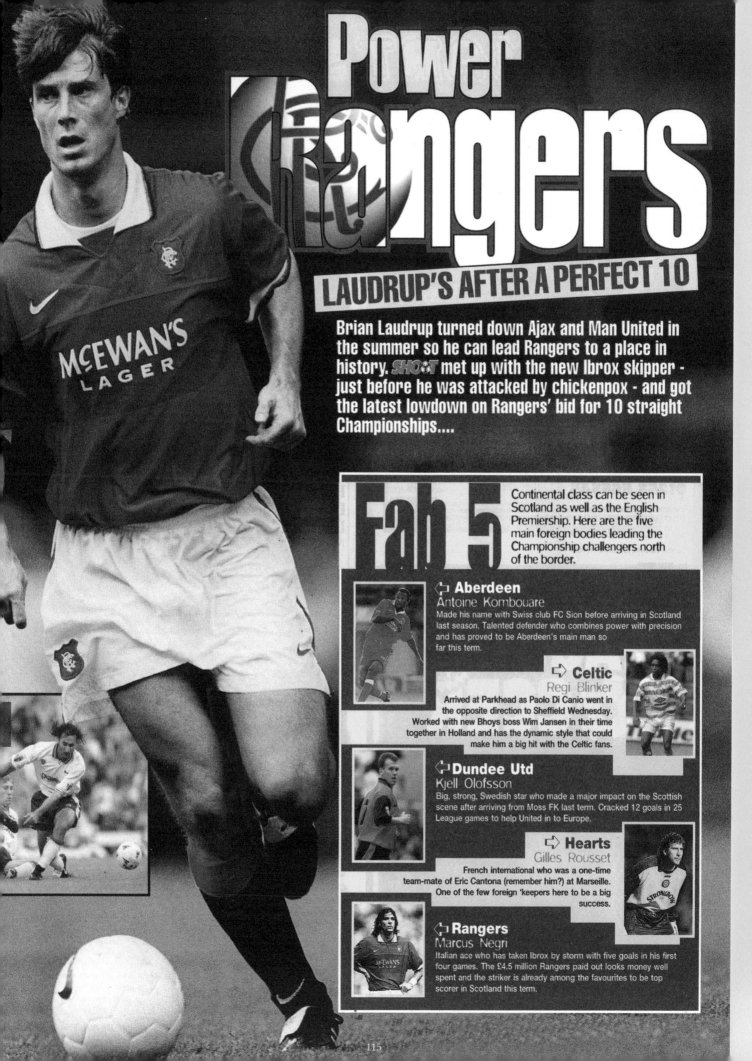

Power Rangers

LAUDRUP'S AFTER A PERFECT 10

Brian Laudrup turned down Ajax and Man United in the summer so he can lead Rangers to a place in history. *SHOOT* met up with the new Ibrox skipper - just before he was attacked by chickenpox - and got the latest lowdown on Rangers' bid for 10 straight Championships....

Fab 5

Continental class can be seen in Scotland as well as the English Premiership. Here are the five main foreign bodies leading the Championship challengers north of the border.

⇐ Aberdeen
Antoine Kombouare
Made his name with Swiss club FC Sion before arriving in Scotland last season. Talented defender who combines power with precision and has proved to be Aberdeen's main man so far this term.

⇒ Celtic
Regi Blinker
Arrived at Parkhead as Paolo Di Canio went in the opposite direction to Sheffield Wednesday. Worked with new Bhoys boss Wim Jansen in their time together in Holland and has the dynamic style that could make him a big hit with the Celtic fans.

⇐ Dundee Utd
Kjell Olofsson
Big, strong, Swedish star who made a major impact on the Scottish scene after arriving from Moss FK last term. Cracked 12 goals in 25 League games to help United in to Europe.

⇒ Hearts
Gilles Rousset
French international who was a one-time team-mate of Eric Cantona (remember him?) at Marseille. One of the few foreign 'keepers here to be a big success.

⇐ Rangers
Marcus Negri
Italian ace who has taken Ibrox by storm with five goals in his first four games. The £4.5 million Rangers paid out looks money well spent and the striker is already among the favourites to be top scorer in Scotland this term.

Strikers. You can't escape from Jonathon Woodgate.

Shoot

ROBBIE RELIANT!

10 FASCINATING FACTS ON THE HIGHFIELD ROAD HIT-MAN.

■ Robbie broke a 40-year scoring record when he became the youngest goalscorer for the Republic of Ireland aged 18 years and 98 days with a goal during the 5-0 victory at home to Malta.

■ Robbie scored twice on his debut for Wolves in a 2-0 win at Norwich. He was aged just 17-years, one month and one day!

■ He certainly likes his sleep and claims he never goes to bed after 11pm.

■ Robbie comes from the Irish town of Tallaght and one of his neighbours was Jason Gavin, who has just broken into the first team at Middlesbrough.

■ Collecting stickers has always been one of his favourite hobbies, although the only album he remembers completing was one for Italia '90.

■ His first football trial was with a club called Fettercairn where 40 young boys turned up hoping to impress. And when the manager picked the 20 biggest boys, Robbie was about to cycle home disappointed. But his older brother, who was a few inches taller, hid his little brother behind him to sneak him into the team and then show exactly what he could do.

■ In 1998 Robbie started on the NuTron diet and after specialists analysed a sample of his blood, he was told he could not eat 18 different types of food! These included beef, rice and chocolate.

■ West Ham missed out on his talents when Hammers boss Harry Redknapp sent him back home after a two-week trial.

■ When Robbie was 13, he was the star player of the school under-16 team. And during one cup comp he scored in every round and even netted a hat trick in the final – but his team lost 4-3 after extra-time!

IS THE GAFFER A MAD SCOTSMAN?

"Nah, not at all. Gordon just loves the game and is one of the main reasons why I came here. Every day he takes part in training and he's still some player. His enthusiasm is second to none and I know he will help me to become a better player."

WHO DID YOU SUPPORT AS A KID?

"I was a big Liverpool fan and was lucky enough to even travel over from Ireland to watch them play on a couple of occasions. I used to love watching John Barnes but Ian Rush was my big hero with all the goals he scored. I went to see United at Old Trafford a couple of times and although I quite enjoyed it, they just weren't Liverpool for me."

WHEN DID YOU LEAVE IRELAND TO COME TO ENGLAND?

"I was only 16 and had just taken my GCSEs when I joined Wolves. Liverpool and Forest both tried to sign me but my parents told me I shouldn't join the club I supported, so I opted for Wolves. I'll never look back and think what might have happened if I'd gone to Anfield as who knows? I certainly don't."

WHAT'S ALL THIS ABOUT THE MATCHDAY ANNOUNCER CALLING YOU ROY KEANE?

"To be honest I didn't even realise it had happened at the time and nor did any of the players. I've been told that when I ran on to the field, the announcer said 'Please welcome our new signing Roy Keane.' But I was so focused to do well on my debut, I didn't hear a single thing. But being compared to Roy's not bad, is it?"

DID YOU EVER GO CAROL SINGING?

"I love singing and even used to be in the school choir! I used to go knocking on people's doors singing a few carols and made quite a bit of money out of it – well, it seemed a lot for a little boy! I reckon me and Noel Whelan could still make a bit of dough if we went out together but that's only if Carlton Palmer stayed away as I've heard him singing in the showers!"

ON THE FOOTIE FRONT, ARE YOU AMAZED AT HOW WELL THINGS HAVE GONE AT COVENTRY?

"I always hoped things would go well but I couldn't be happier with what's happened for me. I was under the spotlight with the price tag and the hype around the move, but I can honestly say the fee never worried me and I never felt under pressure. I'm not the sort of person who lets things like that get to me and since day one I've gone out and played my normal game. It's been great and I suppose you could say Christmas has come early for me."

SO WHERE DOES THE FLIP-OVER CELEBRATION COME FROM?

"It's something I've done ever since I was a kid playing back home in Ireland. And I won't be changing the celebration as I've scored goals throughout my career while doing it. I kind of think that if I did something different the goals might might dry up. People keep asking me whether I've ever ended up on my backside but luckily it hasn't happened yet, touch wood!

"I RECKON ME AND NOEL WHELAN COULD MAKE SOME DECENT CASH FROM CAROL SINGING!"

119

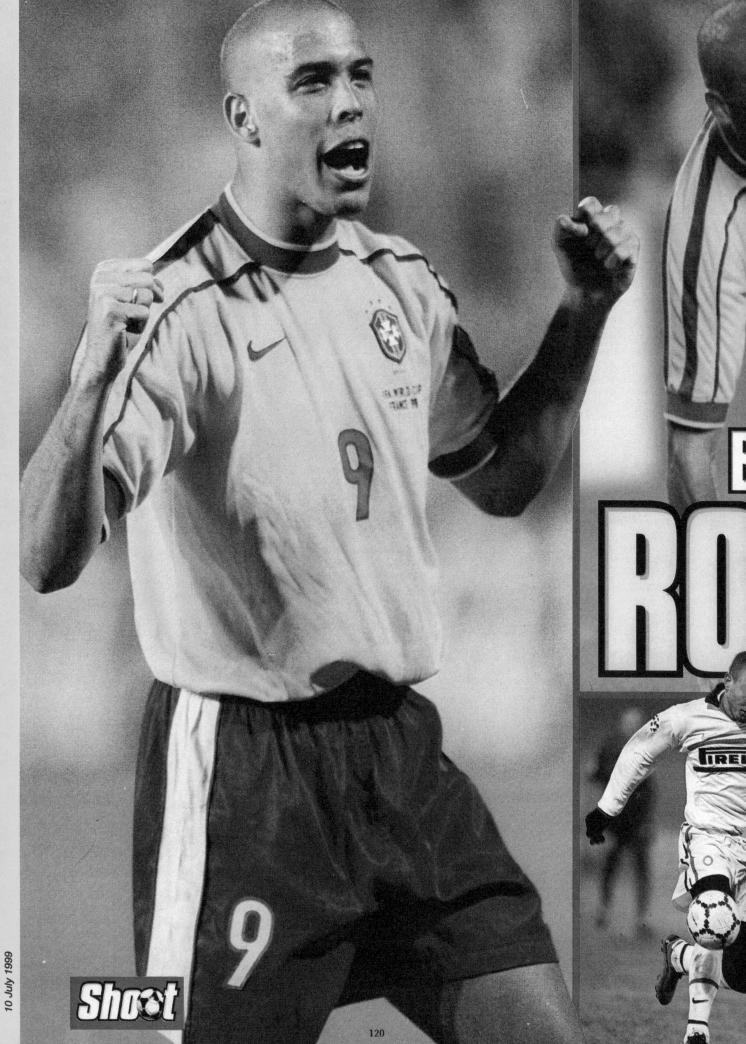

Shoot

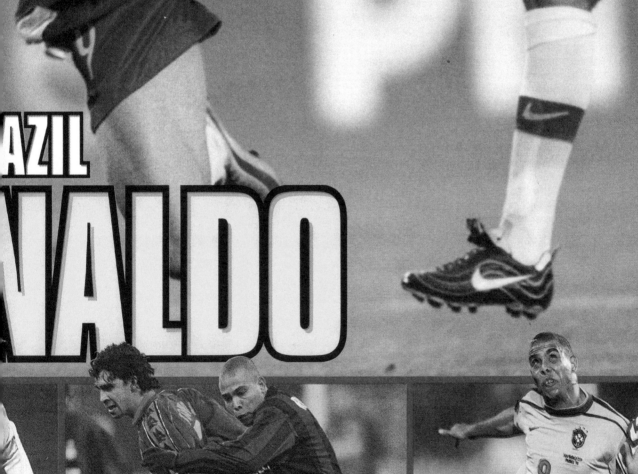

AZIL

NALDO

121

United striker Ole Gunnar Solskjaer talks about life at Old Trafford and last minute European Cup winning goals!

As he prepares for the new season, Norwegian goal machine Ole Gunnar Solskjaer can look back at the past 18 months of his Old Trafford career with mixed emotions.

After finding himself the odd one out as he battled for a role upfront with Andy Cole and Dwight Yorke, he did his best to win back his place by scoring for fun when he was brought on as a sub. But despite a four-goal spree in an amazing final ten minutes at Nottingham Forest, he never seemed to do enough to convince Fergie he was the man to break up United's goal laden front duo.

Unfortunately, poor Ole spent the final few months of last season sat on the bench trying not to get depressed. That was of course until one famous night in Barcelona when he took off his tracksuit and notched the goal that ensured Fergie's dream of winning the European Cup came true.

But now the United manager is worried that the Norwegian hotshot will leave for another club next season if he isn't handed a more regular first-team role.

But Fergie doesn't need to waste too much time thinking about Solskjaer doing a runner, though. Because as far as the nippy forward is concerned, he's here to stay. And as he returned to pre-season training he told SHOOT of his desire to remain a Red for the next few seasons.

"If people still can't understand why I didn't leave United last season, I hope they do now that we've done the treble," he says.

"I'm just so happy at Manchester United and it's just unbelievable to be a part of this incredible team."

GOAL-DEN OLE

WHAT A FEELING!

"I've never had a better feeling than when I scored the winning goal in the European Cup Final against Bayern Munich. I think it'll take a couple of years to sink in. When I came off the bench, 81 minutes of the game had been played, so I fancied my chances to score because I was fresh and I could tell that the Bayern players were tired."

UNITED SPIRIT

"All the players at Man United stick together and everyone looks out for each other. When you look at stars such as Jaap Stam, Ryan Giggs and Dwight Yorke, what else can you feel but self-confidence? The players don't know when they're beaten, as we proved several times last season."

TRANSFER TALK?

"There's been speculation about my future at Manchester United, but what happened to me against Bayern has made me even more committed to the club. I'm 100 per cent committed to staying here. I can't say that feeling will last forever, but right now I can't imagine being anywhere else than at Old Trafford. I've never knocked on the manager's door, I don't think I'll ever do that as I'm not that type of player. It's more like Alex coming to me and telling me why I'm not playing. He's told me he is satisfied with my work and has assured me he will try to get me more games in the future."

STRIKING RIVALS

"Last season the chemistry between Dwight Yorke and Andy Cole was absolutely brilliant. I think there's no partnership in the world that's been better than them. If you look back, Dwight's arrival at the club benefited everyone. His attitude and enthusiasm for the game are an inspiration to us all. But the team is not just about Dwight or Andy. And Teddy Sheringham is also a quality player. It means there's plenty of competition for places at the club. But all of us are in it together and hopefully if I carry on scoring I will get my chance in the starting II every week."

GREAT FUN

"It might sound funny, but I've enjoyed this year a lot, despite being on the bench for long periods. Some people may say I've suffered from not playing games on a regular basis, but I don't believe that's the case. In fact, I think it is quite the opposite. I feel that last year I improved as a player. The first season I was here I finished as top scorer at the club. But I feel I've played better over the past season. I played my part last year and I think I have become a better player from it. Hopefully I will continue to learn and develop at a club like United. The atmosphere around the team is great and winning the treble was a fantastic experience. We have a feeling that we'll win every game. But I must admit it has been painful at times as I have not been on the pitch as much as I would have liked. But you have to look at where you are. After all, if you can't enjoy playing for Manchester United then what can you enjoy as a footballer?"

EURO DELIGHT

ryone's been talking about United and European Cup since I joined the club e years ago. It was a great motivation e players and everyone wanted to win it. were all confident that last season was g to be our year, and all the talk in the s would be laid to rest."

SUPER SUB

"Last season I scored several goals after coming off the bench, like the four against Nottingham Forest and of course the goal in Barcelona. I think that coming on late in a game is a big factor for me. If I can come on in the last IO minutes, the rest of the players are very tired so I'm more likely to score in those situations."

THE ROAD TO THE CHAMPIONSHIP WILL GO THROUGH OLD TRAFFORD NEXT SEASON. SO IF ANY TEAM WANTS TO WIN IT, THEY BETTER MAKE SURE THEY KNOW HOW TO BEAT YORKEY, BECKS, GIGGSY AND CO. READ ON TO FIND OUT HOW TO GET PAST MAN UNITED.

HOW TO...

1

KIDNAP DAVID BECKHAM

Where would United be without the best crosser in the world providing balls for Cole and Yorke to blast in? Well they'd still be pretty good but you're going to stand a better chance of beating them with David Beckham out of the picture. Now he's learnt to tackle and curbed his temper, it looks like the only way Beckham will be left out of the United side is if you kidnap him.
TOP TIP Send out a fake invite to a Gucci party, offering the bearer a chance of winning a pair of designer loafers. Becks will jump at the chance and before he knows he's been framed, you can lock him in a cupboard!

2

PLAY THEM AT THE DELL

If there's one place United have a problem playing, it's at The Dell. Maybe it's the small pitch, maybe it's the small showers – but there's something about the pokey Hampshire ground that the Mancs don't like. Over the last five seasons, United have only picked up four league points and were spanked 6-3 in '96/'97. See if you can get your game changed to take place down south.
TOP TIP With rumours of Southampton moving to a new stadium, the Dell will soon be empty. Petition your chairman to move just one home game – the United clash – to the ground to pay respect to the crumbling old monument.

5

PLAY THEM AFTER A EUROPEAN GAME

Fergie's quest for European silver was the most important of the three competitions United were in last season. And last season, United did suffer a hangover the morning after their European exertions – in the 12 games directly following a Champions League clash. United lost one, drew seven and won only four. If there's ever a right time to play Fergie's men, catch them after Europe.
TOP TIP Hope and pray United have been kicked about the park by some ropey Russian side, were held up in the airport by raving Turkish fans or were food poisoned in the Portuguese capital. That'll help your chances!

6

HOPE FERGIE PLAYS BLOMQVIST AND MAY

United have got the strongest squad in Britain but there are still a few weak links. Not that there's anything wrong with May or Blomqvist but you'd much rather be facing them than Stam and Giggs, wouldn't you? Keep your fingers crossed Fergie wants to rest his top men for more important games and you might catch the reserves a little out of sorts. Maybe...
TOP TIP If you're playing against Blomqvist, try winding him up by reminding him what a 'mare he had in the European Cup Final. Likewise with May, mention that the last time he played, the Titanic was just about to sail!

A STEP BY STEP GUIDE

BEAT MAN UNITED

3

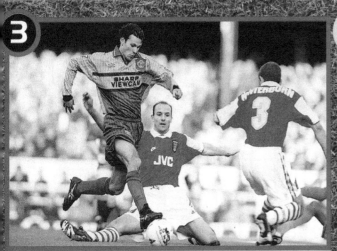

MAKE THEM WEAR THEIR GREY KIT

Whoever came up with the idea for United to play in grey a few seasons ago should never be let near a kit design again... or given a job for life, depending on your view! The Red Devils didn't win a single game in grey, losing to Liverpool, Aston Villa, Southampton and Arsenal on the way. The players said the kit made it hard for them to pick out team-mates. OK, but the goal wasn't grey too, was it?

TOP TIP Try to make the FA play an Old School game each season where sides wear retro kits for one fixture. Of coûrse, your team's game would be against United in their grey kit and a 6-0 win would be the result. Yeah baby!

4

DRAW THEM IN THE WORTHINGTON CUP

Fergie cares about winning the Worthington Cup as much as he does about getting an invite to Arsene Wenger's house for tea. That's not very much at all. When you're facing teams like Juve and Bayern, you're not going to give a rat's arse about some dodgy cup with three handles. Draw United in the Worthington Cup and you'll almost be guaranteed a win, especially next season.

TOP TIP Take all of the United bit-players on loan, so when it comes time for them to play them in the Worthington Cup, they won't have a team to put out. They'll have to play Fergie upfront and get Brian Kidd in on loan!

7

ONLY PLAY FOR 90 MINUTES

What is it with refs and Man United? Do they forget the game only lasts for 90 minutes? Time after time, United have been given a few extra minutes to get themselves out of a sticky situation – watch the European Cup Final if you don't believe us. As the game goes on, subtly remind the ref that the rules clearly state the game is to last just 90 minutes. If not, nick Fergie's stopwatch to prove your point!

TOP TIP If all else fails and you do have to play extra time, make sure you trip up Solskjaer or Sheringham and delay them getting on the pitch. The less time they're on the pitch, the better chance you have of winning.

8

LET THEM WIN EVERYTHING

Yes, this might sound strange but there is a long term strategy. By letting United win every single trophy next season, it will help in two ways. Firstly, all their players will either retire at the top or move to another club for a challenge. Secondly, they'll probably pull out of all domestic competitions to concentrate on international tournaments like the World Clubs Championship in Outer Mongolia.

TOP TIP Obviously if you are going to choose this option, you must totally ignore the rest of our advice. Just hope they're not wearing grey, it's not the Worthington Cup or after a Euro game or you'll have made the wrong choice!

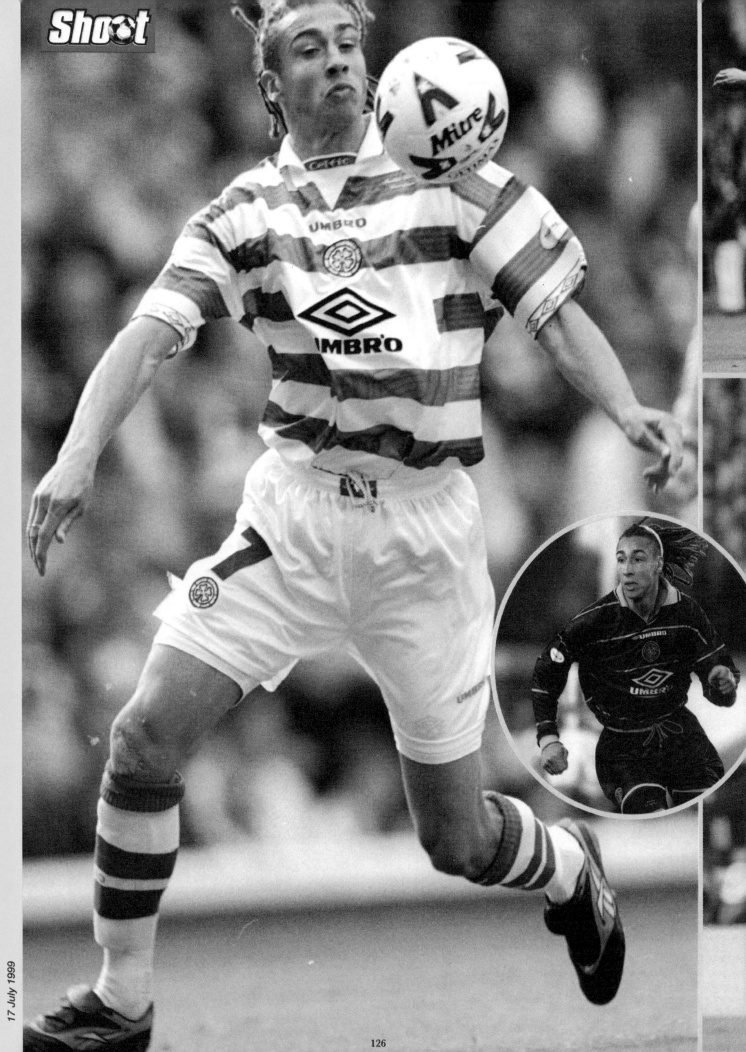

17 July 1999

CELTIC
HENRIK LARSSON

A to Z ARSENAL

WANNA KNOW MORE ABOUT YOUR FAVE CLUB? THEN CHECK OUT SHOOT'S GUIDE. THIS WEEK WE CHECK OUT ARSENE WENGER'S GUNNERS!

A IS FOR ANELKA
What went on with moody Nic? Real Madrid, Juventus and Lazio chased him, and he finally joined the Spaniards. But it left a bitter a taste in Arsene Nic's mouth. Is Arsene Wenger now off his Christmas card list?

B IS FOR BERGKAMP
No player has lit up Highbury like Bergy, who wants to stay a bit longer. Gooner fans rejoice.

C IS FOR CHARITY SHIELD
What's the best way to get over United winning the Treble? Beating them at Wembley helps, which is what The Gunners did. Ray Parlour scored the winner.

D IS FOR DEFENCE
Dixon, Adams, Keown and Winterburn let in 18 league goals last season, the best in Europe.

E IS FOR ENGLISH PRESS
Under George Graham, the press called Arsenal "boring". Now, with Arsene Wenger, they're called "dirty" for the red cards they picked up last season. But the players ain't bothered.

F IS FOR FRENCHMEN
Vieira, Petit, Grimandi, Garde, Grondin, Wenger. And there's been Anelka and Diawara. There are more Frenchmen in N5 than at Paris St Germain.

G IS FOR GUNNERSAURUS REX
He's seven feet tall, has scaly skin and growls. Not Martin Keown but the Arsenal mascot! Every club has one but few are as imposing as Highbury's dinosaur.

H IS FOR HARRY
Prince Harry goes to Highbury often. Unlike big brur, who likes polo.

I IS FOR INJURIES
Every club moans that injuries have cost them but Arsenal have suffered more than most. Seaman, Adams, Keown, Petit and Bergkamp have all been injured. Not so sure when it's Boa Morte and Wreh.

J IS FOR JUDAS
What fans call ex-boss George Graham after he joined rivals Tottenham.

K IS FOR KING'S CROSS
Highbury holds only 38,000, and derelict land near King's Cross station is tipped as the site for a new ground. Arsenal may move say they may move anywhere.

L IS FOR LEGENDS
Baker in the '50s, Brady in the '70s, Bergkamp in the '90s. In the '80s, Arsenal were hopeless.

M IS FOR MONEY
"We have a strict pay policy at this club, and we will not overstep the mark for anybody," says Wenger. Probably why they missed out on Sutton, Dyer, Deschamps, Hamann...

N IS FOR NIKE
They might not have the multi-stadium and the multi-million pound signings but at least they have a flash Nike kit and all the leisure wear that goes with it.

O IS FOR OWN GOAL
"It was the most embarrass-ing moment of my life. I just played the ball back, expect-ing David to be on his line. He wasn't," was Lee Dixon's response when, in 1992, he chipped Seamo from 30 yards.

P IS FOR PENNANT
Poor Notts County. One minute, the England schoolboy's on their books, the next, he's a Gunner.

Q IS FOR QUICK
They've had Perry Groves, and Anders Limpar, now it's Marc Overmars. We are talking about nippy wingers. Just ask Alessandro Pistone.

R IS FOR RENNIE
Not an indigestion tablet but referee Uriah. Gunners think they are one and the same.

S IS FOR SHERINGHAM
Teddy is the most hated player to have visited Highbury. Well, he has played for Tottenham and then Man United, and wound Gooners up by kissing his United shirt in front of them a while ago.

T IS FOR TONY
A legend at Highbury, Mr Adams has won three titles, two FA Cups and the Cup Winners' Cup.

U IS FOR UNDERGROUND
Arsenal are the only club to have an Underground station named after them. In the 1930s, ex-boss Herbert Chapman managed to get the nearest tube changed from Gillespie Road to Arsenal.

V IS FOR VIVAS
Argentine defender Nelson won respect for cuffing Man Utd's Nicky Butt, but let in Jimmy Hasselbaink to score in the penultimate game.

W IS FOR WOOLWICH
Spurs fans hate Arsenal so much because The Gunners aren't really a north London side. They hail from Woolwich in south east London, and were once called Woolwich Arsenal.

X IS FOR X-RATED
That's what people call Arsenal but, amazingly, they finished third in last season's Fair Play league. Although they have thrown the odd elbow.

Y IS FOR YELLOWS
What Arsenal fans sing when playing away, when the kit is sponsored by SEGA. This is a rude word in Italian, so if Arsenal meet AC Milan, expect a very different song from their opponents!

Z IS FOR ZZZZZ
Gone are the days of the long ball. One reason is Ian Wright's departure. Tony Adams says: "We would have never won the league with Ian in the team. We did-n't just look to knock the ball."

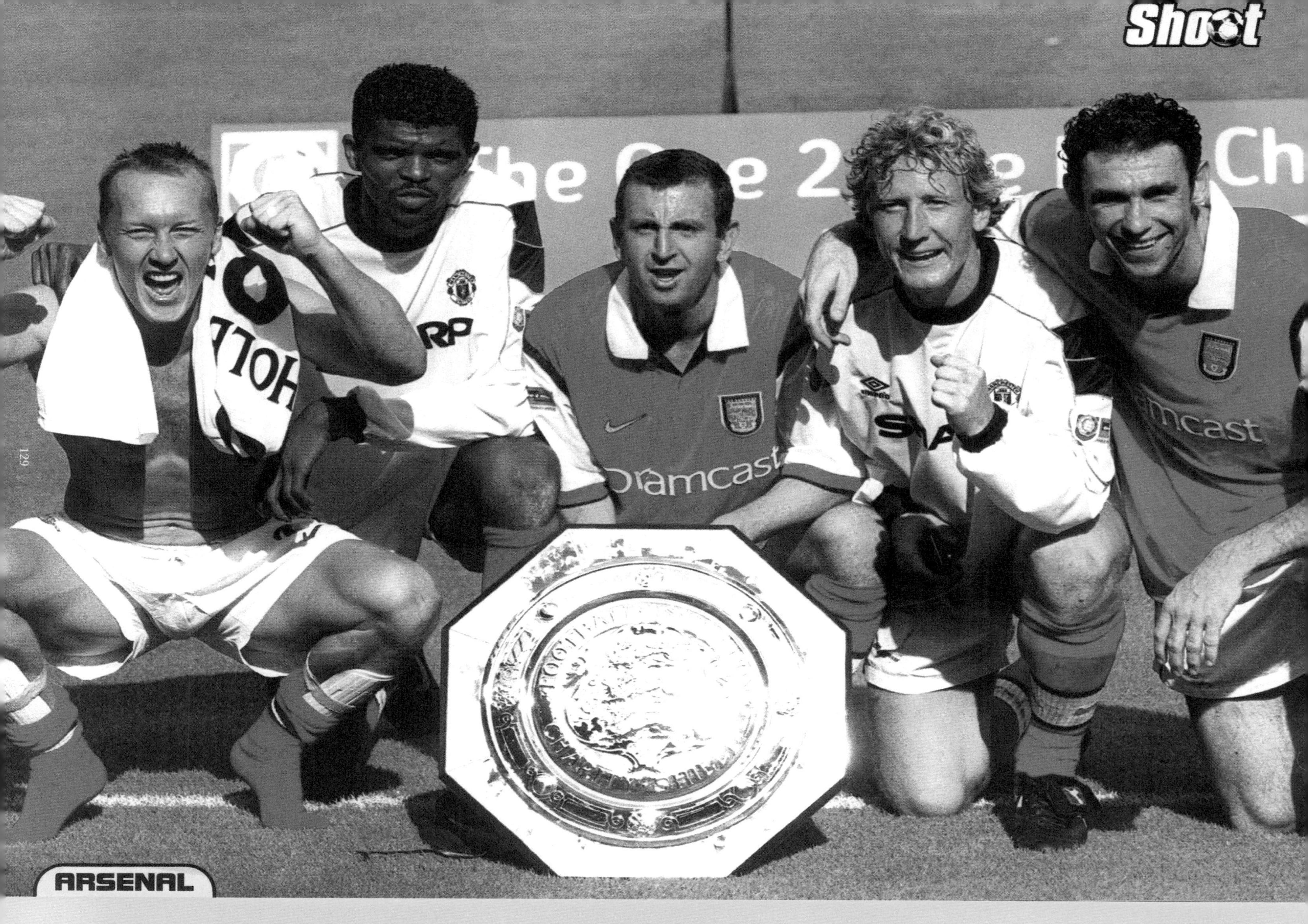

Shoot Hotline

FOOTIE STARS ARE ALWAYS ON THE DOG 'N' BONE TO THEIR FAVE FOOTIE MAG FILLING US IN ON ALL THE TOP GOSS AND BIG STORIES... HANG ON! THERE IT GOES AGAIN. HELLO, SHOOT HOTLINE...

It's **KEVIN PHILLIPS** – and he's inviting us up to his gaff to do another interview with him. "I've finally finished building my house, says Kev. "You know, the one which you ran a story on last season when it was just a pile of rubble! So are you coming up again, chaps?" Sure Kev, we'll do that. Gotta go, the phone's going crazy again. Make sure you put in a couple in against The Scots for us!

"Hello?" It's **DEAN WINDASS** of Bradford. "I've got another funny story to tell yer – and I know how you lot like a laugh," says Deano. Come on then, tell us more. "It's from a few years back when I was with Aberdeen. I was running down

SOUTHAMPTON'S MATTY OAKLEY RINGS IN. HE'S AT SEA WITH DAVID HOWELLS AND JAMES BEATTIE!

the touchline when I heard someone yell, 'Deano, show us your arse'!" What did you do? "What do you reckon? I obliged of course! I must have been mad – the temperature must have been -10c!"

On the subject of feeling cold, **MATTY OAKLEY** has certainly been braving the elements – he's been to sea!! "I'm on the yacht which is joint owned by David Howells and James Beattie and we're going to the Isle of Man for a day trip." Are you a good swimmer? "Yeah, not bad – but I'm still keeping my life jacket on at all times while Beats is sailing the thing!"

Things seem to be getting back to normal at Toon after Ruud scarpered. Well, they must be – even **STEVE HOWEY** is getting close to fitness! "Yeah, I'm getting there," he screams down the blower. "I'm out of plaster now and hopefully it won't be too long. Just keep your fingers – and everything else – crossed for me!"

KICK OFF

RED NOSE'S REVENGE

Anyone who thinks the long-running feud between Peter Schmeichel and Ian Wright has ended now that the former Man United 'keeper no longer plays in England would be seriously wrong. The red-nosed Dane is just about to release his autobiography and in it launches a blistering attack on the ex-Arsenal striker. "There was always something happening when Wright was on the pitch. I have always considered him a bit of an idiot," fumes Schmeichel, who clashed with Wrighty on several occasions over the years. "In my opinion his vulgar behaviour should have been stamped out a long time ago." So there's not much chance of them appearing in a Nescafé TV ad together then, eh?!

BAD OLD LOOK

JOE ROYLE

MINGIN'

GUS IS PLANE BORED

Posh Spice can complain all she likes about the fact her beloved David works 300 miles from London but that's nothing compared to the distance Chelsea star Gustavo Poyet has to travel to spend time with his family. The Uruguayan says: "I first have to fly from London to Sao Paolo which is almost 11 hours then wait two hours in Sao Paolo for a connecting flight. From there to Montevideo is almost another three hours. So in total it's around 15 hours worth of travelling!"

A DAY IN THE LIFE OF...

DENNIS WISE*

7am Get up early and leg it downstairs for a row with the postman. He always bends my copy SHOOT before sticking through the letterbox.

9am The missus sends me out into the garden for arguing with the dog. Find the cat and kick off with him instead.

12pm Phone my top mate Nicky Butt for a slanging match. He isn't there so I give his answer phone a right mouthful.

3pm My agent Eric Hall comes round. I kick him up the bum then pinch him – just for a laugh.

7pm Next door neighbour comes round moaning that I've made his kids cry again. Accidentally elbow him in the face.

11pm Go to bed and have a horrible dream about never being picked for England again.

* Not THAT Dennis Wise, obviously!

BOSS

100°

KEVIN PHILLIPS
Who said he'd struggle in the Prem?

CHAMPIONS LEAGUE STICKER ALBUM
Which is totally free with this issue of SHOOT!

PHONING WEMBLEY
... and getting through to flippin' Autoglass instead!

MANAGERS SLAGGING EACH OTHER OFF
Keep it up, it's a right laugh!

MOANING ABOUT REFEREES
Shut up, they're only doing their jobs!

STAN THE MAN
Villa don't want him, Fulham don't want him – any takers?!

0°

DEAD LOSS

FRANKLY SPEAKING

LE MOAN

Was it only a couple of weeks ago that Frank 'The Plank' Leboeuf was slagging off the Prem for being too violent? Only the arrogant Frenchman (he's won the World Cup, y'know!) has now changed his mind and decided that he 'prefers English players' after all. "They give their all," says Letwit. "Someone like Pippo Inzaghi of Juventus will dive 25 times a match without anyone touching him. I sometimes wonder if the guy has any balls at all." Blimey, first the English, now the Italians – who's Frank going to slag off next?!

WELCOME TO THE CRAZY GANG

This big pile of smoking clothes in the picture on the right is the remains of ex-Bolton star Hermann Hreidarsson's clobber after the Crazy Gang welcomed him Wimbledon style to his new club – by setting fire to his garms then chucking them out of the dressing room. Bless.

STOP PRESS
If you want to buy a bit of Wembley Stadium get online. The stadium will be demolished next year and everything will be auctioned off piece by piece on www.qxl.com

SPARE 10p FOR POTLESS PALACE?

SKINT!

Things are worse than we first thought at Potless Palace as hard up boss Steve Coppell tries to make ends meet. "It's coming to the end of the season in Scandinavia and I'm presuming there are players available on a Bosman," reveals Copp, "so I intend to get in touch with a few Scandinavian newspapers for some names and say, 'listen, we can't pay you but we can give you a stage'. And what a stage... food parcels can be sent to Steve c/o Selhurst Park.

SMART!

BECKS' FASHION TIPS

NO.3 IN A GREAT NEW SERIES!

"Get yerself into a jumper like the one Alan Shearer wore on the cover of last week's SHOOT. They're only a tenner from the market!"

GO ON YOU KNOW YOU WANT TO!

GOSSIP

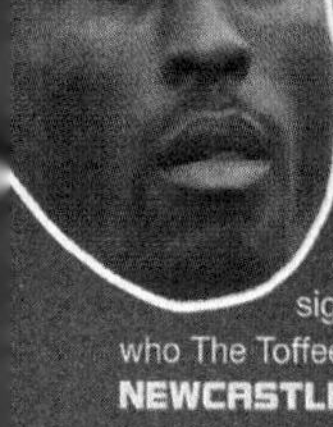

TOTTENHAM... and England star Sol Campbell is being targeted by Real Madrid again. John Toshack, boss of the Spanish giants, is said to be ready to splash out £15 million to secure the services of the 25-year-old defender, a player they've been chasing for the last 18 months.
EVERTON... youngster Michael Branch could be on his way out of the Premiership. Both Birmingham and Bristol City are interested in signing the out-of-favour 22-year-old who The Toffees value at under £1 million.
NEWCASTLE... defender Warren Barton has been fined two weeks' wages – £30,000 – for getting sent off against Coventry for fighting recently.

"I have no excuses, it was my fault entirely," said the former England man. "I have never been sent off before, even as a schoolboy. I have let everyone down and I owe them an apology." Too right! 
LEICESTER CITY... boss Martin O'Neill won't be able to make any new signings for the forseeable future because the club's financial backers are fed up with the club's continuing problems in the boardroom. That means O'Neill's plans to swoop for Sheffield Wednesday striker Andy Booth are now on the back burner.

THE S
WIT

THE RULES: In the kit bag there are 50 footie obje
with a tough question attached. Lee must pick out a few of
objects randomly then answer the corresponding question.
make it tougher he also has to pick a tricky question (socks
team question (plastic player) and three from SHOOT reader

WHAT'S YOUR MOST EMBARRASSING MOMENT DURING A FOOTBALL MATCH?

"That was when I scored my first goal for United – a right footer from just inside the box. I ran towards the Stretford End and went to slide on my knees. But my knee got stuck in the ground and I went head first into the turf – right in front of the fans!"

HOW DO YOU SPEND YOUR SPARE TIME?

"Oh, doing lots of exciting things. Today, for example, I'm going up to Manchester to pick some curtains up from my old house! It's nearly the golf season so I'll be playing that a bit. I did plan on a bit of tennis this winter but that never happened. The lads down here usually go on the odd night out."

SHOOT KIT BAG

LEE SHARPE

WHO'S THE WORST ROOM-MATE THAT YOU'VE EVER HAD?

"Dean Windass. He farts, snores, talks in his sleep – he's horrible. He's a busy bloke round this place. He likes the radio, TV, press – anything, he loves it. With a face like his though you'd think he'd keep away!"

WHAT HAS BEEN THE HIGHLIGHT OF YOUR CAREER?

"I would say beating Barcelona and winning the European Cup Winners Cup with United was good. The best though was winning the league title for the first time in years. It was such a long wait and the team had been building towards it. We just missed out the year before to Leeds – so it was a great moment."

WHO'S YOUR BEST MATE IN THE GAME?

"The only one at United that I still keep in touch with is Roy Keane. I was quite good mates with Ryan Giggs for a time but we went our own ways. He's always had his own mates and when mine weren't coming up that much I used to knock about with Ryan and his mates. Gary Kelly at Leeds is also a good mate. The two Irish lads, I think I must be the calming influence on them! I was also at Manchester United with Neil Whitworth, who plays at Hull now, and we're good mates."

HAVE YOU EVER HAD A ROW WITH A BOSS?

"I've never actually rowed with a manager, at any club I've been at. They've had a go at me and I've never said a lot back. You just let them get on with it – you don't want to fuel the fire! Alex Ferguson lost it with me a few times – round my house, at half-time, full-time, and the training ground. I think that with some managers it's just their passion inside, they just have to let it go and it doesn't matter who gets it."

ARE YOU A PRACTICAL JOKER?

"No, no! I just sit, listen and watch. You want to speak to Dean Saunders – he's the joker around here, but he plays by the law of averages. He tells that many stories so that, hopefully, one of them might be funny!"

WHAT'S THE BEST HOLIDAY YOU'VE EVER HAD?

"Oh my god, I couldn't tell you one – there's been that many. I've been to Ayia Napa for the last two years and that was really good. The best would have to be when we went during the last World Cup. The atmosphere was great. Everyone was singing Vindaloo and all that – it was a great laugh."

WHAT IS THE FUNNIEST THING YOU'VE SEEN IN FOOTBALL?

"Hmm, probably Dean Windass's face! Mr Potato Head! Actually, I was reading SHOOT the other week and I saw that you had him in there. He was saying that I had a bad old look, but I'm sure that was just to cover for himself. Dean wears some bad stuff, as does David Wetherall and Robbie Blake."

CAPTAIN

YOUR SHOUT

WHO'S GOING TO BE THE BRIGHTEST STAR AT EURO 2000?

> I reckon it could be Alan Shearer. He'll want to finish his international career on a high.
> David 14, London

> David Beckham. He will be keen to wipe away the memory of being sent-off in France '98.
> Frank 12, London

> Thierry Henry has taken the Premiership by storm with Arsenal – he could do the same with France.
> Aaron 12, London

> Zinedine Zidane is the best midfielder in the world and he'll show that he's the best.
> Nicholas 12, London

> I reckon it could be Zidane. He scores great goals and is the most skilful player in the tournament.
> Joe 12, London

> Alan Shearer. He always shows his best form in major tournaments and he'll fire England to the Final.
> Tommy 12, London

Two years ago the balding bonce of Zinedine Zidane put France on the way to the biggest, most triumphant night in the proud footballing history. Arsenal's Emmanuel Petit, who is far more flowing when it comes to the locks department, was also on the score sheet, but it was the two goals from Zidane which had everyone talking after their 3-0 World Cup Final win over Brazil in Paris.

Zidane, by his own very high standards, has had a couple of indifferent years since the greatest night of his career. A succession of injuries haven't helped matters but the whisper coming out of the French camp is the Juve star is almost back to his best – and now he's ready to show it. So can France add the European crown to their World title? SHOOT asked the 27-year-old when we met him in Paris recently for the launch of the new Lego Football Game.

WAS SCORING TWICE IN THE WORLD CUP FINAL THE PEAK OF YOUR CAREER?
"It was, but what happened afterwards will stay with me forever. The celebrations in Paris were just unbelievable but to have my face projected onto the Arc de Triomphe meant something words can't describe. It really touched me and I felt the proudest man on earth that night."

ARE YOU FEELING TIRED AFTER ANOTHER LONG SEASON WITH JUVENTUS?
"I feel OK. I'm sure there'll be players at Euro 2000 who'll be suffering from fatigue more than me. I've had quite a few injury problems since France '98 and this has meant I've missed a few games. No one likes missing games, but at least they've given me time to relax from football."

HOW DO YOU THINK FRANCE WILL FAIR IN THE EURO 2000 TOURNAMENT?
"It won't be easy, as we're the World Champions and everyone will be out to beat us. Our preparations have gone well, but you never know what will happen in a major tournament. The expectation levels are high, and if we perform we know we have the players to win it."

WHAT WOULD IT MEAN TO FRANCE IF YOU BECOME EUROPEAN, AS WELL AS WORLD CHAMPIONS?
"It would be unbelievable. Michel Platini was one of my heroes and he wore the No. 10 shirt when

he led France to success in the European Championships of 1984. I was only a young boy but I can still recall everyone singing and dancing in the streets. I'd love to be part of the next French side to become European Champions."

FRANCE HAVE SUFFERED WITH INJURIES DURING THEIR PREPARATIONS. COULD THIS EFFECT YOUR CHANCES?
"I don't think so as everyone has injuries and, luckily for us, they've just been little niggly ones. Any problems the players have we can play on with. I've had too many problems to count. After the World Cup I had been playing continuously for over a year and my body couldn't take it. It's only logical for problems to arise. But now I've rested and have no lasting problems."

HOW DO YOU RATE ENGLAND'S CHANCES IN EURO 2000?
"I think England are probably on par with someone like Italy. And I believe both of them have a genuine chance of winning it. England have so many talented individuals but it all depends on how they work together as a team. I wouldn't say they are one of the favourites but they are definitely amongst a group of teams who are capable of taking the trophy home. English teams always seem to have a good spirit and I'm sure they're a country many people will try to avoid if they reach the Quarter-Finals. "

WHICH ENGLAND PLAYERS IMPRESS YOU THE MOST AT THE MOMENT?
"I really enjoy watching David Beckham and his Man United team-mate Paul Scholes. I've played against them with Juventus on a couple of occasions in the Champions League and I rate them very highly. Beckham is a great player with

so much skill, while Scholes is always looking to get forward and score goals. Alan Shearer and Michael Owen are both good goalscorers and will always be a threat. But you could take any nation and go right through the squad and pick out good players. That's why I believe it will be a very open tournament."

HOW IMPORTANT IS IT TO HAVE PLAYERS WHO CAN PLAY IN MORE THAN ONE POSITION?

"It's very important. Each manager can only name 22 players and when you play games in quick succession you are bound to pick up a few injuries along the way. You have to have a squad of players who are comfortable in a number of different positions. We're lucky to have people like Marcel Desailly who is a world-class player at either centre-back or in midfield."

IS IT TRUE YOU'RE CALLED 'THE BOSS' BY YOUR TEAM-MATES?

"Yes, and I don't like it. If there was someone in the team who deserves a name like that it should be Didier Deschamps, my Juventus team-mate. I like being able to input different things to the team even if I'm not the skipper, but my main job is to create scoring chances for the strikers. That is my responsibility for the French team and it's something I like doing."

TELL US ABOUT YOUR TOUGH UPBRINGING AS A CHILD?

"There was always football to keep me away from trouble but the area of Marseille I grew up in, Castellane, is rough. My family still live there. They made a lot of sacrifices so I could become a footballer. My dad was unemployed and there was not a lot of money. When I was 14 I moved to Cannes and lived with a nice family, that a club found for me. The family treated me like their own son. I could go home to see my real family once a month."

VIVA ZIDANE!

top bhoys

→ **CELTIC PARK** was a sea of green as more than 60,000 fans celebrated only their second Scottish Premier League title in 12 years. With the CIS League Cup won in March and an impending Scottish Cup Final appearance against Hibs at the end of May, Celtic are looking to win their first domestic treble since 1969. Martin O'Neill, in just under 12 months, has been hailed as the most successful manager at the club since the great Jock Stein, and with Swedish striker Henrik Larsson looking likely to win the Golden Boot as the leading goalscorer in Europe, it is difficult to argue that Celtic have been the British success story of the season. The Bhoys' supporters think so anyway.

THE SAME OLD STORY

Managers change, results vary but one thing stays constant at West Ham – they keep producing brilliant youngsters. One of the latest exciting products of The Hammers' academy, is England Under-21 striker **Jermain Defoe**. **Words: Eddie Kelly Pictures: Paul Webb**

JERMAIN DEFOE did not so much arrive on the scene last season, as sensationally burst on to it. Nobody expected West Ham's teenage hotshot to take the old adage "start as you mean to go on" quite so literally.

In coming off the bench to superbly smash home the winner, on his first team debut, in a Worthington Cup tie at Walsall, the diminutive striker had dramatically announced his arrival in the professional game.

At just 17 years-old, that goal started an inaugural season, that more experienced pros could only dream of. Following his promising debut, then West Ham boss Harry Redknapp surprisingly loaned the zippy front man to out to Second Division Bournemouth.

But far from sulking his time away on the South Coast, Jemain decided it would be far more fun to set about breaking goal-scoring landmarks, and duly obliged by calmly slotting home in ten consecutive league games – a post-War record.

Although he recalls that time with some affection, Jermain admits it was a move which came as a bit of a shock.

"To be honest, I wasn't expecting it. I thought that I was still a bit young for a move, and could continue learning my trade at West Ham.

"But Harry was always very good at explaining things, and he told me that I would gain a lot more from playing in Bournemouth's first team than in the West Ham reserves.

"He also told me to go with an open mind, and learn as much as I could. He said playing for a first team regularly I would be among the big boys and it could only benefit me in the long run. He was right of course, and I'll always be indebted to him for guiding me through my early career."

With his name now firmly etched in the archives of Bournemouth FC,

Main: Jermain at the Umbro kit launch. **Left:** Holding off Chelsea's Graeme Le Saux.

Jermain returned to the East End with another more immediate goal – making a name for himself in the England Under-21 set-up.

His opportunity came in the May encounter with Mexico, when, you've guessed it, he scored again on his debut. His penchant for international goals didn't stop there, with a further three in his next four appearances.

With such a fairytale start – and progress which has seen him not only become an England Under-21 regular but also notch up his first League goal for The Hammers this campaign – you could forgive the Beckton-born teenager for being a wee bit cocky.

But when *Shoot Monthly* caught up with the West Ham No.25 at an Umbro boot launch, we discovered that his feet are still firmly on the ground.

"I'm delighted to be part of the set-up at West Ham," said Jermain. "But we do have some real quality strikers here and that makes it difficult.

"I guess that Paolo [di Canio] and Freddie [Kanoute] will be the manager's first choices, but the rest of us have just got to keep plugging away and prove to the boss that we can do a job too.

"I have come on as a sub in a few games and have felt very comfortable. I had been told by some of the Bournemouth lads that I would find the

pace in the Premiership to be a bit quicker, but that hasn't really been the case so far.

"Of course there is some real quality here, and when you are constantly training with such talent, it kind of prepares you for what awaits in the Premier League."

Undeniably, The Hammers certainly have a fair smattering of gifted players. Historically known as "The Academy", the club continue to churn out young players who appear destined for future stardom.

Following hot on the heels of England's centre-back Rio Ferdinand, lavish entertainers such us Jermain, Michael Carrick and Joe Cole all eagerly await the call to take their place in the England revolution.

"I speak to Joe and Michael all the time, and we are always willing to help each other out," revealed Jermain.

"Michael has told me what it was like training alongside players of the calibre of Beckham and Owen. He says it was a great experience, and if I keep working hard my chance will come.

"At the moment I am relishing the opportunity to play for the Under-21s, as it's really helping to develop my game. I have tremendous respect for the manager, David Platt. He has been there and done it himself, and you can't say fairer than that."

Clearly the feelings of respect are mutual. Platt, himself, has made the remarkable claim that young Jermain may be one of the best products *ever* to emerge from the Under-21 set-up.

He said: "Jermain excites me and I think he is absolutely without weakness, I just can't find one. Every time I think of the future, my mind is drawn back to Defoe. He's unique.

"How many players can I name

West Ham

If Jermain steps up to full England honours he'll be in good company. Here are a few of the other stars to graduate from the West Ham academy.

BOBBY MOORE England's captain in 1966. Played a total of 108 games for his country and respected throughout the world as probably the greatest defender ever.

MARTIN PETERS Midfield maestro and World Cup winner who scored 20 goals in 67 appearances.

GEOFF HURST Another World Cup-winner, he scored a total of 24 goals in 49 England appearances.

FRANK LAMPARD SENIOR Full-back who played for his country twice – against Yugoslavia in 1973 and Australia in 1980

TREVOR BROOKING Made his England debut in 1974 and played 47 times for his country.

TONY COTTEE Failed to score in seven appearances for his country, starting with a debut in 1987.

PAUL INCE Won a total of 53 caps and became the first black player to captain England.

RIO FERDINAND Sven Goran Eriksson's first choice centre-half in the current England squad.

FRANK LAMPARD JUNIOR Made debut against Belgium in 2000.

MICHAEL CARRICK Awarded his first cap against Mexico earlier this year when he came on as a sub.

JOE COLE Joe also came on as a substitute in the 4-0 win over Mexico.

without a weakness? Not many. Maybe Michael Owen. Maybe Luis Figo. That could be it."

Whether or not Jermain can join these giants of the game remains to be seen, but clearly the latest product from West Ham's conveyor belt of talent knows that he is well placed to challenge for honours at the highest level…eventually.

"Sven Goran Eriksson has also shown that age is no barrier to selection for the full squad," he smiled.

"If you are good enough, age is irrelevant, and hard work and the right attitude could earn you a full cap. Even just to train with the full squad would be a marvellous opportunity.

"But ultimately, I really want to establish myself in the England team, and eventually help to win the World Cup! Why not?," he asked.

ENGLAND'S FINEST

WHAT A WONDERFUL YEAR it has been for England captain David Beckham. Apart from masterminding the World Cup miracles against Germany and Greece, he also scooped two very prestigious individual awards. In December he was voted Sportsman of the Year by the sports writers of Great Britain, the first time since Bobby Moore in 1966 that a footballer had been awarded this honour. Then a week later he carried off the prestigious BBC Sports Personality of the Year award. In fact the only pot not to grace the mantlepiece at Beckingham Palace is the FIFA World Player of the Year. Shortlisted alongside Raul and Luis Figo, Beckham was beaten into second place as the Portugese won the ultimate individual prize in football. Maybe not the best in the world, he is certainly England's finest footballer for a generation, and for that we salute him.

March 2002

This month: A new manager and a stadium in transformation, but **West Ham** still can't get it quite right out on the pitch.

SPECTATOR: Duncan Bond

PLAY AWAY

WHEN SHOOT MONTHLY'S editor asked if I would like to go as a guest of our good friends at Fila and spend the day in their hospitality box at Upton Park, I did not need much persuading.

I had never before experienced the corporate day out at any sporting event, so to be wined and dined and then watch a top Premiership football match, was too good an opportunity to decline.

Plus, if truth be told, this ardent Southend United fan, once possessed claret and blue blood and could be found on the terraces cheering on the likes of Bonds, Brooking, Lampard (the older one!) and Devonshire.

The first thing that caught my eye was the stunning new stadium. Guarded by twin towers, the new Doctor Martens Stand is a most impressive structure and is cleverly built around the old West Stand. It boasts 70 luxury boxes which double up as hotel rooms on non-matchdays – there's more than one

way to score at Upton Park these days!

We were served a delicious four-course meal prior to the game and, needless to say, The Clarets' own brand of claret was flowing freely throughout the afternoon.

Looking across from my seat outside the corporate box, the last remnants of the old West Stand had been flattened leaving a gap of about 15 metres between the side of the pitch and the new main stand. This will eventually be turfed and the pitch will be moved sideways so the East Stand can also be upgraded. Work should start this summer.

The impressive Bobby Moore Stand is to the right and opposite that is the slightly smaller Centenary Stand. The stadium will boast a capacity of just over 40,000 when all the work is complete. Quite impressive, I must say, for someone who used to stand on the North Bank and Chicken Run terrace.

As for the match, it was about as flat as the rubble from the old demolished West

Stand. Suffice to say that Tottenham won 1-0 thanks to an early second half Les Ferdinand header that was missed by your correspondent who was finishing his cheese course! It's a hard life for some.

AROUND THE GROUND

THE STROLL along Green Street from Upton Park tube station was like being in a timewarp. Nothing much has changed in the past 20 years.

The souvenir traders still stand in the front gardens of terraced houses selling anything from player posters to badges, scarves and old programmes. I am pleased to say Ken's Café can still be found halfway between station and stadium. This used to do the best hot dogs and hamburgers money could buy en route to the main event. The queues suggested standards have not deteriorated.

As for watering holes, it would be advisable to steer clear of the two main

HAMMERS

OFFICIAL PROGRAMME £2.50

WEST HAM UNITED
Saturday November 24, 2001 – Kick off 3.00pm
v TOTTENHAM HOTSPUR

Guarded by twin towers, the new Doctor Martens Stand is a most impressive structure.

pubs in the vicinity. The Queens, a few yards from the station, and the more famous Boleyn on the corner of Green Street and Barking Road are strictly for Hammers fans only. Enter them at your peril.

JUST THE TICKET

AWAY FANS are well treated at Upton Park and use the Centenary Stand, behind the goal opposite the Bobby Moore Stand.

Spurs fans had accommodation in both tiers offering unrestricted views of the whole stadium. As this was listed as a category A match the cost of a ticket was £32 for adults, otherwise category B matches are priced £26 for adults and £15 for children or over 65s. Category A matches include the likes of Arsenal, Chelsea, Liverpool, Manchester United, Tottenham etc.

BOG STANDARD

TO GO FOR A half-time break and find a shower cubicle in the toilets and a hand towel embossed with club crest was a refreshing change. I then remembered I was with the "prawn sandwich" brigade. I have been informed the toilets, as befitting any new stadium, are of the highest quality.

TRANSPORT

THE EASIEST WAY to travel is by London Underground. However, be warned, the journey home is hugely delayed by the local Constabulary who direct you around the perimeter of Queen's Market before they make you double back on yourself to Upton Park station.

The stench of rotten cabbages accompanies you all the way onto the platform. I left a good 40 minutes after the end of the game and it was still a nightmare.

By road: If travelling from the north or west take the North Circular (A406) to A124 (East Ham), then along Barking Road for two miles turning right into Green Street at the cross-roads. From the south go through the Blackwall Tunnel and take A13 to Canning Town. Follow signs for East Ham (A124) and after two miles turn left into Green Street.

By rail: Take Central Line to Mile End and change onto the District Line eastbound to Upton Park station. Alternatively take the Jubilee Line extension and change at West Ham. Take the District Line to Upton Park.

READ ALL ABOUT IT

AT THE STANDARD PRICE of £2.50 and with 64 pages the matchday programme is a good read. Packed with information, stats and good pictures it also includes a regular column from former Hammer turned radio pundit Tony Gale.

However, like all programmes it really only appeals to home supporters. For them it is an excellent read, but money could be better spent elsewhere for away fans.

August 2002

Fred alert

He's the main man behind Arsenal's Double triumph and a crazy Swede who secretly supports Brazil. Fresh from his World Cup exploits, Freddie Ljungberg takes a trip down memory lane.

 Can you tell *Shoot Monthly* readers something about the place you grew up?

"I am born in a city called Halmstads and it's in the south of Sweden, what we call the beach side. It's a bit of a tourist town and yeah, I love the beach. My family supported me while I was making my way in the game and I can't really complain about anything.

My life's mostly been about football all the time so I haven't seen that much."

What role did sports play in your family?

"We're very interested in sports, my father played football, my brother plays football and I play football. So there's been a lot of football talk at the dinner table!"

Can you can you remember the first sports event that influenced you?

"I don't know to be honest. I just know we were moving to another city when I was five years-old. I just said: 'I'm not moving if you don't get me to a club', and they eventually did and I agreed to move."

And your room as a child, did you have any hero posters on the wall?

"I somehow got hold of Socrates' shirt (Brazilian midfield legend pictured right), so

I had that on my wall but otherwise there wasn't really that much stuff."

Tell us a bit about your first club?

"I stayed at the same club (Halmstads in Sweden) from the ages of five to 21, so I have a lot of heart for the place. The president and some of the coaching staff were like my extra fathers. I eventually turned professional and stayed there until I left for London."

Did you make any sacrifices for your career as a youngster?

"Of course. When friends went on a skiing holiday or something, I couldn't go, because I had to play. But I think in the end it was worth it. You need talent and determination and you have to be able to put football first, enjoy yourself and be positive. I've always tried to be that way."

When did you really think you would become a very good player?

"It's difficult to say. I was just trying to be as good as I could. I realised when you're under 15 or 16 and start in the national sides, you maybe have a chance to be a good footballer. I have never really been a dreamer; I just tried to do it as best as I can."

Which trainer influenced you the most?

"Mostly I think it was a guy called Ole Eriksson who I worked with when I was between, maybe, eight to 12 years-old. He let me know how to develop the skills that I have and he was really a good coach. He had been a national coach before and when he trained me he was about 70 years-old."

What did he teach you?

"In Sweden they only want to teach the tactical game when you're young, but he said: 'It's better to grow your own skills and when you get older, *then* we're going to fix the tactical stuff'. His training was more for the individual instead of the whole team which helped me."

What are your best footballing qualities?

"I don't like to talk about myself too much but I suppose I'm pretty fast and I like to dribble with the ball. I play attackingly from midfield and score goals every now and then."

Do you have any weak points?

"Yeah, of course, everybody has weak points. I'm not that tall and sometimes the bigger players can move me aside. And maybe my heading in front of goal is not the best."

Do you think today's football needs a different type of player than in the past?

"I think so. I mean, it's so much quicker than it used to be and especially now with all the Champions League games, you need to recover fast and be very, very fit. I think that's the difference."

People talk about your versatility, but what's your favourite position?

"I love to play behind the strikers, but at the moment we don't play like that at Arsenal. I like a free role on the right wing because you

Left: Freddie gets to grips with Ipswich Town's Titus Bramble during Arsenal's Double-winning season. **Below:** In action for Sweden against England in the 2002 World Cup. **Inset:** Freddie in a recent Nike ad.

see a lot of the ball, which I like. I played in that position as a youngster, which also helps. It's very different in Sweden. We maybe play a bit more defensively sometimes and I like to play a bit more offensively, but that's life. It is a different style of football."

Do you have any stand-out moments in your Arsenal career so far?

"One of my favourite moments is, of course, when we won the League, that's very nice. And when I came to London, I scored in my first game (Manchester United, September 20, 1998) after I had been on a pitch for five minutes. That, of course, was very special and a good memory."

If you become a coach, what's the first thing you would teach your team?

"Teach my team? At the moment I think most professional players know

I ALWAYS SUPPORTED BRAZIL AS A KID BUT NOW I ONLY THINK OF SWEDEN.

what to do, so the key is to try and get them motivated. To get them in a positive mood like Sven Goran Eriksson has done with England. Although I'm not sure I should be thinking about coaching just yet!"

Do you have many friends among your fellow football players?

"Yes, of course we are friends and

sometimes we socialise outside of football, but I think it's important as well to have other friends that don't talk football and have other jobs. My friends away from the game usually come to London and stay for a week or so and that is brilliant for me."

You are straight out of a World Cup with Sweden but this campaign aside, which World Cup do you remember the best?

"The Italian one in '90, where I was very disappointed because Brazil lost against Argentina in the second round. I didn't understand how, but they did. And then probably when Sweden played the United States in '94, They came third, and it was a very big thing for my country."

You mentioned Brazil again and you had that Socrates shirt on your wall as a kid. Have Brazil always been a favourite side?

"For sure. There was always something about Brazil, the yellow shirts, and the way they tried to play the game. As a kid I always supported them or tried to see their matches. Now I play in the Swedish National team so I stopped thinking about the Brazilian team quite so much – I support the Swedish team and the Swedish team only!" ↻

CRAZY FOR YOU

Wimbledon supporters pulled no punches to protest at the possible move to Milton Keynes.

WORDS: Eddie Kelly

THERE'S ALWAYS BEEN something unique about Wimbledon FC. Noted for odds-defying victories on the pitch and high jinks off it, history dictates that you underestimate The Dons at your peril.

A 1988 FA Cup Final win over Liverpool, a giant-killing cup run in the mid-1970s when still a non-league club, and being an established member of the Premier League throughout the 1990s all adds to a memorable past.

But perhaps the greatest achievement of all during the existence of this spirited little club has not been accomplished by 11 men on a football field. We are, of course, talking about the supporters, the men, women and children who have backed an unfashionable side.

These fans are now the lifeblood of the new AFC Wimbledon. The trigger for their new side came on May 28, 2002, when they fell victims to what they claim was "the final betrayal."

After months of debate an FA Commission granted permission for the owners of Wimbledon FC to relocate to Milton Keynes, 70 miles away from the club's home town.

Two days later some 1,000 outraged fans attended a Wimbledon Independent Supporters Association (WISA) meeting, and agreed that whilst continuing to oppose the move to Milton Keynes, they would launch a new football club – AFC Wimbledon was born.

For many, AFC would be the continuation of the club that, for them, died on May 28.

Fast forward to July 10, 2002, and Sutton United's Gander Green Lane. AFC kicked-off their inaugural game in a pre-season friendly against their old South London rivals, in a leafy Surrey suburb. A packed stadium didn't know what to expect – until the first-ever AFC Wimbledon team was announced.

"You've heard of Ronaldo, you've heard of Rivaldo, you've heard of Ronaldinho, but now please give it up for ...Trigger!"

As loud cheers greeted the arrival of the Fashanu-esque figure of "Trigger" the star striker's infectious grin was soon mirrored on the face of every supporter in the ground.

The spirit of the original Wimbledon Crazy Gang had been reborn.

THE A TEAM

Even though co-founders and life-long Wimbledon fans Kris Stewart and Ivor Heller were instrumental in launching the new club, AFC is essentially owned by The Dons Trust.

This is a democratic, not-for-profit organisation, committed to strengthening the voice of the club's supporters.

Kris Stewart told *Shoot Monthly*: "The important thing about AFC is not so much who is in what position, but that the club is owned and controlled by the fans. No businessman will be able to try and drag this club half way across the country to play our games, and we will always maintain our identity.

"We are very proud to have a large number of hard-core Wimbledon fans with us, and we have also attracted back fans who drifted away from the club when it moved to Selhurst Park."

Ivor Heller added: "The time came to fight back against all the negativity surrounding the old club. We now have a set-up that true Wimbledon fans are proud of, and we firmly believe the supporters will now vote with their

VIEW FROM THE TERRACES

What the fans think of the moves:

KEITH FONTYN (supporter 26 years).
"When the FA Commission gave their approval for the Milton Keynes move, I was so gutted that I just disowned the club. Many fans feel the same and I think that Wimbledon will just wither away and die. For the first time in ages, true Wimbledon fans can enjoy watching football again with the advent of AFC. Terry Eames is a Don through and through, and we are in the right hands to progress to bigger things."

XAVIER WIGGINS (supporter 18 years).
"My aims for AFC are to get promoted and get a ground! It would be a dream to move back to Plough Lane but the realistic aim is a ground as near as we can get to Merton. We now have a club whose support won't get ruined by unrealistic expectations of its owners. I haven't met a fan who will watch the other lot at Selhurst Park this season."

feet and come to watch AFC. This is a club that belongs to the community and we are striving to get a ground in the Borough of Merton.

"An amazing amount of hard work has gone into the formation of AFC and we will continually have people working on a daily and weekly basis to achieve our aims."

Following a rejection by the Ryman League the new club have been elected to the Combined Counties League for this season. They will share Kingstonian's Kingsmeadow ground but want their own facilities in Merton as soon as is reasonably possible.

The team will play in the traditional Womble kit of Royal blue and yellow, and even have a former Wimbledon player, Terry Eames, as their manager.

Eames, who appeared for The Dons between 1977 and 1981, said: "It was a very emotional moment for me when I took charge of team affairs here, as well as being a real honour.

"I formed a great affinity for the club, and am very excited about the future here. If I was not the manager I would be on the terraces

with the rest of the supporters, that is how much the new set-up means to me.

"We have come a long way in a relatively short space of time and with the players that I now have at my disposal I am very confident about what we can achieve."

Sports Interactive, the electronic games publisher, has announced a six-figure, three-year shirt sponsorship deal with the club, the largest in the history of non-league football.

COMMON PEOPLE

Remarkably, less than two weeks before AFC's first match, they lacked a vital ingredient crucial to the success of any team – players!

The solution to the problem came on Saturday, June 29, when an open trial was held on Wimbledon Common. By mid-day some 230 players hoping to be the new Vinnie Jones or Dennis Wise were being put through their paces by Terry Eames and his right-hand man Lee Harwood.

Pick of the bunch was former Chelsea player Joe Sheerin, whose only outing for The Blues

had, ironically, been a 20-minute substitute appearance against Wimbledon. He honestly admits he can't remember touching the ball!

Add to the mix a trialist who had flown in from Finland, a former Oxford United youth player and a gaggle of lads with non-league experience and the next generation of the Crazy Gang were on their way to selection.

WATCHING BRIEF

Even the most die-hard of Wimbledon fans would be hard pressed to remember a Dons game delayed due to crowd congestion!

But the Sutton friendly had to be put back three times! Nearly 5,000 eventually squeezed in to the ground. When the Combined Counties season gets underway AFC hope to attract an average home gate in excess of 2,000, in a league where attendances peak around 250. On the eve of the Sutton game AFC had sold 600 season tickets.

The Dons hold the record for the lowest top-flight attendance since the War, with 3,039 at Selhurst Park in 1992/93 to see Everton play. ↻

October 2002

THE EMERALD SMILE

After a summer of football he will never forget, Republic of Ireland hero Gary Breen reflects on how the World Cup changed his life. **INTERVIEW:** Frank Tennyson

THE REPUBLIC'S SECOND ROUND EXIT

WE SHOULD HAVE WON the match against Spain, no doubt about that. They were hanging on looking for penalties. I remember when I took over as captain after Steve Staunton came off and I had to toss up with Hierro for the first period of extra-time. He wouldn't look me in the eye. I've since watched the team and the Spanish bench had their head in their hands. They were a beaten team.

REGRETS

IT STILL DOESN'T FEEL GOOD knowing that we could and should have done better. After Spain it would have been South Korea in the quarter-finals and we certainly would have fancied our chances. The semis would have thrown up Germany and, again, who's to say we couldn't have beaten them? Brazil in the final? We would have given them a game. We feel that we have some unfinished business and this team is determined to show the world how good we are.

THE SURPRISE PACKAGE

I THINK WE SHOWED a few people that Irish football isn't all about the long ball game, after all you can't play that way when you have skillful lads like Robbie Keane and Damien Duff up front. I even had English fans come up to me and say that they preferred watching us to England. They responded to our kind of football – it was excitement all the way.

THE IRISH FANS

WHEN WE GOT BACK it was amazing. Some 100,000 people came out to see us and we were treated like heroes. But it was tinged with disappointment for a lot of the lads because we thought we could have gone further in the World Cup. The Irish fans are brilliant though. There were thousands out in Korea and Japan they supported us every step of the way, despite it being so expensive to get there. They were a credit to themselves and their country and gave us a real spur to do well.

THAT SAUDI GOAL

IT WAS WITH THE OUTSIDE of my foot as well! Actually it's no big deal, I keep telling the lads I can score those with my eyes shut – if only they would give me the right service!

THE REPUBLIC'S FUTURE

THINGS ARE LOOKING GOOD. Okay we've lost a few players through retirement but we've got such strength in depth that there are ready-made replacements waiting in the wings. There's such character and talent among this bunch of lads. You can perhaps argue that when the likes of Andy Townsend and Paul McGrath went off the scene a few years back, there wasn't that same quality in the squad to compensate.

ROY KEANE

NONE OF THE LADS really like to get involved with all this. During the World Cup we just closed ranks and worked for each other. The belief was there that we had the talent in the squad to do well, irrespective of the build-up and al the fuss that surrounded the Roy Keane thing.

THE IRISH CAPTAINCY

OF COURSE SKIPPERING your country is the highest honour in the game and I would be delighted to do the job. Some people have spoken about me as a possible candidate to take the armband but to be honest there are a lot of strong characters in the squad who would do a good job. It would be easy to captain this lot anyway because there is such a great team spirit and belief throughout.

MOVING TO WEST HAM

I HAD TURNED DOWN a new contract at Coventry because I felt it was time to move on. I showed some loyalty when we were relegated but we couldn't get back up. I knew Glenn Roeder from when he was my Gillingham coach and was keen to hook up with him again at West Ham. They did well last season after a tough start to finish seventh but no-one is content with that. I wouldn't have come here if that was the case. We're all looking to push on that bit more and perhaps look for a European spot.

IN THE SHOP WINDOW

FOR ME IT WAS A GREAT WORLD CUP, it was everything I dreamed about as a kid. I really enjoyed it and luckily I stayed fit. I suppose playing on that stage did bring me to the attention of a few clubs. I don't like to talk about it too much but, yes, I got a few amazing offers from abroad but at the time thought it would be better for my career (particularly with Ireland) that I stayed in this country.

EURO 2004 QUALIFIERS

As I said before, the Irish lads think we have some unfinished business after the World Cup. We want to go through another tournament unbeaten although we know it is going to be tough, especially in terms of the geography. We have to travel to some far flung-places (Russia, Switzerland, Georgia, Albania). In the last three international campaigns we've done well in the opening games. It's a trend we're obviously keen to continue.

21 THINGS YOU WANT TO KNOW ABOUT WAYNE ROONEY

He's been showered with praise from every angle. He's scored wonder goals and is being tipped as English football's biggest hope. But just who is Everton's Wayne Rooney? **WORDS:** Colin Mitchell

1 **THE EVERTON STRIKER** was born on October 24, 1985. At that time Wham! (right) were top of the pop charts with Wake Me Up Before You Go-Go.

2 **WAYNE WAS PROMOTED** to the first-team squad this season after scoring eight goals in eight games in last season's FA Youth Cup.

3 **HIS PREMIERSHIP DEBUT** was in the 2-2 home draw with Tottenham Hotspur on the opening day of this season when he created the first goal for Mark Pembridge. He became Everton's youngest-ever goalscorer in the 3-0 Worthington Cup win over Wrexham.

4 **HE SCORED A HAT-TRICK** against SC Weiz during the club's pre-season tour of Austria and another three when he encountered Queen's Park the following week (right).

5 **HIS FIRST PREMIERSHIP GOAL,** which earned him the title of youngest-ever Premiership scorer, was in October when he ended a long unbeaten run by Champions Arsenal. He also received the Barclaycard Premiership Goal of the Month award for that stunning last-minute winner.

6 **DEPUTY GOODISON PARK** chairman Bill Kenwright has admitted that he wouldn't like to over-promote the potential of the youngster but added: "How can you play down the greatest thing around in football today?"

7 **AMAZINGLY,** he is not The Toffees youngest-ever player, despite making his debut at 16 years and ten months. That title goes to former Everton boss Joe Royle (right) - but only just! (16 years nine months).

8 **WAYNE MADE** nine appearances for Everton's Reserves last season but he also turned out for the Under-19 side despite being only 15 years-old.

9 **WAYNE HAS ALREADY** been called up by England Under-21s. Some pundits suggest he could even make his full debut in the friendly against Australia in February.

10 **WHEN HE SCORED** in last season's Youth Cup Final against Aston Villa he pulled off his strip to reveal a T-shirt (below) with the words: "Once a Blue always a Blue."

11 **WAYNE WAS REPORTEDLY** rejected by big rival Liverpool, despite scoring a number of goals during a run out at The Reds' training ground when he was just nine.

12 **ALL OF WAYNE'S FAMILY** are true Blues and his younger brother John is also on the books at Goodison Park.

13 **WAYNE HAS STILL** to sign a contract to keep him at Goodison but there are likely to be no problems in him staying. The hold up has been caused by him changing agents and he is likely to pen the deal before the turn of the year.

14 **ARSENAL BOSS** Arsene Wenger said of Wayne: "He is the biggest English talent I've seen since I arrived in England. There has certainly not been an Under-20 player as good as him since I became a manager here."

15 **FORMER EVERTON PLAYER** and boss Colin Harvey, now in charge of the club's youth side, has said that the

THE KIDS ARE ALRIGHT!

Wayne follows in the footsteps of other young stars who made the grade

STEVE WATSON
THE TYNESIDE-BORN defender - who has also played in virtually every outfield role - became Newcastle's youngest-ever first-team player at the age of 16 years and 223 days.

He made his debut in November 1990 when The Magpies played Wolves. Stunned fans even saw him do a flip as he took throw-ins at some games.

Moved to Aston Villa for £4m in 1988 and then was snapped up by Everton two years later for £2.5m. Recently returned to his home-town club in the Worthington Cup and scored a goal.

MICHAEL GRAY
THE SUNDERLAND SKIPPER recently signed a new three-year deal which, if he sees it out, would mean he has been with The Black Cats for an amazing 14 years! Born on August 3, 1974, he is the club's

longest-serving player, notching up more than 350 appearances for the side.

In 1999 he became the first Sunderland player to play for England at Wembley for more than 23 years

But the Sunderland-born defender will want to forget the national stadium for another reason. In season 1997-98, he missed in a play-off final penalty shoot-out. However, the following season he helped the club to a record-breaking promotion.

JERMAINE PENNANT
A GALAXY of big name stars have held back the progress

youngster has a footballing brain "years ahead of his time."

16 **A WORRIED FAN** is reported to have phoned Everton boss David Moyes to tell him he had seen young Wayne kicking a ball against a wall in a street near where he lives. The gaffer said he wasn't too concerned, because the teenager still needs to mix with his friends.

17 **HE MIGHT BE ONE** of the biggest rising stars in the country, but Wayne has already been warned about his future conduct. Yellow cards against Villa, Newcastle (right), Charlton and Middlesbrough during the current campaign suggest that this lad isn't going to duck any challenges.

18 **WAYNE SCORED** a brilliant hat-trick last May when England demolished Spain 4-1 to clinch third place in the European Under-17 Championships.

19 **APPARENTLY YOU** can see Wayne's bedroom walls - plastered with all things Everton - walking down his street in Liverpool.

20 **REDS FAN RICKY TOMLINSON**, star of England Manager Mike Bassett, and BBC TV's Royle Family (left), reckons Wayne will partner Michael Owen up front for England but says the youngster will have to give up the paper round so he doesn't get injured falling off his bike!

21 **TEACHER JOHN HENNIGAN** presented Wayne with a record of achievement award in May when he left De La Salle School in Croxteth - then a few months later the Everton fan was watching him turn out for his favourite team.

of wide man Jermaine Pennant at Arsenal but he is still their youngest-ever debutant, having turned out for the first-team at the tender age of 16.

Signed from Notts County for £2m he has helped The Gunners to two Youth Cups and is an England Under-21 regular.

Nottingham-born Jermaine, who will be 20 in January, made his Arsenal debut on November 30, 1999, against Middlesbrough in the Worthington Cup when the Londoners drew 2-2, but lost on penalties.

RYAN GIGGS
JUST HOW LONG has Man United's flying winger Ryan Giggs been playing at the top level? Forever and a day it would appear!

Ryan, who was 29 in November, signed for United on December 1, 1990.

Always named by fellow pros as one of the biggest talents in Britain, Ryan became the youngest-ever player to turn out for Wales when he made his debut at the age of 17 years and 321 days.

MICHAEL OWEN
STILL ONLY 23, Michael became the youngest player this century to represent England when he played against Chile in February 1998 at the age of 18 years 59 days. Three months later he became England's youngest-ever goalscorer.

He scored 21 times during his first season in the Premiership and got 23 goals

the following campaign.

The PFA Young Player of the Year for 1997-98 and BBC Sports Personality of the Year in 1998 for his great form in the World Cup finals.

SAD END TO AN ERA

THE ENTRANCE TO the "stadium of legends," the last reminder of the days of Matthews, Finney, Moore, Hurst and Gascoigne, Wembley's twin towers stand alone They once greeted the throngs of football fans as they descended down Wembley Way on FA Cup Final day. The spine of every supporter tingled as the towers came into view. Now they are to be lost to the national game, to be replaced by an illuminated arch. How sad that they cannot be used to form a gateway to the new modern Wembley. Instead, they will be removed and another chapter of the English football history will come to an end.

MAKING A DIFFERENCE
www.kanuhea...tion.c
FOR AFRICAN CHILDREN

KANU BELIEVE IT?

Arsenal striker Kanu reveals why Arsene Wenger's men are the flag-bearers for what could be a new era of Premiership football. **WORDS:** Gemma Thompson

SPEAKING FROM THE HEART

IT'S THE END OF AN ERA. With Arsenal leading the charge for Premiership honours and Manchester United struggling to assert their old authority, we're told the dramatic power shift to North London is here to stay.

Gunners' striker Nwankwo Kanu, although reluctant to get carried away with the talk of United's demise, confirmed that his Arsenal side are setting a new footballing standard for the Premiership to follow.

"The way the team are playing at the moment I would have to say we have taken over from Manchester United," the 26-year old exclusively told **Shoot Monthly**.

"But football is always changing and you never know what can happen between now and the end of the season. For me it's important for us to wait until then before we can say, for definite, that we are the best team in England. But at the moment, I would have to say yes, we are on top of everybody."

Arsenal are currently leading the way in the Premiership as they have done for much of this season, whilst the FA Cup has proved an enjoyable distraction. The Champions League wasn't so fruitful after their departure during the second group stage.

Kanu has made just over 20 appearances for The Gunners this season, having missed much of the campaign through injury. However, speaking at a charity match in aid of the Kanu Heart Foundation, he confirmed he is still enjoying life at Highbury.

"We are in good form at the moment and are winning most of our games so everybody's happy," he added. "But that's what football's all about. If you're winning everybody's always happy and when you're not it's a bit more difficult. We've got a big squad of players and everyone has got to contribute. That's what we're all doing.

"I've had a few injuries this season but I managed to play in a charity game a few weeks ago before I came on against Roma. That was the foundation for my fitness and I was happy with how I came through.

"The season's not over yet and there's still a lot we want to do in the league and the FA Cup and hopefully I can be a part of that."

So what's been the reason behind the switch in Premiership punching power? Kanu believes it's down to one factor – a certain astute Frenchman who talks sense.

"Arsene Wenger is an excellent trainer and all the players believe in him," revealed the Arsenal striker. "If you haven't got that confidence in your manager it makes it very hard for the players. But the way he does his work means we all have great confidence in him which really helps us all to keep going.

"Whoever comes into the side always does a good job for the team and not only is that

AS ARSENAL ENTER the final and toughest period of the season in search of a second successive Premiership title and possible European glory, Kanu is as relaxed as ever.

The pressure of football is something he enjoys for he, more than most, knows just how tough life can be away from the game.

It's almost seven years since Kanu underwent life-saving open heart surgery to correct a weak heart valve at Cleveland Hospital in America, just days after signing for Italian giants Inter.

Since the operation he has set up his own charity, The Kanu Heart Foundation, entrusting the likes of Patrick Vieira, Thierry Henry and Arsene Wenger to act as trustees and patrons.

The Kanu Heart Foundation was set up in August 2000 and the recent charity game at Bolton's Reebok Stadium (below) involving the likes of Jay Jay Okocha, Joseph Yobo and Kanu himself, will go some way to giving hope to the 2,236 children who are on the Foundation's waiting list.

"The friendly match we held at Bolton's ground last month went really well," said Kanu. "I was really grateful to all the players who turned up, as well as my manager Arsene Wenger who came to support the evening.

"The supporters were great and it was a very good atmosphere which was the most important thing."

Kanu has organised a number of fund-raising events to help other African children with heart problems over the past few years and he is hoping many more can be saved in the future as a result of his work.

For more information on Kanu's charity check out: www.kanuheartfoundation.com

Above: In action during the Kanu Heart Foundation game. **Left:** Lauren, Bolo Zenden, Mario Melchiot, Marcel Desailly, Winston Bogarde, Carlton Cole and Kanu ready for a spot of fund-raising.

the sign of having good players, more importantly it tells you all about our manager. That's what makes the difference."

And strength in depth? One assumes that Wenger's focus on building a *squad* rather than *team* has stood them in good stead?

"Absolutely. I think the experience we've all gained from each season has made us a better side," Kanu added.

"We've got some superb players in the squad who can't even get into the team at the moment because the others are playing so well. The fact that we've not just got more than 11 great players to call upon is the key.

"And when you're on a good run you're full of confidence and you want to win every game. That's the way we are feeling at the moment and we want to keep that going because all the players are enjoying themselves.

"Every player in the team knows each other well and we all know what we are capable of.

"For me the most important thing is for players to believe in themselves, as well as the whole team. If you can do that and if you also have a great manager like we have, you've always got a chance of doing well." 🔥

Arsene Wenger is an excellent trainer... we have confidence in him which helps us all to keep going.

LIFE IN THE LEAGUES

BARCLAYCARD PREMIERSHIP

JOHN TERRY CHELSEA DEFENDER

Life at the top

 WHAT A WEEKEND! I scored a goal, felt I had a brilliant game and then got called up for the full England team. It doesn't get much better.

I've made no secret of my desire to play for England, and hopefully the dream will soon become a reality.

Add the fact that my goal came in a 5-0 home win against Manchester City to keep us on course for a Champions League spot and you can imagine that I was on Cloud Nine.

But my feet are going to be firmly on the ground as we approach the climax to the season, because the progress and standing of the current Chelsea side means we are still maintaining our push for that vital European place.

Our exploits in the quarter-finals of the FA Cup highlighted the tremendous team spirit and belief that has been instilled in the players at Stamford Bridge by Claudio Ranieri.

In the first game at Highbury, we took the game to Arsenal in their own backyard and, particularly in the second-half, dominated for long periods against a great side.

Although we only salvaged a draw with

Frank Lampard's late strike, a replay was the least we deserved.

In last season's final in Cardiff, we under-performed when it mattered most and on a personal level, was the most disappointing moment of my career. On the morning of the game I felt really dizzy and needed an injection from the club doctor to put me back on an even keel.

Although I declared myself fit for the game, I failed to make the starting line-up and although I eventually came on in the second-half, I didn't do myself justice. It still grates with me to see the TV replays of Arsenal scoring their goals.

It remains a big ambition of mine to exorcise the ghosts of that day and, hopefully, I will get a chance sooner rather than later.

But let's hear a few words of praise for Sheffield United. Neil Warnock's side have proved with their cup exploits this season that they live for these one-off cup games and victories against Leeds twice, Sunderland and Liverpool says a lot for their credentials and the attacking instincts of their side.

The momentum of the cup can also have a positive effect on our league form, although I think our hopes of qualifying for the Champions League will go right to the wire.

Everton are still in the hunt for fourth spot, having enjoyed a fantastic season so far, but I think it will be Liverpool (above) who will prove to be our closest rivals.

Their Worthington Cup win against Manchester United has acted as a catalyst in their season, although with their obvious quality I always knew it would only be a matter of time before they returned to form.

Yet our destiny lies in our own hands. With four of our last six games at Stamford Bridge, I feel we have a fantastic opportunity to be playing in the top European competition and

Above: John heads home in the 5-0 drubbing of Manchester City at Stamford Bridge, on the eve of his England call-up.

May 2003

What's it like to play professional football? What goes on behind the scenes?
Shoot Monthly has signed five players, from the Premiership down to the Conference, to reveal what the job entails.

SKILLS: DEFENDING CORNERS

AS A CENTRE-BACK, defending corners is an integral part of my game.

When the ball is swung over, it's vital that you stay within touching distance of the player you are marking and although that doesn't mean pulling your opponent's shirt, you need to be tight on him.

As a general rule, I stay on my toes at all times and also put my arms out so that I can get some extra elevation as I go to attack the ball.

I also position myself to the side and slightly behind the player as this gives me a clear sight of the ball. But if my marker should have reacted quicker, then I'll try to give him a little nudge, within the laws of the game, to give myself the advantage.

Invariably, you'll find yourself marking someone different at corners than you would for the rest of the game, and that's why pre-match preparations are vitally important.

Although we don't practise a specific drill in training, defending corners naturally happens in training games. Although I confess I do spend time just heading the ball which tends to help with elevation.

against the very best sides next season. It's up to us to keep our quality and our nerve.

I don't think anyone else will doubt that Arsenal, Manchester United and Newcastle will contest the top three places but in what order they finish will also go to the death.

At one stage, it appeared Arsenal had the title wrapped up, but you write off Man United at your peril and at this moment in time there is nothing to separate the sides.

I believe the game at Highbury towards the end of April will go a long way to determine the eventual Premiership winners, although Sir Bobby Robson's side also appear ideally placed to make the most of any slip ups.

Trouble at the bottom

FOR SUPPORTERS of all the top sides, it's a real nail-biting time of year but spare a thought for the fans, and players for that matter, of those teams at the wrong end of the table.

It's the time of year when strong characters and positive minds are needed and there are a number of teams who could still find themselves drawn into trouble.

The general consensus is that Sunderland and West Brom are in deep trouble, and I would tend to agree but, those sides directly above them – West Ham, Birmingham, Bolton and maybe now Leeds will also be living on their nerves at the moment.

I wouldn't wish relegation on any of my fellow professionals but of all the teams down there, I hope that The Hammers survive.

I've got a few friends at the club, including Michael Carrick, Joe Cole and Jermain Defoe, and I think that Glenn Roeder is a very positive and forward-thinking coach.

As a Barking-born lad, they are also my local team and although I didn't support them as a kid, my brother Paul takes a keen interest in their results.

It's also important for London football that they stay up, especially for Chelsea where games between our clubs always make for a fantastic atmosphere.

Giving something back

ALTHOUGH I NO LONGER live in the Essex area, I often pop back home to see my family and friends.

Footballers lead a privileged life, so it's important to remember where you came from and who helped you along the way.

I can remember kicking a ball around and gaining many representative honours during my time at Eastbury Comprehensive in Barking and that was one of the reasons why I returned there recently to meet the pupils and some of my former teachers.

In my day, we had to wear our rugby shirts for football, so I felt it was only right to supply new kits for all five teams at the school, although they could have chosen blue instead of the claret shirts they wanted!

If I can give something back to the community and the next generation of footballers coming through, then that is just as important to me as scoring an FA Cup goal against Arsenal.

When I was a kid, we never really had any players come to see us and I certainly can't remember collecting autographs, so it was important for me to spend some time with the boys and girls, and they seemed to appreciate my presence.

In my days at Eastbury, it was always my dream to become a professional footballer and then play for England and it now looks as though it might not be too long before I finally make the progression onto that international stage.

Above: Children from Eastbury Comprehensive in Barking receive their free kit from John.

FACT FILE
MARCEL DESAILLY

BORN:
GHANA, SEPTEMBER 7, 1968
HEIGHT:
6ft 1in
WEIGHT:
13st 5lb
CLUBS:
NANTES, MARSEILLES,
AC MILAN, CHELSEA
HONOURS: FRENCH
LEAGUE 1992, EUROPEAN
CUP 1993 (MARSEILLE);
SERIE A CHAMPIONS 1994
AND 1996, EUROPEAN CUP
1994 (AC MILAN); FA CUP
2000, (CHELSEA)
INTERNATIONAL:
WORLD CUP 1998,
EURO 2000
BET YOU DIDN'T KNOW:
MARCEL'S NICKNAME IS
"THE ROCK"

YOU AIN'T SEEN
NOTHING YET!

He's reached a significant French milestone but veteran Chelsea
defender Marcel Desailly maintains there's plenty more to come.
Words: Jean-Marc Azzola

Marcel, what does it mean to you to have equalled Didier Deschamps' international record number of caps (103) for France?

"Actually the key figure was definitely when I reached 100. At that time It was hugely emotional looking back to my career and what I had achieved. But I have to say that to equal Didier's record is a great landmark. For a long time, I wanted to equal that of my hero Maxime Bossis (former France defender capped 76 times). This time it is a bit different. I've equalled a friend of mine."

Looking back, what are the proudest moments in your international career?

"Nothing specific. Just to have been able to play at the highest level for my country for so many years. That is really what makes me feel so happy and proud. After that, whether I have achieved 101, 102 or 104 caps is not the major factor to me."

Do you remember your first international cap?

"Very well. It was ten years ago against Sweden. When I started to play for the national team I would have never imagined I could still be here a decade later at the age of 34. I wouldn't have imagined I could be so competitive with my club either."

Has success at Chelsea helped prolong your French career?

"I'm fortunate to play for a wonderful team like Chelsea which allows me to remain at the top and permits me to carry on playing for France. I feel relaxed with The Blues, I can completely express myself and enjoy what I'm doing. But when I eventually retire (from Chelsea in 2004), I will be happy to spend time with my children, to see them grow up."

Would you say consistency is the key factor in your career?

"Completely. And it is not that easy to do in football because many factors like injuries can slow you down. If I had faced a problem like Robert Pirès did recently, maybe things would have been different. I was fortunate not to undergo such a situation. I have always played as a regular with all my clubs so it kind of followed that I would be selected to represent my country very frequently. I never really had huge highs and lows which can happen in a career. But luck plays a big part in the way you perform."

Has your approach to football changed after so many years in the game?

"Not at all. Representing my country is still a magical experience for me. If that was not the case I would've quit after 16 years as a pro (first game Nantes/Bordeaux in 1986). I still have the same desire to work hard through my club and the national team. I could have left after the World Cup but I didn't want to. I am still strong physically so why leave? And you know, retirement has nothing to do with death! Even retired I will carry on playing with old players. Football is my passion but as I said before, it is not everything in life."

What is your feeling regarding the next Confederations Cup which takes place in June? With the club v country rows rumbling on, isn't it just a waste of time?

"We are one of the contenders and it is being held in France so it's another trophy that we want to win. But I have to say that the way things have been planned is a bit strange. The Premiership will be over for a month, same as the French League but the Spanish one will not. This situation is not ideal. But we have no other choice. We have to go for it."

Does being at the veteran stage mean that you want to play in all the competitions, no matter how minor?

"I don't think like that. After the World Cup I still wanted to prove I was able to give my best. The French team failed

last summer but I wanted to come back to show that our lads were capable of bouncing back, fighting for the qualification for the next European Championships. It is not the end of a generation as too many people have been saying. This team will go on and we will see where we are after this tournament."

So how do you see the future panning out for you and the team?

"There will be a sort of break inside the team with the leaving of key players after Euro 2004. But it is not a problem. The new generation is very talented and ready to step in. The quality is there for everyone to see but it is quite far away. Many games have to be played before this happens. We will see..."

Presumably you've welcomed the return after injury of Robert Pirès'?

"Oh yes. He is so important to us. He is so influential in the system. He can be a very dangerous attacker but is also very rigorous in a defensive role. We have a new coach and the system has changed a bit. I am convinced Robert will be able to integrate very quickly in this team, he is such an essential player for us. David Trezeguet and Bixente Lizarazu are also back from injuries. The coach has many wonderful choices to make."

And William Gallas? He's been playing right-back for Chelsea, will this affect his international chances?

"Claudio Ranieri has decided to make that move very recently. The competition is very harsh in the club. William has the potential to cope anyway. It cannot affect France."

And would you like to become a coach?

"No, no... you must be joking" (laughs)

REMEMBER

He may be regarded as the forgotten man of English football but Man City's Steve McManaman has not given up hope of a shock international call-up. **WORDS:** Simon Johnson

Above: City Slickers - Macca in tandem with pal Robbie Fowler. Left: Four successful years at Real did not guarantee any rewards at England level.

DAVID BECKHAM MAY HAVE already won the hearts of fans at Real Madrid but he can only dream of matching Steve McManaman's success in Spain.

Yet it was the England captain's decision to leave Manchester United for Madrid in a £25m deal in the summer effectively brought Macca's reign in Spain to an end.

For four years he had been the English representative among the world-class talent at the Bernabeu, but in August he joined Manchester City on a free transfer.

While Beckham's every move has been monitored by the English press since he left Old Trafford, Macca's stint went largely unnoticed. Yet the 31-year-old midfielder picked up two Champions League winners' medals and a Spanish Championship.

Not only that, but he was even named man of the match after scoring in Real's 3-0 victory over Valencia in the Champions League final of 2000 in Paris.

It was the stuff of dreams for a player who began his impressive career in Liverpool's youth ranks (see pages 28-31). But - perhaps surprisingly for such a talented individual - Macca reveals the secret behind his success in Spain was being one of the few players at the club who could *defend!*

He said: "Playing at Madrid actually helped me improve defensively in a strange kind of way. We had that many attacking players, we had left and right-backs who wanted to play centre-forward.

"At Liverpool I was one of the only attack-minded players and always had six or seven players behind me. But at Real Madrid I only had two or three people behind me so I had to be more aware of what was going on.

"There were no discussions about defending or anything really. Before games the team would be put up on the board and that would be it. It was just a case of 'these are the players, these are the strengths and weaknesses, we're the best so let's get on with it!'"

But Macca paid a huge price despite his impressive term of office abroad. While his skills were deemed good enough for arguably the most successful club in the world, they were not for England.

His international career stagnated and he was only awarded brief cameo roles. And it has culminated in him losing his place in the squad altogether during Sven Goran Eriksson's reign.

But Macca insists he has no regrets. "Playing at Real taught me how to be successful. We had a real winning mentality. At the start of every year there was pressure on us to win things, which we always did.

"It doesn't bother me that I haven't had much recognition for what I have achieved. I think it is the English way to be honest. We tend to concentrate on players who haven't succeeded abroad rather than the other way round. We like to talk about unlucky losers."

Madrid's and England's loss is already starting to prove to be Manchester City's gain. City have begun the season in impressive form and have been tipped to qualify for next season's Champions League.

Macca has certainly played his part in that renaissance, pointing to City's expansive style as the reason for his immediate acclimatisation to Premiership football.

He added: "I joined City because I wanted a different challenge in my career. The likes of Man United and Arsenal are at the highest level in the Premiership and they sustain it year after year. Their new level is in the Champions League, but I think there is a good chance that we can get City to a level they haven't been for some years.

"It's very exciting. There is a very good team spirit among the players and the boss. It's nice to win games in a style of scoring lots of goals. The fans pay their money and it's nice to know that they go away knowing that they have seen a good game.

"They love the fact we can win against Bolton 6-2 rather than watching a boring 1-0 game." He has also been helped by the fact he has

MEN WHO REIGNED (or didn't) IN SPAIN

GARY LINEKER
BARCELONA (1986-89)
Scored 44 goals in 99 games in three years at Barcelona, but left in 1989 after boss Johan Cruyff played him on the wing.
MARK HUGHES
BARCELONA (1986-88)
Struggled to settle in

Barcelona following a £2m move from Manchester United in 1986 and was back at Old Trafford just two years later.
GERRY ARMSTRONG
REAL MALLORCA (1983-86)
The Northern Ireland striker was a big hit

during his three years at Real Mallorca in the early 1980s and was top scorer in La Liga in his first season. Now a Sky pundit for Spanish football.
STEVE ARCHIBALD
BARCELONA (1984-86)
Shot the club to the Spanish title in 1985 and

in the following season helped them to the European Cup Final.
VINNY SAMWAYS
LAS PALMAS (1996-2002)
Former Spurs man played for the Canary Island club throughout the late 1990s. Nicknamed "Mr Vin" he joined Seville for six

months before returning to English football at Walsall.
MICHAEL ROBINSON
OSASUNA (1987-89)
Currently a TV broadcaster in Spain, the ex-Liverpool striker joined Osasuna with former team-mate Sammy Lee. Failed to make an impact and was

ME?

been reunited with two of his former team-mates. Nicolas Anelka spent one year with Macca at Madrid in 1999 before leaving for Paris Saint Germain. Macca also had a close relationship with striker Robbie Fowler during the seven years they were together at Anfield and also in the England camp.

Both strikers have not always had the best of reputations on and off the pitch during their careers, but Macca is adamant they are both remain world-class operators.

The Liverpool-born midfielder explained: "Nicolas got a bad press but I think that was unfair. He scored two goals in the semi-finals of the Champions League against Bayern. So he had one year at Madrid and won the European Cup - you can't say any better than that."

Fowler has yet to find his best form since joining Manchester City for £6m from Leeds last January, but Macca is confident he can bring out the best in his old mate.

He said: "Strikers are judged on scoring goals and if they are going in everything is great even if your overall game is not as good as you want it to be. It's not easy to get it back just by joining a new team and having different players around you.

"You can't score 30 goals for Liverpool and then think I can go somewhere else and do the same straight away. Robbie has had a tough couple of years and I would like to help him."

It has also been two years since Macca played his last game for England - an incredible statistic for a squad not exactly blessed in the left midfield position in which he can excel.

But with the Euro 2004 Championships fast approaching, and despite not receiving a sniff in the qualifiers, he is still hopeful of a recall. Not even Tord Grip's assertion that "he has never played a really good game for England" has dampened Steve's optimism.

Macca added: "I'd like to play in Euro 2004 like everybody else. I don't think it's a closed door to me. If I play well I'll be happy, but it is not up to me. I definitely think I am one of the best 25 English players in the country." ⚽

forced to retire two years later with a knee injury.
LAURIE CUNNINGHAM
REAL MADRID (1979-83)
Scored a goal on his debut, and played a part in Real's league and cup double in that same season. In 1989 (then at Rayo Vallecano) he was killed in a car crash just outside Madrid.

JOHN ALDRIDGE
REAL SOCIEDAD (1989-91)
Signed by John Toshack alongside Dalian Atkinson and Kevin Richardson, the Scouse striker finished second-top scorer in Spain in two successive years. Returned to Tranmere in 1991, a club he later managed.

KING HENRY

WHAT A YEAR IT'S BEEN for Arsenal's star striker Thierry Henry.

After just missing out on the Premiership title and Golden Shoe he was voted by fellow professionals and football journalists as double Player of the Year in April. He then starred for France on home soil in the Confederations Cup, scoring four goals including the golden goal winner in the final against Cameroon.

In November, with Arsenal on the brink of Champions League elimination, Thierry showed all of his "va va voom" and a bit more to help The Gunners to a 5-1 mauling of Inter Milan. Last month he was runner-up in FIFA's World Player of the Year award, pipped by France team-mate Zinedine Zidane. A fantastic year for a fantastic player.

PICTURE: ACTION IMAGES

HOT SEATS

THE FIRST SEATS on offer at Arsenal's new £357m Emirates Stadium have almost sold out.

More than 100,000 supporters, who are members of the club's official membership scheme, were given the chance to register their interest in the Club Level seats at the 60,000 capacity ground which won't be ready until August 2006.

The Club Level, which will form 6,700 seats in a separate tier encircling the directors' box level, will provide supporters with quality hospitality and some of the best views of the pitch.

Buyers will be guaranteed seats for all competitive home matches, including European and domestic cups. There will be bars, restaurants and lounges.

Gunners' managing director Keith Edelman said: "Club Level seats can be purchased on one to four-year contracts.

"The pricing structure of matchday and season tickets, which we assure fans will be comparable with Highbury ticket prices, will be announced in Spring 2005."

Two pints? Certainly Sir, that'll be £357m...

Even Gunners' fans win!

STEPHEN DOWNES could rightly claim he is one of Arsenal's top fans are forking out more than £50,000 for TWO personalised car number plates!

The life-long Gunner first forked out £5,000 for **AFC1X** and then coughed up a further £45,500 for **AR53NAL** and a special auction.

After fighting off a series of bids from other supporters,

Stephen received a round of applause from the opposition as he got the plates.

"Once I knew the plates were coming up for auction, I had to have them. I think I've got a bargain," said season ticket holder Stephen, from Nazeing, Essex.

Asked if he would sell the plates for a player-sized pay packet, Stephen, a Gunner for 35 years,

claimed: "Not in a million years."

Damian Lawson, auction manager for the DVLA Personalised Registrations, said: "That is a true football fan. The auction was a success and a lot of people went home with their ideal plate." Wonder if Stephen has two cars!

■ **More details on similar auctions at: www.dvlaregistrations.co.uk**

GET YOUR KIT ON!

FORGET THOSE FOOTBALL kits that look like nightshirts on your wife or girlfriend.

The growing popularity of the game with the fairer sex now means they even get their own designer

Nice kit! Villa also have casual gear in their range.

shirts. Aston Villa report that tops are "flying off the shelves" since they introduced specialist clothing for women supporters.

Villa Park merchandising manager John Greenfield said: "Villa are one of the few teams in the Premiership to have introduced a new replica kit especially created for women.

"The initial batch of ladies shirts we had sold out within three weeks and the popularity of the shirt has yet to wane.

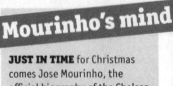

"Most women who come into our club store now opt for the ladies' replica shirt once they realise just how good it looks!"

England kit manufacturers Umbro already produce a version of the national shirt, as worn by England ladies, which is also designed to better fit the female form!

Mourinho's mind

JUST IN TIME for Christmas comes Jose Mourinho, the official biography of the Chelsea chief written by his close friend Luís Lourenço.

The Bridge boss wrote sections of the book, which features photos from his personal collection.

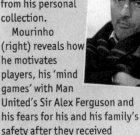

Mourinho (right) reveals how he motivates players, his 'mind games' with Man United's Sir Alex Ferguson and his fears for his and his family's safety after they received a death threat.

QUICK KICKS

■ A new exhibition "The gentle giant" about former Wales legend John Charles (below) has opened at Wrexham Museum. Entry is free and there is lots of memorabilia about the former Juventus and Leeds star.

■ Liverpool are the latest club to sign with mobile phone operator Orange, to provide news, views and interviews through their Orange World service.

■ Littlewoods Football Pools is the first recipient of The National Football Museum Special Achievement Award for outstanding contribution to the game. The firm has been involved with football for 80 years and has given more than £500m to various projects.

Are they related?

PETER REID?   MATEJA KEZMAN?   MONKEY?

IVOR CREATED HISTORY

IVOR VERDUN POWELL has gone into the history books as the longest-serving coach in football.

The Team Bath assistant coach is an amazing 88-years-old and has received a long service award from the FA for his 53 years in coaching and management.

Ivor's feat has been lodged with the Guinness Book of Records.

FA Historian David Barber said:

"There is no record at this level of anyone having coached a team for a longer period of time. It's a phenomenal achievement."

An RAF physical training instructor during the Second World War Ivor said: "I haven't done anything more than I would have asked of my players.

"Determination, will-power, work rate and will-to-win. They have been my watch-words all my life."

Ivor joined QPR at the age of 17 after he had begun his working life down the coal mines. He went on to play 14 times for Wales.

The best man at his wedding was the legendary Sir Stanley Matthews and in 1948 Ivor set a national transfer record when he joined Aston Villa for £17,500.

He later joined Port Vale and Bradford City before being a coach and trainer for Don Revie's all-conquering Leeds United side of the 1960s.

Ivor then became the first manager to win promotion for Carlisle United before he moved to Bath City in 1964.

QUOTE ME... SAYINGS FROM THE PAST FEW WEEKS

"There is a little bit of yoga, pilates and acupuncture. I am even trying to make love to the wife more slowly."
Wolves striker DEAN STURRIDGE has discovered a great way to bounce (or should that be bonk?) back from injury.

"If I go on holiday at the end of the season and come back with a big, fat belly and bald head I will pack it in."
Millwall player-boss DENNIS WISE reckons his annual trip to the sun could lead to his playing retirement.

"People not at the game will think it is another hammering but those here will see it differently."
Whichever way you look at it, Scotland skipper JACKIE MCNAMARA should accept that a 4-1 loss to Sweden *is* yet another hammer blow.

"I must be annoying him. It's like being at school. It's like I am 20-years-old and playing football for the

very first time."
ROBERT PIRES has a classroom problem with the head, France boss Raymond Domenech.

"I will tell anyone planning to cause trouble that I have a very nice B&B waiting for them."
Cardiff police chief BOB EVANS offers a Welsh welcome for any West Ham fans who misbehave at Ninian Park.

"Rooney was like he was on another planet. He didn't know what he was doing. When I looked into his eyes there was nothing."
Spain star JOAQUIN reckons Wayne really was out of this world during his shameful performance for England during the recent friendly.

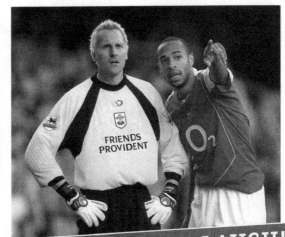

YOU'RE HAVING A LAUGH!

SO JUST WHAT is Thierry Henry pointing out to Southampton keeper Antti Niemi? Premiership survival or St. Mary's exit door? The funniest caption sent to us by the closing date of December 20, 2004. wins £25. You can email us at shoot@ipcmedia.com

Last month's winner was Ian Whalley from St. Helens on Merseyside. He said Robbie Williams was saying: 'You're so bad you wouldn't even make Port Vale's reserve team,' to Jonathan Wilkes after Sky One's *The Match*.

GROWING P

ONE MINUTE WAYNE ROONEY WAS A HAT-TRICK HERO, THE NEXT HE WAS SUBSTITUTED IN DISGRACE. THE TEENAGER SAYS HE CAN HANDLE THE PRESSURE. **WORDS: Chris Hatherall**

WAYNE ROONEY'S LIFE is currently in a hole. Or, to be more precise, two holes – one bitter and one sweet!

The bitter hole the Man United striker dug for himself was during England's recent friendly with Spain when the boy wonder had to be substituted before he was sent off.

He added to his woes by allegedly swearing at coach Steve McClaren and also throwing to the ground the black arm band all the team were wearing in honour of former skipper Emlyn Hughes, who had died days earlier.

His acts of petulance during the game in Madrid could cost him when it comes to player of the year awards.

Yet all of those actions were in stark contrast to the previous few weeks of his young life when he celebrated his move to Old Trafford in some style, and discovered that playing in the hole behind England's front two was tailor made for him.

The country went Rooney-mad again after the 18-year-old striker made an astonishing United home debut by scoring a hat-trick in

the Champions League against Fenerbahce.

Then he was back to his international best for England in World Cup qualifiers against Wales and Azerbaijan.

It wasn't just his performance in those games that made the headlines, though. England tried out a new and exciting three up-front policy against Wales, and it appeared to work a treat.

The system saw Wayne play slightly deeper than his strike partners, lurking "in the hole" behind Michael Owen and Jermain Defoe.

Former England striker **Gary Lineker's** verdict on Wayne's new World role.

"Rooney's been brilliant for England in that deeper position, the one most of the world's great players favour.

"You look back in time, and there's the Maradonas, the Cruyffs, the Zicos and the Platinis. I'm not saying Rooney's as good as them yet, but he's certainly got the potential to be something along those lines," said the former England striker, now a successful BBC TV presenter.

"I think we'll get better at it," added Wayne. "It was good to have three of us up front and I think it worked well. We have a lot of pace between us and I had loads of space to try and play other players in.

"I had lots of possession behind their midfield and, though it's disappointing when you don't score, we won and that's the important thing.

"I didn't think we ever looked like losing the game and I don't think Wales had too many chances, to be honest. I think we played well and we did the job that was required.

"I don't know if we'll use the system all the time but if we do I'll enjoy it. Hopefully we can go and qualify for the World Cup finals."

The England manager looks to have found the answer to his left midfield dilemma forced by injury to Steven Gerrard and the explosive start to the season enjoyed by Michael Owen, Jermain Defoe, Alan Smith and Rooney.

The coach was impressed by Wayne's performance in the international double header. "He is a phenomenon," said Eriksson. "Doing what he did on his United debut and in Portugal is incredible at 18.

"He's complete - he can do everything. He can play as a target man and if the ball comes to his feet it's very difficult to take it off him. He can also beat people, he's quick, he can shoot with right foot or left and although he's not tall he's a rather good header of the ball!

"On top of that he's clever, so it's very difficult to see where he's weak."

Eriksson used the same system in his club days at Lazio with Roberto Mancini playing in the hole. That side went 17 games unbeaten and ended up winning the Italian League.

But Eriksson likens Rooney most to another great player – Robert Baggio who he played in the same role at Fiorentina.

"Of the players I've managed, only Roberto Baggio could compare in terms of cleverness. But I don't know if he was as clever as Rooney. Wayne is more complete because he's strong as well, Baggio was not that strong but he beat people and gave a pass and scored. With Rooney it's very difficult to see where he's weak. He's not arrogant at all, but his confidence is incredible."

It's not the only compliment Rooney has received this season, of course. But coming from his international manager it clearly means a lot to the teenager rapidly becoming one of the biggest names in football.

At club level, United boss Sir Alex Ferguson has looked long and hard for a replacement for Eric Cantona, and believes Paul Scholes and Rooney can open up space for each other on the attack. Scholes is at his best going forward and Rooney dropping deep.

Rooney believes he can cope with the extra weight. "I know the spotlight is going to be on me a lot more because I have signed for the biggest club in the world by leaving Everton for Man United," he said.

"That will bring more pressure but I am big enough and strong enough to handle it. No-one has to tell me how to behave on or off the pitch. I know myself. I think I've changed a lot as a person on and off the field over the last year. I'm much more mature than I was 12 to 18 months ago, but that all comes with playing, especially for England in Euro 2004.

"Hopefully I can keep my head down, do my job well and go out and do my best for Man United and for England."

Sven took the microphone, but point blank refused to do his impressions of Abba songs for the media.

Not only did England win 2-0 but they created a string of chances with Wayne so close to getting on the score sheet on his return to international football after injury.

"I think I played pretty good in there," said Wayne. "I like playing that role and I had a lot of space to work in. But all I want to do is play for my country and it's a great feeling to be in the team – whatever the formation."

Having said that, there is no doubt that defenders across the world will have watched Wayne's performance and got nervous. After all, this was the first time England had played the formation, with only a couple of day's practice.

FAB FOOTY FACTS!

BIG MATCH SPECIAL!
Ronny

Cristiano Ronaldo and Cesc Fabregas are both playing out of their skin this season! But as United face Arsenal at Old Trafford, who looks most like the perfect footballer?!

I'M THE KING OF THE PREM, CESC!

NO CHANCE MATE. YOU'RE MORE LIKE THE CLOWN PRINCE!

HEAD
Ronny's learnt a lot at United and is now more of a team player!
SHOOTY'S SCORE: 8/10
YOUR SCORE: ☐/10

HEART
You've gotta be brave when you're kicked around as much as he is!
SHOOTY'S SCORE: 9/10
YOUR SCORE: ☐/10

LUNGS
Has proved his stamina this season by often scoring late, late goals!
SHOOTY'S SCORE: 9/10
YOUR SCORE: ☐/10

LEGS
With or without the ball, he's one of the fastest in the Prem!
SHOOTY'S SCORE: 10/10
YOUR SCORE: ☐/10

FEET
No-one's cleverer with the ball at his feet than the step-over king!
SHOOTY'S SCORE: 10/10
YOUR SCORE: ☐/10

FACT! RONNY IS HAVING A DREAM SEASON. BOSS FERGIE SAYS: "HE CAN PLAY ANYWHERE IN THE LAST HALF OF THE PITCH!"

SHOOTY'S TOTAL: 46/50
YOUR TOTAL: /50

MAN U v ARSENAL
PREM HEAD-TO-HEAD
PLAYED 31
MAN U WINS 12
ARSENAL WINS 9
DRAWS 10

FACT! CESC DOMINATES THE MIDFIELD DESPITE BEING SMALLER THAN MANY OF HIS OPPONENTS. HE ADMITS: "I AM NOT THE STRONGEST MAN IN THE WORLD!"

SHOOTY'S SHORTS!

PLAYING BY NUMBERS!

Boro defender David Wheater knew just how to celebrate his shock call-up for England. The 20-year-old's favourite night out is to take his girlfriend out for a game of... BINGO!

WHAT'S COOKING SHOOTSTERS?!

Dishing it out!

Everton's Mikel Arteta loves to cook for Liverpool's Spanish stars Pepe Reina and Xabi Alonso. Wonder what he served up after the derby defeat at Anfield?!

y Fab

HEAD
uick thinker who can spot
openings sooner than most!
SHOOTY'S SCORE: 10/10
YOUR SCORE: ☐ /10

HEART
ways refuses to admit defeat and
ads by example on the pitch!
SHOOTY'S SCORE: 9/10
OUR SCORE: ☐ /10

LUNGS
ttacks, defends and works as
ard as anyone all over the pitch!
SHOOTY'S SCORE: 9/10
YOUR SCORE: ☐ /10

LEGS
overs every blade of grass and can
eep up with the best of 'em!
SHOOTY'S SCORE: 8/10
OUR SCORE: ☐ /10

FEET
antastic passer of the ball who
ery rarely wastes possession!
SHOOTY'S SCORE: 9/10
YOUR SCORE: ☐ /10

SHOOTY'S TOTAL: 45/50
YOUR TOTAL: /50

THE KEY BATTLES

WAYNE ROONEY v WILLIAM GALLAS
Wazza's much happier up front on his own for United than he is with England — which means Gallo could be in for a busy afternoon!
VERDICT Who can stop Roo?!
....

RIO FERDINAND v EMMANUEL ADEBAYOR
Manu's been struggling since he chopped off his braids, but he's smart enough to give Rio a few hair-raising moments!
VERDICT Rio is a cut above!
....

OWEN HARGREAVES v MATHIEU FLAMINI
With both players happiest winning the ball and giving it to a team-mate, expect some tasty tackles in midfield!
VERDICT Owen up to the challenge!

NET LOST RUUD!

Ruud Van Nistelrooy used to climb over the fence at his local stadium when he was a boy 'cos they had nets on the goals. He was often chased away by the groundsman!

HELP ME! I'M STUCK!

LEND US YOUR MOWER JT?

HOW D'YA WANT IT JT?

MAKE IT LOOK LIKE WEMBLEY PLEASE, RIO!

You'd think Prem rivals and England team-mates Rio Ferdinand and John Terry would be sick of the sight of each other, but no — they've bought holiday homes next door to each other in the Caribbean!

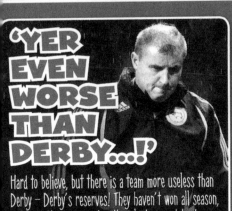

'YER EVEN WORSE THAN DERBY...!'

Hard to believe, but there is a team more useless than Derby — Derby's reserves! They haven't won all season, and haven't even scored in their last six matches!

BRAZIL NEED OWN GOALS!

I'LL NEVER LET ONE IN NOW!

NO GOAL!

When Brazil players ignored pleas to stop training at Arsenal's Emirates Stadium recently, the only way ground staff could get them off the pitch was to take down the goalposts!

MORE FAB FOOTY FACTS OVER

HEAVEN

Being Captain!

> "LEAST I WON'T SINK!"

"It gives me a really big boost, confidence-wise, wearing that armband for Liverpool. I enjoy putting it on every time. As for England, I don't want to push myself forward as that would be disrespectful to John Terry or whoever – but ask any England player if they'd like to lead their country on a permanent basis and they'd say yes."

> "HALO! WHAT'S ALL THIS ABOUT THEN?"

ENGLAND

ANDORRA
V
ENGLAND
28 03 2007

Best Moment In Football!

The Final 2005

> "TOLD YA IT WAS THE BIGGEST!"

"As a player you want to win as many trophies as possible and the Champions League is the biggest. Winning it in 2005 was the best night of my footballing life. I went through all the different emotions that you can go through in 120 minutes that night. But it's all in the past now – I want to experience it again!"

England Fans' No.1!

"If I wasn't playing I'd be an England fan myself, so it was a fantastic honour to be voted as the England Supporters' Player of the Year. To come out on top was a tremendous feeling. I'll admit it, it gives me a real buzz when I hear my name being chanted by the fans. And that feeling is the same now as when I first broke into the team. I think every player listens out for their name being sung!"

> "ING-ER-LAND!"

Most Impressive Team-Mate!

> "I LOVE YOU NANDO!"

> "GET OFF ME, YA BIG GIRL!"

"The way Fernando Torres has been playing is frightening. Everyone talks about the goals he scores, but you shouldn't lose sight of all the hard work he puts in off the ball. He defends from the front and that makes a big difference. I've got to be honest, I'm made up to have him in our team."

Rompin' Rafa!

> "HMMM! FOOTBALL! YUMMY!"

"Benitez is a manager who EATS, breathes, sleeps football. He is 24/7. He loves the game, he is always trying to improve himself and he's always trying to improve every player. I've got total belief and confidence he can continue to take us forward and bring success to this football club. I think the future is looking bright."

HELL

Liverpool and England midfielder STEVEN GERRARD

> THIS IS A RIGHT TAIL OF WOE!

Stuck-Up Stars!

" There is nothing worse than seeing a footballer who thinks he's something special, who thinks he's more than he is. I don't think I've ever had a problem keeping my feet on the ground."

Transfer Blunder!

> SHOULDA SIGNED ME SCOUSERS!

" Every club makes a couple of mistakes in the transfer market and we made one when we didn't sign Nicolas Anelka in 2002. Nicolas was top class for us and I thought he'd done enough on loan to stay. I've always thought it's a shame he's not still with us. I don't think anyone will deny we got that one wrong!"

No England Silverware!

> LOOK WHAT WE WON!

> I'M GREEN WITH ENVY!

" England haven't won a major tournament for many, many years and all the players want to be part of something that matters – especially after the rugby boys won their World Cup in 2003. I think the football lads are a bit jealous of what they acheived. We want some of that."

Euro 2008 Exit!

" Losing to Croatia at Wembley was the worst night I've had in an England shirt. To lose in front of 88,000 people really hurt. It's going to take a long time to get that out of our system."

> D'OH!

Prem League Failure!

" You don't get any prizes for finishing in second place – never mind fourth – in football. I don't think the fans would accept fourth as an accomplishment and, for me, it's not nearly good enough. I'm a Liverpool fan and I believe the league is the most important trophy going. I'm pretty gutted every time I look at the table and see the gap between us and the top three. We've got to improve."

> BOO-HOO!

FAB FOOTY FACTS!

FACT!
Cristiano Ronaldo is only the second player ever to win the award two years in a row – the other was Thierry Henry!

2 BACARY SAGNA ARSENAL
Transfer Value: £10m

5 RIO FERDINAND MAN UTD
Transfer Value: £20m

THE BEST IN THE PREM!

These are the stars the Prem players themselves voted the TEAM OF THE SEASON! But if anyone fancies buying this lot, be warned – it'll cost nearly a QUARTER OF A BILLION POUNDS!

8 STEVEN GERRARD LIVERPOOL
Transfer Value: £30m

7 CRISTIANO RONALDO MAN UTD
Transfer Value: £50m

TOTA £2

WHAT WOULD £236m BUY YOU...?

3 EUROFIGHTER JET PLANES!

1,475,000 XBOXES!

2,385 PORSCHE 911 TURBOS!

7,866,000 COPIES OF PRO EVO 2008!

FACT!
Ronny's own vote for Player Of The Season went to Arsenal striker Emmanuel Adebayor!

10 EMMANUEL ADEBAYOR ARSENAL
Transfer Value: £12m

FA CUP FINAL BONUSES?! BAH, HUMBUG!

Pompey's John Utaka has revealed he spends his spare time reading classic novels by Charles Dickens. Does that make boss 'Arry Redknapp Scrooge?!

SHOOTY'S SHORTS!

WHAT THE DICKENS?!

HAPPY FAMILIES

Newcastle star Geremi must have a nightmare trying to remember everyone's birthday – he's got 17 brothers and sisters! Imagine having that lot round for Christmas dinner?!

MES OUTH
: £7m

6 NEMANJA VIDIC MAN UTD
Transfer Value: £15 m

3 GAEL CLICHY ARSENAL
Transfer Value: £10m

FACT!
Cesc Fabregas was voted PFA Young Player Of The Year – the first Arsenal star to win it since Nicolas Anelka in 1999!

4 CESC FABREGAS ARSENAL
Transfer Value: £35m

COST: M

11 ASHLEY YOUNG ASTON VILLA
Transfer Value: £12m

FACT!
Arsenal had the most players in the team with four, while Man United were next with three. Chelsea had NONE!

FERNANDO TORRES LIVERPOOL
Transfer Value: £35m

I MIGHT HAVE TO REDECORATE MY ROOM!

HOUSE ABOUT THAT?!

TOTTENHAM new boy Luka Modric had a shock for Spurs fans when he announced that when he moves to London he'll probably live with one of his Croatia mates – ARSENAL star Eduardo!

DISCUS KING!

Dean Ashton might have become an Olympic champion – at the DISCUS! He says: "I could have had trials for England at discus when I was at school but I opted for football"

The Wigan and Reading players weren't happy after they came off the pitch at the JJB Stadium following the 0-0 draw recently – there was no hot water coming out of the showers!

WHAT A SHOWER!

GIGGS IS TOP DOG!

EVEN AT MY AGE I STILL DON'T FEEL "RUFF"!

Sir Alex Ferguson reckons 34-year-old Ryan Giggs can play another three years for Man United. "Look at him," says Fergie. "There's not an ounce of fat on him! He's like a WHIPPET!"

MORE FAB FOOTY FACTS OVER

CHAMPO LEAGUE

THE BIG MATCH
MAN UNITED V BARCELONA

WE'RE GOING TO MOSCOW, LEO!

NO CHANCE, RONNY! WE'VE COME HERE TO WIN!

BLIMEY! HE'S A BIT TASTY!

HAVING DRAWN 0-0 AT HOME, LIONEL MESSI GETS OFF TO A FLYING START AT OLD TRAFFORD!

BUT AFTER **14 MINUTES** PAUL SCHOLES PUTS THE HOME SIDE AHEAD WITH A SCREAMER FROM 25 YARDS!

I NO GET IN THE WAY OF THAT, AMIGO!

NOT THIS TIME, PAL!

GOAL!

'AVE SOME OF THAT, BARCA!

SIX MINUTES LATER EDWIN VAN DER SAR DOES WELL TO KEEP OUT A SHOT FROM MESSI, WHO'S IN GREAT FORM!

AFTER **52 MINUTES** GABRIEL MILITO FOULS CRISTIANO RONALDO BUT THE REF WAVES PLAY ON!

ARRGH! C'MON REF! THAT'S GOTTA BE A PEN?!

WITH **HALF AN HOUR** TO GO, BARCA BRING ON THIERRY HENRY AS SUB! CAN HE SAVE THE DAY?!

NO WORRIES, DUDE! I'LL SCORE!

PHEW! THAT WAS CLOSE!

I CAN'T BELIEVE I MISSED!

TWELVE MINUTES FROM TIME HENRY PUTS A CLOSE-RANGE HEADER STRAIGHT INTO THE ARMS OF VAN DER SAR!

WE'VE DONE IT, BOYS!

ER, RIO?! YOU'RE CHOKING ME, MATE!

AND THAT'S IT! MAN UNITED HAVE WON! THEY'RE IN THE FINAL!

FINAL SCORE (agg 1-0)
MAN UNITED 1-0 BARCELONA

6 May 2008

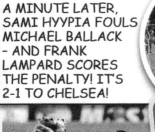